The English Teacher's Drama Handbook

The English Teacher's Drama Handbook is a rich, thought-provoking introduction to teaching drama within the English classroom. Divided into two sections, the first part of the book explores ideological influences that have shaped drama's relationship with English over the past 250 years and aims to help you locate your own practice within a theoretical and historical context. Starting with Rousseau's seminal text *Emile*, it considers the theories of key thinkers and practitioners and a range of complex issues including the construction of 'childhood', children's play, the teacher and student relationship, the implications of linking drama and English and the impact of national curricula on drama and English teaching.

The second half of the book offers a collection of comprehensive, practical schemes of work to inspire and support you and your students to realise the power of drama in bringing English language and literature vividly to life. Suitable for a range of ages and abilities, each activity makes explicit links to the key thinkers and issues explored in the first part of the book and explores a particular aspect of work in English – from grammar and spelling to poetry and play texts. Together with guidance on how to begin and progress the activities, each sequence includes ideas for exploring issues further in the English classroom.

Written for English teachers at any stage of their career, *The English Teacher's Drama Handbook* offers new ways of looking at drama and English that will ensure meaningful and enjoyable teaching and learning.

Nicholas McGuinn has trained teachers of English and drama for twenty years and is an honorary fellow in the Department of Education, University of York, UK.

'This is a highly reflective, stimulating and thought-provoking book. The critical overview of key practitioners and writers in the field offers fresh perspectives on their work. The sequence of practical activities that follow links back skilfully to the earlier discussion.'

Mike Fleming, Emeritus Professor in the School of Education, University of Durham, UK

'Nicholas McGuinn supports the English and Drama teacher to see the developing context in which they are working and offers a wealth of ideas and resources to shape pre-teaching thinking. This is an absolutely invaluable resource for all those intent on making their drama-based learning challenging and enjoyable.'

Martin Illingworth, consultant teacher with NATE and lead lecturer in English Education, Sheffield Hallam University, UK

The English Teacher's Drama Handbook

From theory to practice

Nicholas McGuinn

Routledge
Taylor & Francis Group

LONDON AND NEW YORK

First published 2014
by Routledge
2 Park Square, Milton Park, Abingdon, Oxon OX14 4RN

and by Routledge
711 Third Avenue, New York, NY 10017

Routledge is an imprint of the Taylor & Francis Group, an informa business

British Library Cataloguing in Publication Data
A catalogue record for this book is available from the British Library

Library of Congress Cataloging-in-Publication Data
McGuinn, Nicholas
  The English teacher's drama handbook : from theory to practice / authored by
  Nicholas McGuinn.
     pages cm
  1. Drama in education—Handbooks, manuals, etc.   2. Drama—Study and
  teaching (Secondary)   3. English language—Study and teaching (Secondary)—
  Foreign speakers.   I. Title.
  PN3171.M354 2013
  809.2'00712—dc23

                                                            2013043510

ISBN: 978-0-415-69380-6 (hbk)
ISBN: 978-0-415-69381-3 (pbk)
ISBN: 978-0-203-15278-2 (ebk)

Typeset in Sabon
by RefineCatch Limited, Bungay, Suffolk

Printed and bound in Great Britain by
TJ International Ltd, Padstow, Cornwall

Contents

Preface

I took part in my first drama lesson when I was studying to become an English teacher. Every Wednesday afternoon of our postgraduate certificate in education course was given over to learning how to work in drama. As someone who had experienced a very conventional education, I was amazed and excited by the fact that, for two hours a week, we were invited to learn by exercising our imaginations through what seemed like play. We worked together as a group, rather than as a collection of individuals. There was a lot of laughter and a lot of concentrated, often moving and uplifting, work which depended on collaboration for its success; not that words like 'failure' were ever used in that drama space. I had never experienced anything like it before and was determined to find out more.

Where did these ideas and activities come from? People made generally vague references at the time to Rousseau and Froebel. They talked about children's play and about a debate involving terms like *process* and *product* drama. I learned that this subject, which seemed to be such a powerful tool for learning, was deeply contested by practitioners.

This book is an attempt to find answers to those questions I started to ask over thirty years ago. It is divided into two sections. The first attempts to trace some of my encounters with the theory and practice of drama. The second attempts to suggest practical ways in which those theories and practices might be applied in the English classroom. I am deeply aware that educational politics has not always been as helpful as it might in strengthening the potential connections between the two subjects. The activities in the second part of the book attempt to describe ways of engaging with English while at the same time acknowledging the power of drama as a medium for learning and a subject in its own right.

Nicholas McGuinn
York, September 2013

Part I

Influences and issues

Chapter 1

Early influences
Rousseau and Froebel

No teacher enters the classroom without an ideological agenda, be it consciously or subconsciously addressed. This is as true for English teachers interested in the educational potential of drama as for any other subject practitioner. Part 1 of this book explores some of the ideological influences that have shaped drama pedagogy over the past 250 years. Its aim is to help teachers locate their own practice within a theoretical and historical context and to gain an understanding of the conceptual frames in which the practical activities of Part 2 are embedded. First, it is necessary to consider some of the metanarratives that have contributed historically to the construction of the concept of 'childhood'.

Exploring contemporary attitudes towards childhood during the period 1640–1800, Stone (1977) identifies four fundamental approaches. There is the biological view that a child's character is genetically determined at birth. In contrast to this, the philosopher John Locke (1632–1704) argues in his influential study *Some Thoughts Concerning Education* (1693) that the child is a blank slate, or *tabula rasa*, which is 'written upon' by experience through interaction with the environment. Important though these two positions are, it is Stone's two remaining categories that are of immediate relevance to this contextual section of the book.

Although very different in ideological perspective, both of these categories have been heavily influenced by Judeo-Christian metanarratives. On the one hand, there is what might be called in today's jargon a 'deficit model'. According to this account, brought to prominence by the teachings of the early Christian theologian, Augustine of Hippo (354–430), the child, afflicted from before birth by the *original sin* of our *first parents*, Adam and Eve, enters the world in a state of moral as well as intellectual inadequacy. In the words of the educationalist and Evangelical Christian Hannah More (1745–1833), children 'bring into the world a corrupt nature and evil dispositions, which it should be the great end of education to rectify' (More, 1799, p. 64).

The duty of responsible adults is to try to make good the deficit as quickly as possible by hurrying the child into sober and industrious adulthood. Almost 2,000 years ago, Plutarch (c. ACE 46–120) warned that 'the mind requires not like an earthen vessel to be filled up' (1704, p. 429); but his simile has resonated through time and still serves to describe the transmissive educational processes that are assumed to make this remedial work possible. The child is constructed as a passive recipient of received codes of knowledge and ethical behaviour. Thus armed, he or she must shoulder the burden of Adam's Curse – work – and struggle with patience and endurance towards salvation.

The famous opening lines of the French philosopher Jean Jacques Rousseau's (1712–1778) educational treatise, *Emile* (1762), offer a very different perspective:

> Everything is good as it leaves the hands of the Author of things; everything degenerates in the hands of man. . . . In the present state of things a man abandoned to himself in the midst of other men from birth would be the most disfigured of all. . . . All the social institutions in which we find ourselves submerged would stifle nature in him and put nothing in its place.
>
> (Rousseau, 1979, p. 37)

If, as Coveney claims, 'the eighteenth century . . . turned from the Christian doctrine of original sin to the cult of original virtue in the child' (1957, p. xiii), *Emile* had a major part to play in that paradigm shift. Coveney notes: 'The vital genius of the book inspired the whole progressive school of educational thought in the nineteenth century . . . it is Rousseau's *Emile* that dominates the eighteenth and nineteenth centuries until Freud' (p. 9).

As Coveney's comments suggest, Rousseau's words speak to a construction of childhood that is diametrically opposed to the Evangelical position represented by Hannah More. Its metanarrative, too, tells a story about salvation and is informed by Christianity; but the Christ it evokes is not the wrathful prophet who claimed to bring 'not peace but a sword' (Matthew 10:34); it is rather the teacher who, as Friedrich Froebel (1782–1852), the founder in 1837 of what was to become the first *kindergarten*, put it: 'says, "Suffer the little children to come unto me, and forbid them not: for of such is the kingdom of God." Is not the meaning of this', Froebel continues, 'Forbid them not, for the life given them by their heavenly Father still lives in them in its original wholeness – its free unfolding is still possible with them' (Froebel, 2005, p. 280).

The story this alternative metanarrative tells is of movement away from, not towards, paradise. It reaches back to the pre-Christian era, at least as far as the writings of Plato (429–347 BCE) where, first in the *Meno* and later in the *Phaedo* (e.g., Sedley and Long, 2010), Socrates expounds his concept of *anamnesis*: the idea that human beings have an immortal soul; that the soul exists in possession, from before birth, of ideal knowledge and that this knowledge is forgotten at the moment of entry into the terrestrial world. All subsequent striving for knowledge throughout life becomes therefore an attempt at *recollection* of what was once known.

Early and medieval western thinkers' attempts to accommodate Platonic philosophy to Christian theology led to the neo-platonic idea that the soul journeys *from* God or heaven at the moment of birth. This in turn invites the suggestion that the younger the human being, the closer he or she must be to divine perfection. Far from being deficient, therefore, children, in what Richardson describes as a 'transcendental' (1994, p. 11) expression of this position, are regarded as a source of natural wisdom and holiness. The 'transcendental' vision of childhood is presented vividly in the mystical writings of Thomas Traherne (1636–1674), particularly in poems like *Wonder* and *The Salutation* (Traherne, 1903); but it achieves perhaps its most radical articulation in William Wordsworth's (1770–1850) *Intimations of Immortality*:

> Our birth is but a sleep and a forgetting:
> The Soul that rises with us, our life's Star,

Hath had elsewhere its setting,
And cometh from afar:
Not in entire forgetfulness,
And not in utter nakedness,
But trailing clouds of glory do we come
From God, who is our home:
Heaven lies about us in our infancy!
                    (Wordsworth, 1807/2012)

The pedagogical implications of this 'organic' (Richardson, 1994, p. 11) approach to childhood are significant. It asserts, in the words of Rousseau, that 'Childhood has its ways of seeing, thinking and feeling which are proper to it. Nothing is less sensible than to want to substitute ours [the ways of adults] for theirs.' It insists on taking childhood – and the activities of children – seriously: 'Love childhood; promote its games, its pleasures, its amiable instinct.' (1979, pp. 90, 79). It requires the power relationships between adult and child, teacher and student, to be reconfigured. To take children seriously, to acknowledge that they are different from and not merely imperfect imitations of adults, to 'promote' their 'games' – to adopt this ideological position implied a willingness to pay attention to something children appear to engage in the world over: (Roopnarine *et al.*, 1994) play.

Play has an ancient heritage (Lowenfeld, 1935; Courtney, 1989). As Frost observes, 'Records of children's play date back to antiquity, even earlier than classical Athens and Greece' (2010, p. 9). However, it is the discussion of the value of play presented in two particular educational treatises – one written at the dawn of the so-called 'Romantic' period (Richardson, 1994, pp. 3–4) and the other towards its close some sixty years later – which merit particular attention for the purposes of this book.

Not only did the influence of Rousseau lie behind 'the whole progress of interest towards the child in the second half of the [eighteenth] century' (Coveney, 1957, p. 5); his *Emile* helped to shape the course of drama teaching in Britain almost 200 years later (Hornbrook, 1989, p. 5). Froebel's *The Education of Man* (1826) also deserves consideration by anyone interested in the heritage of drama teaching. While Rousseau is happy to 'promote' the 'games' of childhood, to suggest that learning can be constructed by tutor and student engaging in play together (1911, p. 109) and even to recruit ancient authorities like Plato and Seneca as witnesses to the pedagogical value of play (p. 71), he does so largely because a child at play is a child in harmony with nature: 'Is there anything better worth seeing, anything more touching or delightful, than a pretty child, with merry, cheerful glance, easy contented manner, open smiling countenance, playing at the most important things, or working at the lightest amusements?' (Rousseau, 1911, p. 126).

Froebel is charmed by the same image into using a very similar rhetorical question: 'Is not the most beautiful expression of child-life at this time a playing child?' (2005, p. 55). Whereas Rousseau, in one of his many contradictory statements, is not averse to using 'child's play'– *jeux d'enfant* – in a dismissive context (1911, p. 173), Froebel endows play with a sacred quality infused by his deep Christian faith:

Play is the purest, most spiritual activity of man at this stage, and, at the same time, typical of human life as a whole – of the inner hidden natural life in man and all things. It gives, therefore, joy, freedom, contentment, inner and outer rest, peace with the world. . . . To the calm, keen vision of one who truly knows human nature, the spontaneous play of the child discloses the future inner life of the man.

(Froebel, 2005, p. 55)

Through the medium of play – including the use of 'gifts' (such as balls, cubes and building bricks) and 'occupations' (such as drawing, paper cutting and wood work) (Lawrence, 1952, pp. 238–239) – Froebel insisted that children 'were to be placed *at the centre* of their world, there to act directly on their world' (Walsh *et al.*, 2001, p. 98). Rousseau would certainly have agreed that children should act directly on their world and that play is an essential element of this engagement (see below); but *The Education of Man* presents a far more sustained pedagogical engagement with play than does *Emile*. It is difficult to think of an earlier work in the western canon that takes play so seriously. Froebel attempts to identify and classify the different phases and characteristics of play, argues for the importance of playrooms and playgrounds and, in the latter sections of the book, describes a detailed curriculum informed by play and games (Froebel, 2005, pp. 303, 107, 236).

From a drama practitioner's perspective, one of the most significant points on which Rousseau and Froebel are particularly united is their insistence that, from birth, children are actively engaged in the construction of meanings. A child's play, Froebel argues, 'is not trivial, it is highly serious and of deep significance' (2005, p. 55). If adults cannot understand this, it is because they do not know how to interpret what they see. 'If you attend carefully', writes Rousseau, 'you will be surprised to find . . .' (1911, p. 37). And Froebel makes the point more forcefully:

We call it [a child's 'quiet, busy activity'] childish because we do not understand it, because we have not eyes to see, nor ears to hear, and, still less, feeling to feel with the child; we are dull, therefore the child's life seems dull to us.

(2005, p. 73)

To those who know what to look for, the hum of a sleepy child is 'the first germ of future growth in melody and song' (p. 71); a baby putting an object in its mouth is seeking to 'know all its properties, its innermost nature, that he may learn to understand himself in his attachment' (p. 73); climbing a tree brings 'the discovery of a new world' (p. 103). 'Let them run, jump, and shout to their heart's content', says Rousseau: 'All their activities are instincts of the body for its growth in strength' (1911, p. 50).

Equally important from a drama perspective is the emphasis that both Rousseau and Froebel place on the idea that children learn by engaging directly with the physical world through the medium of their senses. By apprehending 'the near', the mind reaches out to comprehend 'the remote' (Froebel, 2005, p. 66). The 'objects of thought' are 'attained' by means of 'the objects of sense' so that where once 'we were concerned with what touches ourselves, with our immediate environment . . . all at once we are exploring the round world and leaping to the bounds of the universe'

(Rousseau, 1911, pp. 131, 130). The child's manipulation of the environment through play leads to the comprehension of abstract ideas:

> The ball that is rolling or has been rolled, the stone that has been thrown and falls, the water that was dammed and conducted into many branching ditches – all these have taught the child that the effect of a force, in its individual manifestations, is always in the direction of a line.
>
> (Froebel, 2005, p. 76)

Although it is now considered to mark only the starting point of Froebel's interest in the subject (Frost, 2010), *The Education of Man* contains many examples of how, through play, children can explore, for example, numeracy (counting games), rhythm and voice projection (singing games), concepts of self and not-self (hide and seek), tolerance and co-operation (team games) and higher order cognition (synthesis and comparison through the classification of found objects). Similarly with Rousseau: anticipating by over 150 years the American educator John Dewey's (1859–1952) argument that students learn most effectively when presented with a 'genuine situation of experience' and a 'genuine problem' as 'a stimulus to thought' (2007, p. 167), Emile's tutor regularly seeks opportunities to channel the child's propensity for play into purposeful learning: 'Children will always do anything that keeps them moving freely. There are countless ways of rousing their interest in measuring, perceiving, and estimating distance. There is a very tall cherry tree; how shall we gather the cherries?' (Rousseau, 1911, p. 105).

A third aspect of *Emile* and *The Education of Man*, which is of particular significance in terms of its influence upon the ideologies of drama teaching, is Rousseau and Froebel's configuration of the relationship between teacher and student. Rousseau's work is notorious for the blatantly unequal treatment meted out to Emile's supposed partner, 'Sophie', in terms of her education and life chances. It so incensed Mary Wollstonecraft (1759–1797), the campaigner for women's rights, that she famously declared in her *Vindication of the Rights of Women* (1792): 'The most perfect education, in my opinion, is such an exercise of the understanding as is best calculated to strengthen the body and form the heart. . . . This was Rousseau's opinion respecting men: I extend it to women (1975, p. 21).

It would be easy to forget that, as Cunningham points out, an important component of *Emile*'s radicalism is that it attacks the tradition 'established at the time of the Renaissance that fathers must take charge of child-rearing' (1995, p. 66) and thus challenges the 'foundational narrative', which for centuries had interpreted the story of Adam and Eve as one in which 'a woman mediated fatal knowledge of good and evil . . . plunged humanity into sin and thereby introduced death into the world (Bottigheimer, 1994, p. 51). 'Tender, anxious mothers', Rousseau declares at the beginning of *Emile*, 'I appeal to you' (1911, p. 5). Froebel concurs. 'The child . . . cared for by the mother', he writes, 'is well-conditioned in a human, earthly, and heavenly point of view' (2005, p. 26).

By proposing a model of teaching and learning predicated on the relationship between loving parents and their child, both Rousseau and Froebel replace the transmissive didacticism of those who, supposing 'the child to be empty, wish to inoculate him with life' (Froebel, 2005, p. 70) with the concept of the tutor as someone whose task is 'to guide' the child 'from birth to manhood [sic]' (Rousseau, 1911, p. 18). This is achieved by creating practical situations in which purposeful learning might take place and then by drawing understanding from the child through the careful application of what today's educationalists might describe as Socratic questioning techniques. 'If we do not form the habit of thinking as children', Rousseau writes, 'we shall lose the power of thinking for the rest of our life' (1911, p. 82).

Where Froebel sees the tutor in terms of a loving parent, however, Rousseau – in a description that was to have particular resonance for drama practitioners in the early twentieth century – proposes something far more radical:

> contrary to the received opinion, a child's tutor should be young, as young indeed as a man [sic] may well be who is also wise. Were it possible, he should become a child himself, that he may be the companion of his pupil and win his confidence by sharing his games.
>
> (1911, p. 19)

In an early illustration of the idea that teacher and student might learn alongside each other, Rousseau imagines a drawing lesson shared by Emile and his tutor:

> I [the tutor] shall follow his [Emile's] example and take up a pencil; at first I shall use it as unskilfully as he. . . . To begin with, I shall draw a man such as lads draw on walls. . . . Long after, one or other of us will notice this lack of proportion. . . . In this improvement I shall either go side by side with my pupil, or so little in advance that he will always overtake me easily and sometimes get ahead of me.
>
> (1911, p. 109)

One final point to note is that both Rousseau and Froebel are adamant that children need time and space to grow: the incremental stages of childhood development cannot be rushed. 'Give nature time to work' Rousseau demands, 'before you take over her business, lest you interfere with her dealings' (1911, p. 71).

Upon publication, both *Emile* and *The Education of Man* were well received in England. Rousseau's work was translated into English within a year of its appearance. The first *kindergarten* was established in London by one of Froebel's pupils in 1851 and his theories were soon eliciting praise from Her Majesty's Inspector of Church Schools:

> This system . . . treats the child as a child; encourages him to think for himself; teaches him, by childish toys and methods, gradually to develop in action or hieroglyphic writing his own idea, to tell his [sic] own story and to listen to that of others.
>
> (In Woodham-Smith, 1952, p. 38)

To 'tell his own story and to listen to that of others': that phrase, first written in a report of 1854, still has the power to resonate with drama practitioners today. However, despite the initial reception of their work, neither Rousseau nor Froebel succeeded in setting the educational agenda in nineteenth-century Britain. Coveney records that the 'idealism' of *Emile* either fell victim to 'severe Puritan morality' or Victorian sentimentality (1957, p. 229). Speculating, on the centenary of Froebel's death, about why his ideas failed decisively to shape English education policy, Slight makes a comment that has a depressing ring of familiarity sixty years on:

> the English conception of education – apart from the work of the great public schools [sic] – has always stressed instruction in what have become known, almost officially, as the three R's. To this conception the scholarship system has added weight so that any type of education that was not obviously and avowedly directed to the attainment of scholarships (rather than scholarship) was regarded with the greatest suspicion.
>
> (Slight, 1952, p. 117)

If, as Coveney argues, 'romantic assertions about childhood remained very much a protest' during the nineteenth century (1957, p. 230), Hornbrook's observation that they were espoused by drama practitioners in the first half of the twentieth century and beyond says much about the positioning of drama within the educational landscape of the time.

Chapter 2

Emancipation from situational constraints

Piaget and Vygotsky on play and drama

As the nineteenth century progressed, Rousseau's injunction that adults should 'attend carefully' to the behaviour of children was heeded with increasing thoroughness. Lowenfeld (1991) provides a useful overview of the observational works of the period, the most important of which include studies by Spencer (1855), Grasberger (1864), Preyer (1882), Sully (1896), Groos (1898, 1901) and Hall (1907). *Child Study Associations* were established in the United States (1888) and the United Kingdom (1898). Freudian developments in psychology brought to early twentieth-century studies a closer, psycho-analytical focus on the nature and purpose of play, for example in the works of Freud's daughter, Anna Freud (1927), Isaacs (1930), Bühler (1931) and Klein (1932).

There are two specific studies of play, however, which I want to consider at this point because they provide a particularly helpful context not only for exploring the theories about drama and education prevalent at the time but also for raising some abiding issues of drama pedagogy. One text is the Swiss psychologist and philosopher Jean Piaget's (1896–1980) essay on *mastery* and *symbolic* play, first published in 1951. The other is a lecture presented in 1933 but not published until 1966: *Play and its Role in the Mental Development of the Child* by the Russian psychologist, Lev Vygotsky (1896–1934). I want to include, with these two studies of play, a second work by Vygotsky, first published – again, posthumously – in 1967: *Imagination and Creativity in Childhood* because this work makes explicit reference to the links between drama, education and creativity.

Like Rousseau and Froebel before them, Piaget and Vygotsky regard children as active constructors of meaning from the earliest age; both, however, draw a clear distinction between play and a child's other behaviours. To take Piaget's examples: when a baby grasps a stick or a rattle, it *accommodates* its hand–eye co-ordination to the physical properties of those objects and it *assimilates* the concepts of grasping and shaking to its *schemata* or mental world-view. Why, Piaget asks, when a baby has understood what sticks and rattles do, does it continue to beat the one and shake the other in a sequence of patterned movements? It is, he suggests, 'for the pleasure of being the cause' (1976, p. 170) and because the child delights in its 'power of subduing reality' (p. 168). I will return to the distinctions Piaget draws between play and other behaviours of childhood again later; but for now, I want to note that his attribution of the capacity of even the smallest human beings to take pleasure in patterns, images, movements and sounds simply for their own sake puts a marker down for the power of the aesthetic impulse – an issue that was to play an important part in subsequent debates about the nature and purpose of drama in education.

Vygotsky also draws a forceful distinction between play and other behaviours, arguing that 'in fundamental everyday situations' a child behaves in a manner 'diametrically opposed to his behaviour in play' because in play, 'action is subordinated to meaning, but in real life, of course, action dominates over meaning' (1976, p. 551). In an oblique criticism of *transcendental* and utopian constructions of childhood, he suggests that: 'Only theories which maintain that a child does not have to satisfy the basic requirements of life, but can live in search of pleasure, could possibly suggest that a child's world is a play world' (p. 552).

While conceding that the child 'does what he feels like most because play is *connected* [my italics] with pleasure' (p. 548), Vygotsky, noting that play is 'serious . . . for a very young child' (p. 554) acknowledges the importance of other impulses that might be stronger than mere connections. One of the paradoxes of play, he argues, is that the child is willing to defer its own gratification for the greater good of the play experience – for example, by not jumping the starting gun when playing at racing. Furthermore, in an observation that gestures towards the concept of *dark play* (Schechner, 1993), Vygotsky points out that children can play at situations that are not necessarily pleasant ones. By departing in his description of play from the received wisdom – at least as old as the writings of John Locke – that children will always seek that which gives them the most immediate gratification, Vygotsky suggests that what matters more than pleasure to the playing child is the opportunity to construct meanings: 'the action is completed not for the action itself but for the meaning it carries' (1976, p. 549). One point that drama teachers might take from Vygotsky's teasing out of the differences between play and other childhood behaviours is the idea that the decision to enter into play involves a conscious resolution to cross the border, as it were, between a real and a fictional world. A child playing the part of a patient in this other world, Vygotsky offers as an illustration, is able to weep while at the same time revelling in the fiction of the play activity. In this dual consciousness, one might detect the beginnings of Augusto Boal's *metaxis:* 'the state of belonging completely and simultaneously to two different autonomous worlds' (1995, p. 43).

Like Rousseau and Froebel, both Piaget and Vygotsky believe that play – especially what Piaget terms *symbolic* play – enables the developing child to access higher-order thinking skills. To take again the analogy of the baby repeatedly shaking its rattle for pleasure: Piaget describes this action as 'ludic ritualization' (1976, p. 557), which 'as a result of progressive abstraction of the action' (p. 558) eventually enables the child to grasp the concept of symbolism and to incorporate it into its mental *schemata* or world-view. Thus, a child might move from the ritual of pretending to drink from a cup to the make-believe, symbolic action of pretending to drink from a box. With further development, the child might no longer need the box to represent the cup in order to initiate the symbolic play. The consequences of this move in terms of cognition are profound. Piaget comments: 'With the projection of such "symbolic schemata" on to other objects, the way is clear for the assimilation of any one object to another, since any object can be a make-believe substitute for any other' (p. 567).

Vygotsky also explores this idea. Suppose a child creates a play activity in which a stick is used to represent a horse. The stick 'becomes a pivot for severing the meaning of horse from a real horse'. Thus, 'in play activity thought is separated from objects, and action arises from ideas rather than from things' (1976, p. 546). In Vygotsky's telling phrase, when a child calls a stick a horse, 'mentally he sees the object standing behind the word'. 'Things' start to lose their cognitive hold on the child's mind and instead 'the idea becomes the central point'. In this way, play serves as a stage of transition 'between the purely situational constraints of early childhood and thought which is totally free of real situations' (p. 547). The way is open for the child to begin to access the powerful thinking tools of metaphor, metonymy and synecdoche. The ability to make imaginative connections between seemingly disparate concepts is located in the highest levels of cognition identified by Bloom *et al.*'s famous Taxonomy (Krathwohl, 2002). Vygotsky argues that the ability to 'combine elements to produce a structure, to combine the old in new ways' is a uniquely human skill, which is 'the basis of creativity' (2004, p. 13).

Both Piaget and Vygotsky see play as a medium through which the child negotiates the tensions inherent in its reception as a member of an increasingly widening community. As the child develops its language skills and moves from home to school, so, in the words of Piaget, 'ludic assimilation' is gradually reconciled with the 'demands of social reciprocity' (1976, p. 569) by participation in 'school instruction and work' according to Vygotsky (1976, p. 554) or, as Piaget says, in rule-bound games 'through which competition is controlled by a collective discipline, with a code of honour and fair play' (1976, p. 569).

Piaget does not view this movement towards social integration as unproblematic. A price must be paid. A significant part of that price is acceptance of what Piaget calls 'the collective "sign"' (1976, p. 564) – the socially constructed meanings and values applied to the relationship between signifier and signified by what Saussure calls a 'linguistic community' (2010, p. 854). Given that, according to Saussure, 'each language brings into being, by describing, a world that it then knows as external' (Leitch *et al.*, 2010, p. 846) the epistemological implications are profound. Viewed from this perspective, symbolic play becomes a flashpoint as it were in the struggle between the desires of the child's ego and the claims of the community.

Piaget illustrates the point of conflict by describing two instances of symbolic play. He imagines a child using a shell to depict the movements of a cat walking across a wall. An adult coming upon this scene would not be able to interpret the particular correspondence between signifier and signified that the child's imagination has required the shell-sign to bear. What other people think about this is of no importance to the playing child: the shell-cat is therefore an example of 'subjective' generalisation (1976, p. 561). Symbolic play of this kind, Piaget writes, 'is merely egocentric thought in its pure state' (p. 567). The adult then comes across a playing child who is using a spoon to simulate the action of pulling. Piaget describes this action as an example of 'generalizing assimilation' (p. 561): the relationship between signifier and signified created here by the child can be comprehended by others because it falls within the socially constructed understanding of the uses to which a spoon might possibly be put. The celebration of 'egocentric thought in its pure state' represented by the shell-cat analogy, Piaget argues, represents a transition point on the child's journey towards that adult 'objectivity of thought', which is achieved when 'adapted notions' are in 'permanent equilibrium with accommodation of these same notions to things and to the thoughts of others' (p. 567). He concedes that the 'intervention of the social sign' is a 'decisive turning-point in the direction of representation' (p. 561): conformity to the received, communal interpretations of signs is inevitable and even essential to cognitive development. However – and this point is particularly significant from the perspective of drama – Piaget asserts the importance of the 'ludic symbol' (p. 561) – be it shell/cat or cardboard box/plate – in enabling the developing child who is still a long way from a state of 'permanent equilibrium' to establish its sense of self, to nurture its creativity and to have confidence in its capacity to make those imaginative connections that are essential to the higher order cognitive skills:

> for the child assimilation of reality to the ego is a vital condition for continuity and development, precisely because of the lack of equilibrium in his thought, and symbolic play satisfies this condition both as regards signifier and signified.
>
> (pp. 567–568)

Using words that advocates of the *transcendental* construction of childhood would not have found inappropriate, Piaget declares that 'the function of play is to protect this universe [of the child's ego] against forced accommodation to ordinary reality'. Perhaps it is not entirely fanciful to hear, in his observation that 'the effect of social life is to weaken ludic belief' (p. 569), the echo of another line from Wordsworth's (1807/2012) ode *Intimations of Immortality:* 'Shades of the prison house begin to close/Upon the growing boy'. Saussure argues that 'the individual does not have the power to change a sign in any way once it has become established in the linguistic community' (Saussure, 2010, p. 854); but the young child whose imagination has transformed a shell into a cat does not know this and delights in the powers of invention.

Where Piaget sees the child moving through play towards an integration with and acceptance of a community's rule-bound systems, Vygotsky takes the opposite approach. Arguing instead that children learn 'to behave according to certain rules from the first few months of life' (1976, p. 543), he charts the 'evolution of children's play' as a movement from 'an overt imaginary situation and covert rules to games with overt rules and a covert imaginary situation' (p. 543). There is no hint of Piaget's wistfulness. Where Piaget describes play in terms of protection, Vygotsky uses words of liberation. The creation of an 'imagined situation', he writes, is 'the first effect of the child's emancipation from situational constraints' (p. 548). 'As in the focus of a magnifying glass', he continues, 'play contains all developmental tendencies in a condensed form' (p. 552). Far from inhibiting play, rules increase its intensity and sense of challenge. Moreover, because in play children invent their own rules, they not only have opportunities to make meanings and to see those meanings take effect; they also learn to make moral choices – about sharing or turn-taking, for example – according to internally generated codes of behaviour which make sense in a way that the *don't do it because I say so* strictures of adults cannot. Most importantly from a drama perspective, Vygotsky argues that play teaches the child 'to desire by relating his desires to a fictitious "I" – to his role in the game and its rules' (p. 549). He cites – in what might be seen as another prefiguring of Boal's *metaxis* – the psychologist James Sully's (1842–1923) account of two sisters who used to *play at* being sisters. Whereas in real life the girls behave as sisters without thinking about it, in their play, Vygotsky observes, each child consciously shapes their sisterly role - each one 'tries to be a sister' (p. 541).

Both Piaget and Vygotsky express interest in the relationship between play and drama. As mentioned earlier, Vygotsky's posthumous 1967 paper on creativity devotes a not inconsiderable amount of space to the issue. I want to begin this section by comparing Piaget's and Vygotsky's views with those of a current practitioner, Michael Fleming, in order to try to tease out some of the perceived differences between the two modes of expression.

Piaget acknowledges that there are similarities between drama and symbolic play. Particularly interesting is his observation that, as the child develops, 'the ludic symbol is dissociated from ritual and takes the form of symbolic schemas' (1976, p. 557). Piaget draws attention here, at an individual level, to the relationship between ritual and play. Mitchell (1937) and, later, Courtney (1989) and Frost (2010) extend this connection to the social sphere. 'Many games', Frost observes, 'were of religious significance, dating back to ancient rites of divination' (2010, p. 9). This is important in terms of drama because, as Fleming suggests, it can be all too easy to consider 'the origins of children's drama as being purely in spontaneous dramatic play'. Seeing ritual as 'a natural human inclination' (1997, p. 158) or, as Esslin puts it, 'a manifestation of one of humanity's prime social needs' (1987, p. 10), Fleming continues, can be a 'helpful corrective' (1997, p. 158). Fleming parts company with Piaget, however, by suggesting that, far from falling away as the child begins to engage in symbolic play, ritual remains an important element of both a child's spontaneous play and its engagement with drama. He draws attention to 'the open-ended spontaneous activity of make-believe play and the inclination to ritualise which also characterises young children's involvement with dramatic activity, when for example they repeatedly act out a story' (p. 158).

For Piaget, the key distinction between play and drama is that the participants in the latter – and the plural form is used advisedly here because Piaget acknowledges that drama is a social, collective enterprise in a way that symbolic play does not necessarily have to be – are consciously aware of and reflective upon the fiction with which they are engaged (1976, p. 569). The implications of these distinguishing traits for Fleming are that drama has an aesthetic and moral dimension that dramatic play might not:

> It is not easy to define when 'dramatic play' becomes 'drama' but it lies in the realm of content (when participants have to face up to the consequences of their actions) and form (when they are constrained by its demands).
>
> (1997, p. 38)

Playing at being archaeologists is different from enacting a drama involving archaeologists, which is framed by a specific ideological, social and cultural context – the Sutton Hoo burial in Fleming's example – where the participants are confronted by a particular dilemma and have to craft their response to that dilemma with the aid of aesthetic tools such as tension, contrast and exposition.

Where Vygotsky would disagree with Piaget's position as elaborated by Fleming here is over the suggestion that drama differs from play by obliging its participants to 'face up to the consequences of their actions'. Play, being rule-based from its earliest inception, is also capable of inculcating what Vygotsky – quoting Piaget – calls a sense of 'moral realism' (1976, p. 543) through its doling out of sanctions, forfeits, punishment and rewards. One has only to read some of the chapter titles of *The Lore and Language of Schoolchildren* (1960) by those pioneering ethnographers of children's games, Iona and Peter Opie, to take Vygotsky's point: chapter eight is called

Codes of Oral Legislation and chapter ten *Unpopular Children: Jeers and Torments*. Similarly, Frost's account of the 'street games' played by New York children in the early twentieth century ranges from 'ball games in the street' and 'snowballing' to 'burglary' and 'assault' (2010, p. 86).

Fleming cites Donaldson's (1978) description of the 'point mode' as one of the 'four main modes of mental functioning' available to young children (1994, p. 39). Esslin describes the 'point mode' as 'a way of functioning in which the locus of concern is the directly experienced chunk of space-time that one currently inhabits: the here and now' (1987, p. 3). Fleming continues: 'Whether one is participating in or observing drama it is the absorption in the moment reminiscent of our first mental functioning as infants which gives it its particular potency as an art form and as a method of education (1994, p. 39).

Here, Vygotsky would agree. He quotes his colleague Petrova's observation that 'children's representations of the world are rooted in action' (2004, p. 71) and that in 'dramatic rendering', the 'drive for action, for embodiment, for realization that is present in the very process of imagination here finds complete fulfilment' (p. 70). Like Fleming, too, Vygotsky sets particular store on the aesthetic qualities of drama. It is, he argues, the most 'syncretic mode of creation' (p. 71) because it affords children access to so many of the arts. This is why he values the writing and staging of plays so much. 'Along with verbal creation', Vygotsky writes, 'the dramatization, or staging, of plays is the most frequent and widespread form of creativity practiced [sic] by children' (pp. 69–70). Quoting Petrova again, he offers an account of the benefits to be gained from engaging in theatre: 'Drama, more than any other form of creation', he affirms, 'is closely and directly linked to play':

> The staging of drama provides the pretext and material for the most diverse forms of creativity on the part of the children. The children themselves compose, improvise, or prepare the play, improvise the roles or sometimes dramatize some existing piece of literature. The children understand the need and nature of this verbal creation because it takes on the meaning of a part of the whole; this is preparation for or a natural part of a complete and fascinating game. Making the props, the scenery, and costumes provides a pretext for visual arts and crafts. The children draw, model, cut out, sew, and again all these activities take on meaning and purpose as part of a general objective the children are engaged with. Finally, the game itself, involving the actual presentation of the play by the actors, completes this work and provides it with its complete and final expression.
>
> (2004, p. 71)

Fleming's identification of 'form', 'content' and 'point mode' as the essential aesthetic elements that distinguish drama from play resonates with the aesthetic theories of the German dramatist, poet and philosopher Friedrich Schiller (1759–1805), expounded in the twenty-seven letters he published in 1795 as *On the Aesthetic Education of Man* at a time when the Enlightenment's faith in the power of Reason was being shaken by the violent excesses of the French Revolution. Schiller constructs what Fleming calls content and form as two opposing forces – *Stofftrieb* (*material drive*) and *Formtrieb* (*formal drive*) (1967, p. 101) – which are at conflict within the human psyche. *Stofftrieb* and *Formtrieb* can only be brought into balance by a third force

– *Speiltrieb* or *play-drive*. Schiller regards the development of a 'delight in semblance' and a 'propensity to ornamentation and play' as key evolutionary moments in history, marking humanity's emergence from 'the slavery of the animal condition' and a 'decisive step towards culture' (p. 193). Through *Speiltrieb* – 'what in the widest sense of the term we call beauty' (p. 101) – Schiller believes that the increasing fragmentation and isolation of the modern age wrought by 'the all-dividing Intellect' (p. 33) will be overcome and humanity brought into psychic, moral and social harmony with itself. As Sharpe puts it:

> the ultimate form of play is the contemplation of the beautiful; it is there that man truly plays, and where man truly plays, where he is satisfying no material need nor fulfilling any purposes, he achieves a temporary reunion of the two sides of his nature and thus can be held to be expressing the *Bestimmung* (both purpose and destination) of humanity.
>
> (2006, p. 158)

Aesthetic education is charged with no less a task than to save the world. To engage in aesthetic play is not only to bring content and form into productive harmony, however. Fleming's other aesthetic ingredient – 'point mode' – echoes Schiller's concept of *Schein* or *semblance*. Suzanne Langer writes:

> Schiller was the first thinker who saw what really makes 'Schein', or semblance, important for art: the fact that it liberates perception – and with it, the power of conception – from all practical purposes, and lets the mind dwell on the sheer appearance of things. The function of artistic illusion is not 'make-believe' . . . but the very opposite, disengagement from belief – the contemplation of sensory qualities without their usual meanings. . . . The knowledge that what is before us has no practical significance in the world is what enables us to give attention to its appearance as such.
>
> (1953, p. 49)

To be absorbed 'in the moment', as Fleming puts it, is to give oneself to *semblance*: to set the mind truly free from conventional ways of seeing by allowing it to apprehend 'promptly and undividedly, as wholes, the complex structures of the sensible world' (Wilkinson and Willoughby, 1967, p. xx). Significantly, it was through the medium of the theatre that Schiller chose to articulate his own experience of *Spieltrieb*.

Chapter 3

To feel with her senses awake

The legacy of Finlay-Johnson, Caldwell Cook and Hourd

This review of some early influences upon the relationship between drama and play is necessarily brief and selective. Its purpose is to provide a conceptual map with which to chart the response of early twentieth-century practitioners to the possibilities afforded by drama pedagogy. I want now to focus upon three important texts: one written just before the First World War, one at its height and one several years after the end of the Second World War. I have chosen them because, as well as being published in proximity to a time of global conflict – a point that is not insignificant – each of the three texts shares the fact that its author was a classroom practitioner, and that each author had a particular interest in the ways in which drama principles and strategies might enhance the teaching of English, which had itself only emerged as a compulsory subject of study for state schools by Board of Education Regulations in 1904.

The authors are Harriet Finlay-Johnson (1871–1956) whose book *The Dramatic Method of Teaching*, first published in 1912, describes the curriculum she applied at the village school in Sussex where she was head teacher at the turn of the century; Henry Caldwell Cook (1885–1939) whose book *The Play Way: An Essay in Educational Method*, first published in 1917, gives an account of the teaching strategies he used during his time as an English teacher at the Perse School in Cambridge; and Marjorie Lovegrove Hourd (fl 1949–1980), teacher and university lecturer, whose *The Education of the Poetic Spirit: A Study in Children's Expression in the English Lesson*, first published in 1949, is drawn from her experiences of teaching literature and creative writing in a selective girls' school. I want to argue that these three texts merit close attention because they establish principles of practice and raise pedagogical issues that still inform the relationship between drama and English today.

Each of the three writers shares Froebel's enthusiasm for play as a powerful learning medium. '[A]ll this lasting treasure', Finlay-Johnson exclaims, as she reflects on the language and history learning gained by her students from acting out Shakespeare's *A Midsummer Night's Dream*, 'absorbed from and through a game in school!' (1912, p. 103). For Caldwell Cook, play is nothing less than the means by which human beings 'hold rehearsals' for life, an opportunity for us 'to try our strength in a make-believe big world' (1917, p. 1). Hourd discerns an 'intense inner life being externalised in [the] play activities' of pre-school children and argues that the freedom and space to engage in play is essential for the psychic health of the child:

> He [sic] should be allowed a continued period of full dramatic play in which he can reach the solid things of the external world without feeling that we

want to deprive him of his phantasy protection before he himself finds it unnecessary.

(1949, pp. 25, 26)

To welcome play into the classroom as a powerful learning medium is to endorse a series of ideological principles. It follows, for example, that all three practitioners are implacably opposed to systems of rote-learning – and the examination processes that necessarily accompany them – in which what Caldwell Cook calls the 'repressionist spoon-feeder' (1917, p. 51) employs the '"stand-and-deliver" approach' (Finlay-Johnson, 1912, p. 71) and, as Hourd puts it thirty-seven years later, 'makes it his special task to reveal and probe ignorance'. She goes further: 'This constant questioning before knowledge has had time to grow sure of itself is one of the most destructive processes in the whole educational field' (1949, pp. 13, 113–114).

Opposed to transmissive forms of teaching and assessment, Finlay-Johnson, Caldwell Cook and Hourd argue, like Rousseau and Froebel before them, for a reconfiguration of the power relationship between teachers and taught. They are acutely aware that a teacher can be the gate-keeper of knowledge in the classroom. '[T]hrough him [the teacher] the selection of the effective world reaches the pupil', Hourd writes, quoting the philosopher Martin Buber (1878–1965); and she adds in her own words: 'He fails the pupil when he presents the selection to him with a gesture of interference' (1949, p. 118). Finlay-Johnson argues that children 'know by instinct how to get ideas into their companions' minds where a teacher will fail for lack of the sympathetic touch' (1912, p. 27) and, almost a century before Erik De Corte advocated the principle of 'cognitive and volitional self-regulation' for students (De Corte *et al.*, 2003, p. 25) she sought to invest her pupils with the responsibility for teaching each other. Caldwell Cook organised the boys at Perse School into committees charged with the content, regulation and assessment of their learning.

If students are to assume the status and responsibility of teachers, then teachers need to reposition themselves as co-learners. 'Combined effort and corporate discipline will never be possible in the classroom', Caldwell Cook declares, 'until the master relinquishes the sole command, and until the boys are permitted to undertake some parts of their course of learning in an active form' (1917, p. 87). Finlay-Johnson puts the case in more explicitly civic terms. By substituting '*the relationships of teacher and pupil*' [original italics] for those of 'fellow workers, friends, and playmates', she believes that classroom interactions can be imbued with a more ethical – and therefore enhanced – authority:

because the teacher, being a companion to and fellow worker with the pupils, had a strong moral hold on them [the students] and shared in the citizen's right of holding an opinion, being heard, therefore, not as 'absolute monarch', but on the same grounds as the children themselves.

(1912, pp. 9, 9–10)

This move towards the democratisation of the classroom was driven by an absolute commitment to the principle that the learning needs of the individual child are of fundamental importance in education. Both Finlay-Johnson and Hourd would have concurred with Caldwell Cook's assertion that the teacher should 'regard everything from their [the students'] point of view' (1917, p. 37). Honouring this principle implies that the power structures informing transmissive classroom discourse also have to be challenged. To see something from a student's point of view, to be always 'on the side of' the child – in Hourd's telling phrase – (1949, p. 122) requires a commitment to children's ways of seeing and of constructing meanings, a commitment to taking them as seriously as Rousseau, Froebel, Piaget and Vygotsky do. Again, it is Hourd who expresses the principle most vividly when she describes the effective teacher as someone who 'makes it *safe* through the authority of his [sic] integrity for the child to think and feel. There can be no sincere expression where there is fear'. In order to secure the classroom as a place for self-expression, it is necessary to honour the modes of discourse that children bring to school: 'the teacher is the authority who makes it safe to say what you really want to say, and not the authority who dictates what it is you ought to say' (1949, pp. 128, 129). Caldwell Cook writes eloquently about how a child's encounter with the formal language of school can cause deep embarrassment and even alienation:

> When a boy, for instance, reads such a word as *Antipodes* as three syllables – as any one naturally would do on meeting it for the first time – some jolly teachers laugh. It is such an amusing 'howler.' But after such an experience a boy may for months after be reluctant to read aloud.
>
> (1917, p. 42)

Rather than insist that school learning should be mediated through standard forms of English, Finlay-Johnson encourages the use of the language of the home and locality in the classroom:

> Another strong argument in favour of allowing children to impart knowledge to others is that the pupils in any one class will almost always be from the same neighborhood, and limited [sic] to the same vocabulary; hence they will find the correct terms of expression to convey the necessary intelligence to their hearers.
>
> (1912, p. 27)

If a commitment to play requires a reconfiguration of the power relationship between teacher and student, there is no reason why the same principle should not be applied to the iconic writers of 'high' literary culture. Learning through play means learning by doing. Using an apprenticeship analogy, Hourd argues that the most effective way to help a student appreciate great writing is to 'keep expression free and at the same time put her in touch with the masters of her craft' (1949, p. 141) by giving her opportunities to write in a similar style or genre. Since both master and apprentice share the same common humanity, 'instead of there being a great gulf fixed between the mature and the immature artist, their worlds lie very close together, their meanings are akin and the process by which they reach them is the same' (p. 98). Hourd does not believe therefore that her students should bow down in reverence before the great works of literature. Inviting them to compose their own drama in the style of the *Iliad*, for example, she argues that it is up to Homer to prove that he is worth emulating, adding simply: 'The teacher's creed was: "Write your play: I believe in Homer"' (p. 128). Having written alongside a source text, the student has every right to find it wanting: 'Once the child is set free in this way she is of course free to rebel and dislike the poem as well as to submit to it and accept it' (p. 128). Although more reverential in their attitude to the literary canon than Hourd, Caldwell Cook and Finlay-Johnson both endorse the apprenticeship model as a means of encouraging and refining self-expression. '[T]he boys must themselves come forth as poets' (1917, p. 16), Caldwell Cook writes, and he describes how his students created 'chap-books' for their own poems written in ballad form, doing 'the composition, painting, writing, binding and all, even as did William Blake with his books' (p. 161). 'Surely the best grammar or composition lessons must be long drafts from the well of pure English to be found in our standard authors', writes Finlay-Johnson (1912, p. 105). Proudly displaying several examples of the historical dramas written by her village-school children, she describes what is, in effect, a dialogic exchange between self-expression and the literary canon:

> It was only to be expected that, as soon as the pupils of the school had tried to write their own historical plays (and hence knew the points of a good play), they should soon be on the watch for good ready-made plays illustrating the periods they happened to be studying.
>
> (1912, p. 77)

'Naturally', the quotation from Finlay-Johnson continues, 'they found these in the works of Shakespeare' (p. 77); and it is perhaps in the three writers' engagement with this iconic author that the most significant implications of a commitment to play as a learning medium are revealed. By now, it should come as no surprise that Caldwell Cook, Finlay-Johnson and Hourd are completely opposed to what Caldwell Cook vividly describes as 'the spelling-bee' approach to Shakespeare, which has 'the boys all sitting in the stocks and spouting in turn' (1917, p. 191). 'We simply took a play of Shakespeare and acted it', Caldwell Cook recalls:

> We soon found that certain things had to be done, and that their doing was directed by the dramatist. The boys were interested in acting the play, and soon became interested in observing many things essentially connected with the acting of the play.
>
> (1917, p. 78)

Instead of regarding Shakespeare as some kind of formidable cultural obstacle to be approached with trepidation, Caldwell Cook and Finlay-Johnson greet the plays with the same robust, egalitarian enthusiasm that they bring to other works of literature. Using italics to emphasise his point, Caldwell Cook goes so far as to argue that students should base *all their English studies on their acting of the plays of Shakespeare* (p. 218). He is adamant about this and has no truck with those who might argue that the texts are too challenging for some students: if 'the study of Shakespeare in schools today' fails to be 'a means of encouraging self-expression' or 'the medium of much learning in literature and in life', he declares, 'the fault lies not in any want of appreciative power on the boys' [sic] part but in the ignorance and incompetence of narrow-minded teachers' (p. 221). Concerns that the language of Shakespeare might be an impediment to engagement are dismissed out of hand. They encourage what

Caldwell Cook despises as a 'hunting method' approach to the plays: 'that of taking a slice of thirty lines or so and proceeding to mince it into an unrecognizable slush' (p. 204). The power of Shakespeare's narratives, the depth of his characterisation and his consummate skills as a dramatist, will, Caldwell Cook argues – as Hourd was to argue for Homer – work their own magic on the imaginations of the students. Finlay-Johnson agrees. Observing that fourteen of her students chose copies of Shakespeare for their school prizes, she sees nothing remarkable in the fact that their 'favourites' were the Comedies, Histories and Roman plays (1912, p. 86).

'It would be difficult to over-estimate the emancipating work which Mr. Cook did at the Perse School, Cambridge', Hourd writes ten years after his death (1949, p. 92). She shares Caldwell Cook's and Finlay-Johnson's commitment to active engagement with Shakespeare. 'Children show that they understand the passage [from a particular play]', she argues, 'by their power to act and interpret it'. However, she issues a *caveat* that is particularly significant in terms of its implications for drama pedagogy. While agreeing with Caldwell Cook's dismissal of the 'hunting method' of encountering Shakespeare – a method through which, she writes, children are 'only catechised and rendered ignorant' – she warns that a teaching approach 'by which comprehension is never brought to the text' can be just as 'damaging to [students'] confidence' (p. 111). She is not as sanguine as Caldwell Cook or Finlay-Johnson about the linguistic challenges posed by a Shakespeare text. She cites as an example a critical incident from a lesson in which her students are acting Act Two Scene One from *Macbeth*, focusing on the line: *The labour we delight in physics pain.* Hourd recalls that the actor delivering the line gave an interpretation at the time which suggested that she understood what the word *physics* meant in that context; but later the girl confided that she could not actually define the meaning explicitly. The girl's frustration causes Hourd to reflect upon 'what it feels like to know something and know that you know it, but because you cannot explain it you have to behave as if you did not know it' (p. 113). Two ideological issues emerge from this reflection. One concerns the Cartesian assertion of the supremacy of cognition as a way of apprehending the world – *I think, therefore I am/I can explain, therefore I know* – and the other is to do with the way that powerful cultural voices (in this instance, Shakespeare) can reduce to silence those who are less certain of themselves. Hourd's response to the challenges posed by these issues is to call for the harnessing of art to the service of the imagination so that a child might learn to *feel* [my italics] 'with her senses awake' (p. 84). Let the girl only trust in her instinctive, emotional apprehension of the line delivered by Macbeth. The word *physics* will be thus transformed from 'what is not understood and feared' into 'what is understood and desired' (p. 93). It becomes the verbal equivalent of Vygotsky's stick/horse 'pivot' or – to use Louise Rosenblatt's metaphor – a 'live circuit . . . between reader and text' (1970, p. 25), which enables the girl to reach out to the common humanity she shares with Shakespeare. By so doing, she engages with the text as a source of affirmation and personal insight that will help her to negotiate her place in the world. 'This submission of personal needs to the imperative of reality, of personal meaning to objective understanding', Hourd declares, 'is the whole work of education' (1949, p. 115); and the purpose of literature is to 'provide a means towards a fuller development of personality – a means . . . of growth' (p. 13).

This principle governs Hourd's approach to drama pedagogy. Arguing that 'Audiences have their rights' and that they 'should not be expected to make allowances' (1949, p. 65), she suggests that public theatre performances should not be attempted by young people until they are at least sixteen years old. Until then, the balance of power between what she distinguishes as the *aesthetic* and the *psychological* aspects of drama should be decidedly with the latter. Drama has a 'double psychological function. It acts as a release of phantasy and also as a means of grasping reality'. By acting out ballads and stories, by writing their own versions of the *Iliad*, Hourd's students might well develop a sense of aesthetic appreciation and absorb a greater understanding of drama skills or the writer's craft; but the main purpose is 'to give these adolescents scope for a wider interpretation of their own personalities within these media' (p. 63) and achieve that 'meeting of man's solitary psyche with the reality of life outside him', which, for Hourd, signifies the act of creation (p. 173). This dual emphasis upon 'phantasy' and 'reality' in dramatic engagement is clearly seen in Hourd's approach to the teaching of Shakespeare. On the one hand, she encourages her students to let their imaginations engage freely with the text, rewriting the story in their own words (p. 114). On the other hand, acutely aware – as someone who had lived through a time of global conflict would be – of 'the struggle of man within the realities of his own nature' (p. 159), she encourages her war-time students to a political and ideological interpretation of the plays by inviting them, for example, to identify similarities between Hitler and Shakespeare's *Julius Caesar*. Recalling a reading of Brutus's description in Act Two Scene One of 'exhalations whizzing in the air' through the skies of Rome on the night before Caesar's assassination, Hourd comments: 'It gives a description of the nights now-a-days when the sky is illuminated by the gun-fire and the bombs' (1949, p. 112).

The psychological importance with which Hourd invests dramatic play, and her location of the creative act within a metaphysical landscape, which is the site for 'Jung's battle with the shadow' and 'Bunyan's struggle with Satan' (p. 159), recalls Schiller's advocacy of *Spieltrieb* as a means of healing the 'wound' that was 'inflicted upon modern man' by 'civilization' (Schiller, 1967, p. 33); and indeed, she has Schiller in mind, identifying his search for 'fruitful equilibrium' with what she sees as one of the principle tasks of the teacher: to remain 'alert at . . . a kind of zero-point – ready to move in the direction which will unite and fuse the antithetical points of his pupil's thought and being' (Hourd, 1949, p. 154). Arguing that 'a great deal has taken place since 1917 when *The Play Way* was published' and that 'especially through the findings of the psychologists we have come to understand more about child nature and expression' (p. 92), Hourd criticises Caldwell Cook for not affording the 'psychological' – perhaps, in the light of the reference to Schiller, a more appropriate word might be *metaphysical* – aspect of drama the importance she felt it deserved.

Both Finlay-Johnson and Caldwell Cook are more engaged with drama as a crafted art form than with the deeper philosophical implications of its pedagogy. While appreciative of what today might be called the transferable skills such as 'initiative and self-reliance' (Finlay-Johnson, 1912, p. 72), which dramatic play can encourage, and receptive to the educative potential of spontaneous improvisation (p. 129; Caldwell Cook, 1917, p. 82), they are far more willing than Hourd to include an awareness of the demands of an audience – albeit perhaps not an adult audience – (Finlay-Johnson, 1912, p. 7) in their students' experience of drama. Where Hourd suggests that presenting material effectively to an audience is too sophisticated a challenge for young people, Caldwell Cook welcomes the pressure such scrutiny brings, arguing that it provides an incentive for the players to pay acute attention to the content and form of the dramatised text. 'I consider a knowledge of stage-craft essential', he writes with reference to the teaching of Shakespeare, adding that what he means by this is 'a critical study of the dramatist's art and workmanship' (Caldwell Cook, 1917, p. 77). By interrogating literary texts – not only the plays of Shakespeare but epic poems like *Beowulf*, ballads and even nursery rhymes – from the dramatist's perspective, Caldwell Cook argues that students will engage with important craft issues such as interpretation, exposition, motivation, contrast and counterpoint:

> our purpose as teachers is to ensure that by the exercise of playmaking the boys [sic] shall become familiar with these very artistic conventions, and with the dramatic situations and characters which have become typical from their frequent occurrence in the literature we are taking as our model.
>
> (1917, pp. 271–272)

Like Hourd, Caldwell Cook cites an extract from *Julius Caesar* to illustrate his point; but whereas Hourd's example emphasises personal and ideological engagement, his focuses upon Shakespeare's dramatic craftsmanship: 'You could almost "dress" the whole play "Julius Caesar" correctly in the Elizabethan manner out of all the hats, cloaks, shoes, daggers, nightcaps, leather aprons, kerchiefs, tapers, letters, tools, and musical instruments that are mentioned' (1917, p. 206).

'I did not attempt to teach stagecraft', Finlay-Johnson declares (1912, p. 107); but it is the aesthetic power of the staged production that she focuses upon in her own descriptions of her work with Shakespeare. One can imagine what Hourd would have made of Act Four Scene One of *The Life and Death of King John*, for example, where Hubert and his henchmen enter Prince Arthur's prison cell with the intention of blinding him. Finlay-Johnson confines her commentary on the scene to an account of the aesthetic effects of the visual presentation created by the schoolboy actors: 'The two attendants draped themselves in window curtains (which looked like "villains' cloaks") and wore black paper masks – pieces of paper, with holes cut for eyes, tied round their heads' (p. 87).

Even the instruments of torture are described with the same sense of aesthetic relish: 'They carried a pail of coals such as road repairers use at night, and had two pieces of sharp iron stuck therein. The hot coals and red-hot irons were simulated with red chalk!' (p. 87).

If, as Vygotsky argues, the ability to 'combine elements to produce a structure, to combine the old in new ways' is a uniquely human skill, which is 'the basis of creativity' (2004, p. 13), then an argument could be made for suggesting that Finlay-Johnson's and Caldwell Cook's aesthetically focused approach to drama offers their students plentiful opportunities for creativity by giving them problems of stage craft to solve. As well as the use of 'red chalk' to represent 'red-hot irons' cited above, Finlay-Johnson describes approvingly how inkwells are transformed into 'breathing holes' for seals in a geographical simulation of a voyage to Newfoundland (1912, p. 136), or a chalk pit outside the school is commandeered as the setting for a re-enactment of General Wolfe's scaling of the Heights of Abraham in 1759, or a 'roll-call' is improvised to lend poignancy to a reading of Tennyson's poem *The Charge of the Light Brigade* (p. 118). Recalling how he and his boys 'made use of anything we could lay our hands on' in terms of 'the usual apparatus of a classroom', Caldwell Cook declares: 'If any class of playboys [sic] cannot stage a play with such a wealth of material they deserve to be spoon-fed' (1917, p. 191). The Vygotsky who wrote that the 'staging of drama provides the pretext and material for the most diverse forms of creativity on the part of . . . children' would have approved – up to a point.

The argument can only be taken so far, however. Crucially, what appears to be missing from Finlay-Johnson's and Caldwell Cook's practice is an explicit awareness of, or an explicit pedagogical engagement with, those powerful cognitive and ideological forces that Piaget and Vygotsky identified as at work in a child's manipulation of symbol. To a modern reader, Finlay-Johnson's description of the symbolic representation of a torture implement as if it were nothing more than a visually attractive response to an aesthetic challenge, appears strange to say the least; but her airy aside that *The Merchant of Venice*, performed in school, 'had, of course [sic], no historical connection to teach' (1912, p. 102), and her failure to make any comment at all about the issues of power and justice raised by her students' remarkable dramatisation of 'Wat Tyler's Rebellion' (lovingly reproduced over five pages of text in her book) seem to take Schiller's concept of *Schein* – the 'contemplation' as Langer put it 'of sensory qualities without their usual meanings' – to an extreme.

Even taking Finlay-Johnson on her own aesthetic terms, however, she seems, in her account of her 'dramatic method of teaching', to ignore so many of her students' impressive artistic achievements in manipulating content and form – for example in her 'girls'' creation and performance of a play called the *Execution of Mary Queen of Scots* (1912, pp. 109–116). To read this transcript now – written out from memory by one of the participants – is to note the sophisticated use of stage directions and choreography; the powerful moments of dramatic tension (as when Mary pauses, pen in hand, before signing her will); the subtle insights into motivation (when Lord Shrewsbury enters to tell Mary of her impending execution, he waits on her command to be admitted – on the day of the execution, the Sheriff just barges in); and, perhaps most significant of all, the evocative use of symbol:

> *Kent*: [Looking at the crucifix in the QUEEN'S hand] It would be much better advised of you to have Christ in your heart, and not in your hand, Madam.
>
> *Queen Mary*: I cannot hold such an object in my hand without my heart being attached to the sufferings it represents.
>
> (1912, p. 115)

This brief exchange seems to encapsulate the ideological struggle between Catholic and Protestant that informed the tragedy of Mary, Queen of Scots. Finlay-Johnson makes no reference to the considerable aesthetic skills described above but instead praises the girls for the costumes they created.

Caldwell Cook's failure to engage with issues that Piaget and Vygotsky regard as of prime importance is even more pronounced. One particularly interesting section of *The Play Way* (published the year after the posthumous appearance of Saussure's *Course in General Linguistics*) describes how he and his students explored what we might now describe as the semiotics of gesture and expression, going so far as to create their own symbolic actions to signify concepts and feelings. To read

Caldwell Cook's account of this work is to experience a sense of frustration: he seems to hover on the verge of saying something philosophically and aesthetically profound about the nature of communication:

> The description of gesture is a thankless task, because gesture chiefly exists to save description. Words, in any case, are cumbrous to explain movement. A simple wave of the hand may be talked about for a whole paragraph, and still not be made visible. An action may express hope, desire, anger, fear, despair. Words also may express hope, desire, anger, fear, despair. But the attempt to describe in words the feelings shown in the action is hopeless.
>
> (1917, p. 225)

But Caldwell Cook declines the challenge: 'I will not attempt to give descriptions of those gestures which we have used to express feeling of any kind', he declares, opting instead for something that might be considered easier: 'but will confine my detailed illustrations to those signs and symbols which we have devised to represent persons and things and simple ideas' (p. 225). Even these supposedly simpler challenges are, potentially, enormously rich in the opportunities for cognitive, linguistic and ideological insight that they afford: '*King* is indicated by making a plain circle round one's head. Preceded or followed by the sign for "woman", this means "queen"; and in conjunction with the sign for "boy" it means "prince"' (p. 225).

What might Saussure, Piaget or Vygotsky have made of such material? It was to be another sixty-three years before Keir Elam's first edition of *The Semiotics of Theatre and Drama* was to engage fully with the ideas that Caldwell Cook seems to be groping towards here.

Both Finlay-Johnson and Caldwell Cook take it as a point of honour that they will not try to direct their students' creativity: 'instead of letting the teacher originate or conduct the play', Finlay-Johnson recalls, 'I demanded that, just as the individual himself must study nature and not have it studied for him, the play must be the child's own' (1912, p. 7). 'With such a game as this [drawing a map of an imaginary island] in hand', Caldwell Cook declares, 'a boy will work industriously for hours. "To what end?" I may be asked. I don't know. It may end in anything. Certainly, you cannot claim to have definitely *taught* a boy something' (1917, p. 142).

One of the reasons for this reluctance to assume the teacher's conventional role is that, fundamentally, both Finlay-Johnson and Caldwell Cook subscribe to Richardson's *transcendental* account of childhood authority and wisdom (both Wordsworth and the neo-Platonist poet Henry Vaughan are quoted in *The Play Way*). Liberal as their pedagogy might seem, particularly when located within the context of their times, they are both conservators rather than innovators at heart. 'Your true revolutionary' Caldwell Cook writes in an attempt at circle squaring, 'is only a conservative endowed with insight' (1917, p. 12). Like many other contemporary commentators upon creativity and the arts (Mathieson, 1975) – notably the novelist D.H. Lawrence (1885–1930) – they hankered for a return to what Coleridge describes in the *Anima Poetae* as 'the spiritual, Platonic old England' (1895): an organic community united by shared values and untainted by the Industrial Revolution. 'Heaven forbid!' Finlay-Johnson declares, recoiling from the very idea that she might ever be involved in 'training business men' (1912, p. 17). 'Owing to the blindness of our educators', Caldwell Cook complains, in an oblique criticism of suburban life, 'the gap is ever widening between work and play' (1917, p. 271) so that the one becomes 'mere drudgery' and the other is 'gradually thinned out until little is left to them [children] as adults but a round of golf or a game of cards' (1917, p. 4). Like Piaget, Finlay-Johnson and Caldwell Cook identify play as a means by which children 'protect' themselves against 'forced accommodation to ordinary reality'; but where Piaget sees dynamism, they see stasis. Piaget (1951) regards play as a necessary rite of passage through which the ego must pass on its journey towards accommodation with the external world. To Finlay-Johnson and Caldwell Cook, with their *transcendental* vision of childhood, however, play is a refuge for innocence and imagination; and as such, it should be preserved for as long as possible. 'Am I wrong', Finlay-Johnson asks rhetorically, 'when I claim that childhood should be a time for merely absorbing big stores of sunshine for possible future dark times?' (1912, pp. 13–14). This desire to preserve, to seek refuge, informs their school practice: for Finlay-Johnson, engagement with Shakespeare offers 'a way of escape from a sordid world of toil and worldly gain' (p. 85). Caldwell Cook argues that 'a conscious pursuit of realism is inadvisable for boys' and therefore they 'should not be encouraged to take for their material any themes which are not essentially romantic' (1917, pp. 271, 272). It is significant that both teachers established physical refuges for the students in their schools: *Tig's Shed* for Finlay-Johnson and *The Mummery* for Caldwell Cook. Like all the commentators cited in the book so far, Caldwell Cook and Finlay-Johnson believe that children develop in clearly defined stages: both feel that, by fourteen, the magical time has ended: 'There I shall hand him over', Caldwell Cook writes, 'we must leave our playboy [sic] to become a student' (p. 301). Brief, precious, fragile, inspired and driven by the children's own creative desires – it is understandable why an adult might feel reluctant to enter such territory and attempt to control it.

A second reason for Caldwell Cook's and Finlay-Johnson's reluctance to intervene pedagogically in their students' drama work is because, ultimately, as the subtitles of their books suggest, they regard drama as a means to an end rather than as an end in itself. Finlay-Johnson's drama simulation set in a 'post-office', for example, is designed to teach 'the writing of letters (composition), directing of envelopes, a little geography in the correct placing of the various towns, and arithmetic' (1912, p. 174). 'Playmaking', Caldwell Cook declares, 'is a helpful device by which the study of history and of literature can be brought together and understood in a live relation' (1917, p. 274). Like Finlay-Johnson, he creates a range of simulations both in and outside the classroom for his boys to practise a wide variety of vocational skills.

Much as Hourd might argue that thinking had moved on in the three decades between the publication of *The Play Way* and her own book, she shares her predecessors' reluctance to intervene pedagogically in students' engagement with drama. Partly, as the quotation cited earlier about the need to afford the child a 'continued period of full dramatic play' suggests, this is because Hourd is not unsympathetic towards the *transcendental* vision of childhood. She is just as willing as Finlay-Johnson or Caldwell Cook to set her face against the dislocation of work from creativity supposedly characteristic of twentieth-century industrial society: 'The young child is often compelled to live in a world of postmen and steam engines, "as though his whole vocation were endless imitation"' (1949, p. 11). She neatly evades curriculum issues regarding the 'stagecraft' that Caldwell Cook regarded as 'essential' by, as noted earlier, arguing that young people are not really ready to engage with the aesthetics or the skills of theatrical performance until late into adolescence (1949, p. 63). One consequence of this approach is that, although Hourd advocates classroom use of a wide range of drama strategies and experiences, from play-reading to theatre trips to puppetry – the latter being particularly efficacious, apparently, for the 'backward and difficult child' (p. 69) – she does not provide any details about how these experiences and skills are to be mediated and developed in the classroom. Like Finlay-Johnson and Caldwell Cook, Hourd sees drama, ultimately, as a means rather than an end. As for her predecessors, one of its purposes is to encourage transferable skills. Play reading, for example, will help to develop 'poise and confidence' (p. 69). Most importantly, however, drama is to help unlock literary texts – not, primarily, to encourage that sense of aesthetic and craft appreciation valued by Finlay-Johnson and Caldwell Cook – but so that young people can engage with the powers of *figurative language* and, by doing so, come to a clearer psychological understanding of their own place in the world. 'There is no art form where the sense of our own personalities is more keenly alive than in the drama' she writes. 'It is surely this paradox of losing oneself to gain oneself which has always made drama such a great moral as well as intellectual force' (p. 37). And, again, in words reminiscent of Piaget (whose works she knew) and Vygotsky (whose works she did not know): 'Dramatisation is at once the means by which he [the child] ventures out into the characters and lives of others, and the means by which he draws these back as symbols into the person of himself' (p. 26).

The drama teacher's task is to create propitious opportunities for such encounters – and then stand back. Echoing John Ruskin's (1819–1900) criticism of that 'composing legalism' (p. 82), which allows rules and conventions to dominate imagination and creativity, she asks: 'Have we any right to allow a child to seek her own satisfaction through the subjective distortions of other men's meanings?' (p. 109).

Chapter 4

A high art form in its own right
Peter Slade and child drama

The previous chapter has considered how three teachers with a particular interest in subject English responded to the pedagogical potential of classroom drama in the first half of the twentieth century. I want now to throw their ideas into relief by comparing them with those of Peter Slade (1912–2008), a practitioner whose primary focus was not English but drama itself and whose first book, *Child Drama*, was published five years after Hourd's *The Education of the Poetic Spirit*. Slade's academic background was, initially, in German, Economics and Philosophy; but he became world-famous as a pioneer of dramatherapy, as a champion of children's theatre and as an educator of drama teachers.

Like the works of Finlay-Johnson, Caldwell Cook and Hourd explored earlier, *Child Drama* is unequivocally on the side of children and implacably opposed to the 'bashing-in method of teaching' (1954, p. 98), which compels young people 'to suffer from the stormcloud of the exam, hanging there dark and sinister, night and day' (p. 76). Like Froebel, Piaget and Vygotsky, Slade studies the behaviour of children closely and discerns – from the earliest age – a capacity for the construction and negoti-ation of meanings. Like Piaget again, Slade attributes to even the youngest children a natural impulse towards the aesthetic: 'many of the earliest experiments of the baby', he writes, 'are embryonic forms of Drama, Art and Music, and so differ from mere copying' (p. 20).

If Finlay-Johnson, Caldwell Cook and Hourd reveal sympathy with the *transcen-dental* vision of childhood, Slade endorses it with an enthusiasm bordering on reverence. In words that recall the sentiments expressed in Traherne's poem *Wonder* and Wordsworth's *Intimations of Immortality*, he argues that the 'Child's [sic] world is quite different from ours' (p. 267) and that it is the duty of adults to introduce children to 'our world' (p. 82). Like Finlay-Johnson, Caldwell Cook and Hourd, again, Slade views that adult world with distaste as a place of 'apparently mad demands' (p. 42.) Without that 'boisterous humour' that 'is one of the endearing qualities of Childhood', Slade asks, 'how would they [children] get through?' (p. 222). Even more so than for the three English practitioners described in Chapter 3, Slade's sympathy towards the *transcendental* vision of childhood necessitates a reconfigura-tion of the power relationship between teacher and taught, which virtually positions the adult as an admiring onlooker: 'Any bond built between youth and age is a tender, breakable thing. We are allowed to share more if we do not expect too much. But what we can do is pause to sympathise and admire' (p. 83).

Echoing Wordsworth again, Slade declares: 'it is we who must learn. The Children teach us' (p. 278). This is as true for the drama classroom as for any other school subject: 'all that is wanted is a place where Children go to the Land, [of Child Drama] with the help of an understanding adult' (p. 296). As for Finlay-Johnson and Caldwell Cook, this metaphorical 'Land' of refuge and escape is given a physical expression that radically reconfigures the traditional conception of the classroom as a learning space. Where Finlay-Johnson has *Tig's Shed* and Caldwell Cook *The Mummery*, Slade proposes, as 'an *urgent necessity*' [original italics], the establishment of a national network of 'Play Centres' (p. 243) and fills his own *Pete's Kitchen* with props, costumes and musical instruments – 'things to make you want to be all sorts of wonderful people, and dare most mighty deeds' (p. 293).

Slade's comments on play might have been taken straight from the writings of Caldwell Cook. Like his predecessor, he argues that it is 'inborn and vital' (p. 41), 'one of the most strenuous and creative forms of work' (p. 42), which 'may be the correct approach to all forms of education' (p. 42) and – employing a list of active verbs to emphasise his point – is central to the child's apprehension of the world: 'Play is the Child's way of thinking, proving, relaxing, working, remembering, daring, testing, creating and absorbing. Except for the actual physical processes, it is life' (p. 42).

Child Drama contains several accounts of Slade's play-interactions with young people. They graphically demonstrate the extent to which he was prepared to live by his principles. Perhaps the most 'remarkable experience' (p. 249) – to use Slade's own description – recalls a series of spontaneous role-play improvisations conducted with 'a Child of seven and a half years' (p. 248). Slade, writing here as *Self* – his comments on the action are reproduced in italics below – sets the scene for the improvisation by playing a recording of the music for the ballet *The Three Cornered Hat* by the Spanish composer, Manuel de Falla:

> *Child*:   Ooh, music! Come on, let's play.
> *Self*:   I'm making a pudding.
> *Child*:   That's because you're a wild animal. You eat little children. Spit out the bones!
> *The Child then watched me eating Children, and started to copy rather badly. Through lack of help and practice it had lost some ability to create easily. I stopped, therefore, and the Child stopped too.*
> *Child*:   Go on.
> *Self*:   There are no more bones. *(I hoped the Child would invent the next thing.)*
> *The Child lay on its back. I moved away. Suddenly the Child ran across the room and leapt at me. Things were warming up.*
> *Child*:   Aha! I'm a savijanimal [sic], a very savijanimal. I'm killing you now because you've been naughty.
> *I was dragged to the sofa and eaten in time to the music. I was glad the spitting out the bones was not copied. My bones were pulled out like large fish bones and laid in a row. The record ended.*
>
> (p. 246)

The critical incident Slade recalls here can be described as high risk for all sorts of reasons, some of which Slade himself may not have imagined at the time. One can only speculate as to why a seven-year-old girl would respond so violently to a musical stimulus that is meant to be comic in tone (later, in what Slade calls this 'Play [sic] to Music Background' (p. 249), his role-play character, 'Captain Hook', is 'crucified' – twice). What is clear is Slade's absolute commitment to a reconfiguration of the power relationship between adult and child and his absolute determination to work with whatever context, role or content that child chooses to bring to the drama, no matter how questionable it might seem. No attempt is made to step out of role in order either to reflect upon what is happening in the drama or to reassert adult authority and impose direction: Slade operates exclusively within the power perimeters established by the improvisation. When his rejection of the child's initial invitation ('let's play') is immediately swept aside by her fierce switch of context from domesticity ('I'm making a pudding') to fairy-tale nightmare ('You eat little children. Spit out the bones!'), he accepts both this raising of the dramatic stakes and her imposition upon him of the role of monster and outcast. Slade remains true to his declared principle that the teacher can only guide and suggest a route 'out of eternal blood to hope and constructive adventure' (p. 74). When his attempt to move the role-play in a more positive direction ('There are no more bones') is rejected by the girl, he resigns himself to being 'eaten in time to the music'– the lowest of low-status victims in a particularly striking piece of evidence to support Fleming's assertion that child play and ritual are closely linked. What de Falla would have thought about this response to his music, one can only wonder.

Slade's near reverence for children's dramatic play highlights another important connection between his work and that of Caldwell Cook, Finlay-Johnson and Hourd, which has not been considered here yet: a distrust of theatre. Rousseau fulminated against any kind of education that encourages young people to pretend to feel what they do not actually feel – no matter how such pretence might help to oil the wheels of daily social intercourse. Emile, Rousseau boasts, knows only honesty of expression:

> He has never said, 'I love you dearly,' till he knew what it was to love; he has never been taught what expression to assume when he enters the room of his father, his mother, or his sick tutor; he has not learnt the art of affecting a sorrow he does not feel.
>
> (1911, p. 183)

Where better, Rousseau argues, to learn how to identify and thus protect oneself against such dissembling than in the place where human beings are taught to pretend and to beguile for a living – the theatre? What for Schiller is a site of *Spieltrieb* is for Rousseau something very different: 'The stage is not made for truth; its object is to flatter and amuse; there is no place where one can learn so completely the art of pleasing and of interesting the human heart (p. 309).

Much as Caldwell Cook values the study of 'stagecraft' and Finlay-Johnson delights in her students' performances of Shakespeare and their own plays, one of the reasons why they are both so reticent about explicitly teaching theatre skills is because they fear that to do so would be to privilege what Hourd described as the 'rights' of an audience over the students' personal engagement with their material. Caldwell Cook observes:

> The advice I would offer to the teacher in the matter of the boys' delivery is 'Let well alone.' There are of course scores of things one *could* tell them, but they are

not necessary. . . . The obvious danger is that so soon as you mention delivery, or give any directions, you set the boys thinking of how they are speaking instead of giving their entire attention to what they are saying.

(1917, p. 108)

Finlay-Johnson compares unfavourably the 'trained trickery' of 'many actors' (1912, p. 107) with the untutored performance of Shakespeare's *As You Like It* prepared voluntarily by her own students. Demonstrating something of that tolerance seen in the critical incident described earlier by Slade, she insists that the child's experience is of prime importance:

> instead of letting the teacher originate or conduct the play, I demanded that, just as the individual himself must study nature and not have it studied for him, the play must be the child's own. However crude the action or dialogue from the adult's point of view, it would fitly express the stage of development arrived at by the child's mind, and would therefore be valuable *to him* [sic] as a vehicle of expression and assimilation (which is, after all, what we need), rather than a finished product pleasing to the more cultivated mind of an adult, and perhaps uninteresting to a child.
>
> (1912, p. 7)

Neither Finlay-Johnson, Caldwell Cook nor Hourd would deny for a moment the aesthetic power of theatre. Finlay-Johnson observes that the production of *As You Like It* that she so much admired only '*approached* [my italics] pure art' (1912, p. 107) and even argues that 'the illuminating acting and impressive delivery of some great Shakespearean actor' (p. 105) can inspire a love of the plays. Hourd concedes that 'the final work of art depends chiefly upon the operation of form' (1949, p. 170); but she warns that too early an introduction to its intricate conventions might have a negative effect upon the creativity of a young child: 'Let us take care that we do not force his expression into moulds which are too complicated for his forms. This is a real danger of the public performance of the junior play' (p. 67).

What is, for Finlay-Johnson, Caldwell Cook and Hourd, a matter to be noted with caution becomes for Slade an issue of fiercely defended principle. He shares Rousseau's moral concerns about the theatre, echoing Finlay-Johnson's choice of words in observing that 'in order to provide an interesting picture' (1949, p. 91) on the 'stage of the West End . . . a good deal of trickery has to be used' (pp. 90–91). A child's expression of an interest in theatre should be a cause for alarm because it is a sign that 'audiences and trickery' have entered 'its mental development' (p. 91). Anticipating Boal, Slade argues that the child 'is actor *and* audience in one': to privilege the concerns of the latter is to 'violently upset' the 'balance' between the two so that the three most precious qualities of child drama – absorption, sincerity and commitment – are lost and 'showing off immediately begins' (1954, p. 58). Slade expresses particular antipathy towards the proscenium arch stage that dominated commercial theatres at the time, going so far as to assert that 'the proscenium form of theatre has disastrous effects on the genuine Drama of the Child [sic]' (p. 44). For Slade, the proscenium theatre is the physical embodiment of that ideological force, described at the start of this book, that is antithetical to the *transcendental* vision of childhood and that, literally and metaphorically, seeks to impose adult restrictions upon a child's way of seeing and upon what Slade felt to be its natural propensity for creativity and movement: 'Most people know the type of theatre where you merely sit and watch; when the curtains open you are expected to look, when they shut you stop looking' (p. 84).

The 'showing off' encouraged by acting for an audience might be bad enough; but for a child to be a *member* of an audience is to signal something tantamount to spiritual and moral capitulation: 'Nothing is more cruel than to force Children to sit as audience when others are playing. If they want to, then things have gone very far wrong – we have already suppressed them' (p. 58).

There is a second as yet unaddressed area of connection between Slade, Finlay-Johnson and Caldwell Cook that needs to be considered here. The innate conservatism that Caldwell Cook detects in his own pedagogical philosophy can be seen in each of the three practitioners' attitude towards culture. This may seem surprising, given Finlay-Johnson's welcoming of home literacies or Caldwell Cook's sensitivity to the power that a teacher's language can exercise in the classroom. In addition, Caldwell Cook is willing to range far beyond the English literary canon in search of 'tales fit for playmaking', including the Hindu *Mahabharata* and the Egyptian *Book of the Dead* (1917, p. 273) as well as stories from Greek and Norse mythology. Slade, too, is sensitive to home literacies and, despite his criticisms of staged productions, catholic in his celebration of Chinese and Japanese theatre, *Commedia dell'Arte* as well as the music of the Blues. He even acknowledges the value of popular cultural forms such as cinema and comics, noting that both share a potential for helping children engage with narrative structures.

Having conceded these points, it must be said that Finlay-Johnson, Caldwell Cook and Slade all draw a distinction between what they perceive to be high and low forms of culture and that they consider drama to be a force for the former which has the potential to neutralise the potentially deleterious influences of the latter. Finlay-Johnson writes: 'The workingman need not necessarily – because he is a workingman – blow hideous noises and rude songs on a cornet, and generally make an exhibition of himself while on his annual "outing"' (1912, p. 85).

One of the reasons why Finlay-Johnson values the teaching of Shakespeare is because she believes exposure to his plays can help to tame the working classes:

> I have seen in my own village workingmen – including farm and garden labourers – who could not only sit through an evening of Shakespearean plays as spectators with intelligent enjoyment, but who could and did themselves give a splendid rendering of 'Julius Caesar.'
>
> (1912, p. 86)

There is 'more need for inculcating this love of nature and good literature in the mind of the workingman's child', Finlay-Johnson writes, 'than in that of the child of higher station' (p. 125). The political implications of the 'workingmen's' choice of play seems to have been lost on her. 'The representation of a story without the use of spoken words is all that is common between the two', Caldwell Cook declares, in response to the suggestion that his dramatic mime work resembles the new-fangled silent movie. 'To attempt any closer comparison', he continues, swiping out at a second medium of popular culture in the process, 'would be as false as to compare the cartoons of

Raphael with the cartoons in the *Daily Mirror* because both are drawings!' (1917, p. 228). Like Finlay-Johnson, Caldwell Cook believes that drama has the capacity to neutralise potentially disruptive elements in society. Boys – and he always does mean boys – who experience 'the play way' are less likely to become 'characterless units of a mob' (1917, p. 37).

Writing more than three decades later, in the aftermath of two global wars and Communist revolution, Slade holds to a similar position. Distinguishing between 'cultured Child Drama' and 'the Drama of the street' (1954, p. 70), he uses a Froebelian image to argue that adults must nurture the former 'much as a gardener cultivates a flower' in order to prevent the 'weeds' of the latter – 'fighting, getting hurt, cruelty, rudeness' – which are to be 'found often in the streets and playground' (p. 45). 'Successful Child Drama', Slade asserts, using a topical reference to emphasise his point, can provide 'a legal out-let for the atom-bomb energy of that social group we call the gang' (p. 150). Without its protection, adolescent girls will become 'emotionally unstable, often unreliable, giggly, and often addicted to an inhibited form of jive, bebop or the current craze in hot dancing' (p. 123). As for the 'lad who has had little Drama at school', he is 'quite frankly, in many instances a lout' addicted to cigarettes and 'hot swing' (p. 124).

It can seem too easy to judge a past society by contemporary standards; and English teachers familiar with the writings of F.R. Leavis (1895–1978) will know that the distrust of popular culture and energy displayed by Finlay-Johnson, Caldwell Cook and Slade here was not uncommon in educational circles at the time, particularly among those who, like Slade, had witnessed Hitler's and Stalin's ability to harness the popular will through manipulation of the mass media (Mathieson, 1975). Nevertheless, there were other ways of thinking about culture and society available to these early advocates of educational drama, and the fact that they chose this particular ideological position must be acknowledged as part of their legacy. The same point has to be made about the crude gender stereotyping revealed in Slade's reference to emotionally unstable girls and loutish lads. Finlay-Johnson displays it too when she declares, for example: 'Naturally [sic] in historical plays boys' parts predominated, but the girls did their full share of assisting in the preparation for them and in making notes of all the scenes which had to be compiled or invented' (1912, p. 27). It is probably not surprising that Caldwell Cook takes an even more extreme position. Arguing that 'it is not by any means certain that even Shakespeare's female characters are best acted by women', he declares that to 'have a well-shaped young woman mincing [sic] about the stage on high heels, with her legs clad in pink tights, may be good ballet or "revue," but it is most certainly not Shakespeare.' 'Girls', he concludes, 'have no initiative' (1917, p. 257). Observing that 'There is the masculine component in every girl, and the feminine in every boy' (1949, p. 15), and that 'Teachers whose reading of English literature stops at Thomas Hardy cannot hope to keep pace with the modern schoolgirl or boy' (p. 141), Hourd's discourse on gender and culture is far more nuanced; but even she focuses her girls' attention upon the 'great dramatic writing' (p. 60) of canonical literature.

Slade clearly espoused enthusiastically many of the values and attitudes of Finlay-Johnson, Caldwell Cook and Hourd. He even subscribed to their argument that drama could be put to the service of specific academic subjects and, through the development of transferable skills, to the whole educational experience. 'Children who have frequent opportunities for drama and creating of their own kind', he writes, 'not only equal the success of other Children, but frequently surpass them – even in scholastic attainment' (1954, pp. 54–55). Through Child Drama, Slade asserts, young people can develop emotional and moral qualities such as understanding, sympathy, faith, confidence and resourcefulness (p. 106). Deployed in the music lesson, drama can encourage the understanding of movement and rhythm; while its use in English and history classrooms can help introduce young people to 'the richest material in literature, history and human experience throughout the world' (p. 114).

Having said this, however, it is important to note that Slade made several significant contributions to drama pedagogy that Finlay-Johnson, Caldwell Cook and Hourd did not address. Although not averse to using the *What's in it for me?* argument to buy curriculum favour for drama from more sceptical educationalists, Slade went far beyond his predecessors by boldly declaring – the importance of the statement emphasised by the use of italics – '*Child Drama is an Art in itself, and would stand by that alone as being of importance*' (p. 105). Slade's assertion of this key principle obliged him to confront some difficult tensions. On the one hand, he had a deep distrust of conventional contemporary theatre and its techniques; and his *transcendental* vision of childhood inclined him to a *sui generis* account of the 'Art' of 'Child Drama' – as the following quotation makes clear: '"All our own." That is the best description of Child Drama. It belongs *entirely* [original italics] to them [the child creators]' (p. 224). On the other hand, Slade had to acknowledge that – in the words of Mihaly Csíkszentmihályi – 'Original thought does not exist in a vacuum. It must operate on a set of already existing objects, rules, representations or notations' (1999, p. 315).

One of Slade's major claims to significance is that, reluctantly or not, he took up the challenge of thinking through just what exactly the 'domain' (Csíkszentmihályi, 1999, p. 314) of Child Drama might contain. Thus, like so many writers on child development before him – not least Rousseau, Froebel and Piaget – Slade attempts, in his first book, to create a conceptual map of what that development might look like in terms of a young person's staged, incremental encounter with drama. Focusing his developmental model upon two critical points in a child's life (ages six and thirteen) at which they experience a 'dawn of seriousness' (Slade, 1954, pp. 12, 75), Slade identifies a number of staging posts upon the child's journey into drama. Here – to take just one example as illustration – is his surprisingly catholic account of the young person's 'development towards play-writing':

> Play; Dramatic Play; improvisations; polished improvisations; some words written down; stories and dialogues copied from films, radio and life experiences; improved expression (coming from Language Flow) and improved writing ability mix with improvisation and begin to equal it. Out of this last stage comes a tolerably good written play. The age – *not in the junior school* [original italics], but *circa* thirteen years upwards.
>
> (p. 66)

I have deliberately chosen 'play-writing' as an example here because it is important to note that, for all his mistrust of the proscenium arch and its connotations, Slade devotes a chapter of *Child Drama* to the concept of *Child Theatre*. He is not averse to young people being taught theatre skills when they have reached the requisite stage of maturity and development. In fact, towards the end of the chapter on *Child Theatre*, employing a noun one might not expect someone sympathetic to the *transcendental* view of childhood to use, he lists seventeen techniques necessary for the '*training* [my italics] for the type of theatre we were going to develop'. These include references to movement, body posture, speech, creation of 'atmosphere' and an ability to engage with both 'comedy' and 'serious scenes' (p. 282).

Equally significant is Slade's attempt to provide a metalanguage for the domain of Child Drama. His book opens with a glossary of key terms, ranging from the metaphysical (*happiness-development, dawn of seriousness*) to the psychological (*group intuition, hinterland activity*) to the technical (*in-the-round, language flow*) (pp. 12–14). Most important in this context are Slade's thoughts about the concept of *play*. Where Finlay-Johnson and Caldwell Cook offer consistently enthusiastic but ultimately rather nebulous endorsements of its qualities, Slade attempts a more sustained scrutiny of what he, just as much as his predecessors, believes 'may be the correct approach to all forms of education' (p. 42).

First, Slade describes a young child's *Running Play*: an exuberant glorying in the physical, *point-mode* pleasures of movement and unleashed energy (pp. 13–14). So far, so consistently *transcendental*; but Slade's vision is more nuanced and problematic than this initial account of care free indulgence suggests. Even the 'elementary testing experience' of babies, he observes, 'is often a grim business' (p. 30); and while *Child's Play* (Slade is careful to put the emphasis on the italicised first word) can be 'a state of great satisfaction, bringing with it a feeling of accomplishment' (p. 31), this feeling will only be 'complete' if 'emotional experience balances with exterior experience' (p. 30). Working from this binary, Slade describes a continuum bounded, respectively, by *Personal* and *Projected Play*, the former being more concerned with 'inner Self [sic] and personal mastery, *though outward material things may be used* [my italics]' and the latter reaching towards those 'outward material things' and 'their organisation'. It is 'the flow between them' that 'makes possible, in part, the ultimate process of ideas becoming conscious' and that provides 'the harmony and the intense beauties of the growing Child' (p. 67). For Slade, therefore, play is fundamentally informed by a dynamic tension between an inward and an outward impulse. On the one hand, he can share Piaget's almost Wordsworthian description of play as a means for the child to escape 'the full brunt of a particularly worldly experience which it is not yet ready to face' (p. 42); but on the other hand – and here again he echoes Piaget and, implicitly, Vygotsky, too – Slade concedes that play offers a powerful and necessary means of socialisation and accommodation with others: 'the terrible test', as he so tellingly puts it, 'of sharing what is loved' (p. 32). I have deliberately used the verb 'concedes' in the previous sentence: Slade's ultimate loyalties lie with Personal Play because it focuses inward upon the concerns of the holistic, individual child as absorbed creator and source of innate wisdom; whereas Projected Play reaches outwards to the social and material world and therefore inevitably demands compromise, co-operation and submission to externally imposed rules. The complex and problematic relationship between Personal and Projected Play is highlighted in Slade's account of the advantages and disadvantages of using puppets with children. Like Hourd before him, he acknowledges that puppets can help the shy, unconfident or inarticulate to shift the focus of attention from themselves by *projecting* their concerns and preoccupation outwards onto an artefact which, by standing-in as their representative, as it were, offers the child the chance of a safe, staged entrance into engagement with the social world. Over-reliance on the use of puppets in this way, Slade cautions, is to be avoided because it 'brings the habit of seeking cover' and by doing so, encourages the child to renounce the 'adventures of personal Play' (1954, p. 316). It may be significant that Slade chooses a discussion of puppets – one of the most vivid examples of theatrical artifice with their ideological connotations of conformity and manipulation – to issue a ringing endorsement of Personal Play:

> The Children [for whom puppets become 'a sort of fetish'] spend far too much time in projected Play and can become quiet, wide-eyed and odd, instead of healthily using their whole bodies, speaking out as themselves, or courageously and personally being different people (personal Play).
>
> (p. 316)

The point about 'using their whole bodies' is particularly important. Long before the American psychologist James Jerome Gibson articulated his theory of 'affordance' (1977), Finlay-Johnson, Caldwell Cook and Hourd were thinking radically about how the classroom might be reconfigured as a space owned by children rather than adults. As the earlier description of *Pete's Kitchen* suggests, Slade shared their vision – but he took it much further by identifying, celebrating and nurturing the young child's propensity for free, exuberant physical movement. Furthermore, Slade invested children's use of space with a particular meaning-making authority by linking their use of 'the circle, the spiral, the cross, the square, the S shape, the triangle and the zigzag' with archetypal Jungian symbols such as 'ships, water, cats, men, houses, children, women, stars, the moon, trees and fish' (1954, p. 50). Thus, Slade brought together, through the medium of play, two crucial elements of drama: *point-mode* absorption and engagement with symbolic form. This is perhaps one of the most significant aspects of his legacy to drama pedagogy.

There are however two final contributions made by Slade that ought to be examined here. One is positive, the other less so. To consider the positive first: Slade asserted the claim for drama to be taken seriously as a subject of study and research. Where Finlay-Johnson and Caldwell Cook, particularly, describe their drama practice in a series of uncritical and sometimes self-congratulatory anecdotes, Slade – as the quoted example of his encounter with the 'Child of seven and a half years' explored earlier suggests – offers a more forensic and detached account of his practical work, one that is supplemented by transcripts and a critical commentary that is far from self-aggrandising in tone. Where the reader has to take on trust that Finlay-Johnson's, Caldwell Cook's and even Hourd's classroom practice was as successful as their narratives claim, Slade tries to let the children speak for themselves and to describe what happened without, seemingly, attempting to gloss the events in his favour. The pedagogical implications for future practitioners are important: by transforming critical incidents from his practice into recorded texts, Slade opens them up to deconstruction, replication, scrutiny and reconfiguration. No less importantly, he is suggesting that educational drama is robust enough to bear the weight of discourses more rigorous and objective than personal anecdote.

A more problematic aspect of Slade's legacy, however, is the model of teaching he bequeaths. Perhaps this is inevitably the case when charismatic practitioners with an intensely personal pedagogic vision attempt to share that practice with others less charismatic and less intuitively engaged with that vision than they are. Part of the problem stems from Slade's sympathy for the *transcendental* view of childhood with its implied reconfiguration of the power relationship between teacher and taught: if the child is innately wise, then it follows that 'it is we [adults] who must learn. The Children teach us'; and from that position, it is a small step to declaring: 'A Drama expert is not necessary to help develop Child Drama' or that 'some of the best work with Children is done by experienced teachers *who really understand what they are doing* [original italics], and yet, strangely enough, have very little knowledge of Drama' (p. 271).

Statements such as these sit uneasily beside Slade's sustained attempts to chart the domain of drama as an art form. Although *Part Two* of *Child Drama* is 'dedicated' to 'all teachers' with 'profound respect' (p. 129), one can imagine just how confusing such vagueness and inconsistency might seem to the student teacher faced with a mixed-ability class of thirty or more children – especially if they are not prepared to interpret Slade's exhortation to 'be free and energetic enough to make our *own* [original italics] fare if we want to' (p. 270) in quite the Wordsworthian manner he imagined. It is all very well to tell an inexperienced would-be practitioner that 'Absorption' and 'Sincerity' (pp. 12, 14) are the goals they must aim for in their drama lessons; but if subject expertise is not expected from the teacher and if it is up to the children to make their 'own fare if they want to', where does that leave the key elements of effective pedagogy: content knowledge and application, planned progression, differentiation, classroom management, formative and summative assessment?

Appraising Slade's legacy thirty years after the publication of *Child Drama*, Gavin Bolton argues that the (mis)application of his vision had actually worked against the cause by encouraging the belief 'that pure, undisciplined self-expression should be the basis for dramatic education' (1984, p. 7). 'Even today', Bolton observes, 'vast numbers of schools have no drama at all. This is due in part to a legacy of preciousness that the subject has inherited' (p. 9). Referencing one of two *desiderata* cherished by supporters of the *transcendental* vision of childhood – the second comes in for attack in the quotation below – Bolton suggests that Slade's procedures represent 'Romantic *child-centredness* [my italics] at its purest'. He does not mean this to be taken as a compliment: 'The activity of Child Drama appeared to be without content and without form and the drama lesson without structure apart from a loose sequence of relaxing and releasing activity followed by *unfettered dramatic playing* [my italics]' (1984, p. 35).

Chapter 5

From noun to verb

Growth through English or development through drama?

The years following the Second World War brought an intensification of interest in the pedagogy of English teaching. This was precipitated partly by the war itself – many of the writers had seen active service and been obliged, as a consequence, to rethink their views on the nature and purpose of education – and partly by the introduction, in 1944, of the 'Butler' Education Act, whose tripartite system of schooling gave new impetus to the debate about the kind of English curriculum appropriate for the children of an entire nation, not just for those from an academic elite.

Two events from this period are of particular significance. One is the seminar convened for North American and British teachers of English at Dartmouth, New Hampshire in 1966, the findings from which were reported a year later in John Dixon's *Growth Through English*. The second is the publication in 1975 of the almost 600-page-long enquiry into English teaching entitled *A Language for Life* (DES, 1975) but more commonly known, after its chairman, as *The Bullock Report*. One particularly resonant metaphor encapsulates the thinking represented by these two landmark events: that of the *dais*. Frank Whitehead, one of the most prominent contributors to the debate at the time, employed the term in the title of his influential study *The Disappearing Dais*, which was published in the year of the Dartmouth Seminar; and, in his 1967 report on the latter, Dixon took up the image, observing that one of the aims of the seminar had been to replace the 'disappearing dais' with 'the round table' (1967, p. 34).

The metaphor works on a number of levels. A *dais* connotes authority, separation, the transmission of knowledge from an expert to a novice, whereas a *round table* suggests equality, collegiality and mutual endeavour. One might expect the kind of language associated with a dais to be formal, rehearsed, performative, monologic. The language of the round table is more likely to be dialogic, dynamic, fluid, exploratory, spoken from the heart. The removal of the dais has consequences for the affordances of the classroom: it suggests that the spaces within which formal learning takes place should be active and capable of reconfiguration rather than passive and immoveable. Fundamental, then, to the new thinking about English pedagogy – and it is significant that one of the major theorists of the period, James Britton, was an early advocate of Vygotsky's work in the West – is the belief that children are active *and social* meaning-makers who construct their sense of themselves and their world through language. As Dixon puts it:

> at the level of language we can say this: we make for ourselves a representational world, sense out to the full its ability to stand for experience as we meet it, come

up against its limitations, and then shoulder – if we dare – the task of making it afresh, extending, reshaping it, and bringing into new relationships all the old elements. Learning to use language continues so long as we are open to new experience and ready to adapt and modify the linguistic representation (the world) we have made for experience.

(1967, p. 9)

If these sentiments seem familiar, it is because most, if not all, of the statements – about the pedagogical implications of the removal of the dais or the construction of the world and of personal identity through language – would have been endorsed by the theorists and practitioners reviewed in the previous chapters of this book. It should come as no surprise, therefore, that post-war texts on English pedagogy pay tribute to the learning potential offered by drama, either in the form of whole chapters or appendices (for example Whitehead, 1966; Holbrook, 1964) or substantial references (for example Dixon, 1967; Britton, 1970). Comments about the importance of drama are to be found, too, in contemporary government publications. Often, as in the case of *Half Our Future* (*The Newsom Report*) of 1963 (DES, 1963), they are located within sections dedicated to *English* – even though this particular report covers a range of curricular subjects. *A Language for Life* itself devotes five pages to drama – meagre enough; but at least an official statement of intent.

It is Dixon, again, who most vividly identifies what precisely it is about drama that excites English specialists of the period so much. He notes that the Dartmouth Seminar marks a grammatical shift from focusing upon what English as a subject *is* (in other words, thinking about it in terms of nouns) to English as 'a definition by process, a description of the activities we engage in through language' (in other words, to thinking about it in terms of verbs) (1967, p. 7). Drama, with its emphasis on action, absorption and *point mode*, is the ideal medium for the exploration of English-as-verb because, Dixon continues, '"Drama" means doing, acting things out rather than working on them in abstract and in private. When possible it is the truest form of learning, for it puts knowledge and understanding to their test in action' (p. 43).

Putting 'knowledge and understanding to their test in action' rather than 'working on them in abstract and in private' foregrounds the importance of learning as a social enterprise and challenges learners to use language – particularly spoken language – in authentic contexts for real purposes of communication, analysis and problem-solving. Declaring that 'Real communication begins when the words are about experience, ideas, and interests which are worth putting into language' (1963, p. 153), *The Newsom Report* asserts, as if stating an undeniable truth: 'It is *of course* [my italics] within poetry and drama that the use of language goes deepest' (p. 156). *The Bullock Report*, significantly, includes its dedicated section on drama within a chapter entitled *Oral Language* and endorses its predecessor's claims for drama as a powerful medium for language development by asserting:

its potential in helping the child to communicate with others, to express his [sic] own feelings and thoughts, and to gain confidence in a variety of contexts. Both in its close relation to literature and in its inherent shaping powers for speech, drama is a powerful instrument to this end.

(DES, 1975, p. 161)

Improvisation is held in particularly high esteem by the English specialists of the period because, as the Vygotskian James Britton argues, it is a 'concerted undertaking' relying upon 'spontaneity, sensitive interaction and cooperation' (1970, pp. 225, 149) as opposed to that 'abstract' and 'private' engagement with 'knowledge and understanding' criticised by Dixon. Britton cites, as an example, an improvisation undertaken by ten-year-olds and based on *The Great Plague* of the seventeenth century. The planning and analysis required by the children's work provides them, certainly, with plentiful opportunities for out-of-role discussion and problem solving; but once they enter into role as participants in that drama, something transformative happens:

> there comes a point at which the situation takes over. Since it is the situation that is being explored, its demands will be not for histrionics, not for audience response, but for greater penetration by each of his role, and by all of the developing action as a whole – in fact for a more sensitive and energetic exercise of insights.
>
> (Britton, 1970, p. 146)

Instead of discussing the ethical issues at one remove in a classroom debate, the children are obliged to think and respond from within the fictional situation; and this obligation charges their language with power and authority:

> when the scene is enacted, the physical situation itself – the sick man lying there – pushes them to the point where something must be decided, something must be *done*. In interacting with each other it is to the demands of this situation that they are responding.
>
> (p. 146)

Work of this kind plays persuasively to the 'personal growth' model of English advocated by the participants at the Dartmouth Seminar. The ten-year-old contributors to *The Great Plague* improvisation are learning to negotiate their sense of identity within a culture on what Bronfenbrenner (1979) might call a *microsystemic* and a *macrosystemic* level. At the *microsystemic* level of the classroom, the children conduct this negotiation through the give-and-take of preparatory discussion with their classmates; but beyond this, at the *macrosystemic* level, by trying to imagine what it might have been like to have been exposed to the intense moral pressures faced by the people who lived through a major historical event like the Great Plague, they are attempting to come to terms, as citizens of Britain, with an aspect of their cultural heritage. For Whitehead, this learning to think about one's own identity in relation to the identities and needs of other people is crucial to learning: 'If we observe children sensitively and sympathetically', he writes, 'we cannot fail to realise that this process of identification lies at the heart of all their intellectual and emotional growth' (1966, p. 126). Drama is a most powerful medium for such 'identification'. Quoting Slade's observation that play provides opportunities for 'trying out bits of real life before it comes to them', Whitehead argues that drama can encourage a child to 'step outside the circle of his own ego' and that it is the task of the drama teacher to foster the process of identification of self within the world by helping the child 'to move in his acting towards a keener grasp of reality (the reality of human speech, behaviour and emotions) by stimulating livelier and more accurate imagining' (p. 126).

English specialists of the period were also particularly taken with the idea that drama could reach out to what the *Newsom Report* describes as 'weaker boys and girls' who are in danger of being condemned to a state of 'apartheid' in which they are 'debarred by lack of ability from the great things of our civilisation' (DES, 1963, p. 152). Using language that, sadly, would not sound out of place today, the writers of the report continue:

> many of the weaker pupils never seem to reach the point at which real English begins. Some teachers, including many who have never been trained for teaching English, give them a watered down version of what they remember from their own grammar school experiences. Much use is made of textbooks providing endless exercises in comprehension, composition and the like.
>
> (p. 152)

Geoffrey Hawkes, who contributed an unfortunately named section entitled *Dramatic Work with Backward Children* to David Holbrook's (1964) publication *English for the Rejected*, argues his case for drama by emphasising its affinities with the affective, rather than the cognitive domain. No matter what score they might achieve on an intelligence test, his argument runs, everybody is capable of feeling and thus everyone is capable of engaging with what Newsom calls 'real English' through the medium of drama, which is, Hawkes asserts, 'One of the loves of all children, anywhere'. He writes: 'the emotions cannot be graded, perhaps because they are older by a million years than the intellect' (1964, p. 248) and, pushing further the egalitarian argument against the rigid ability-groupings then prevalent in schools, he suggests that 'in such work as drama children would probably benefit most if they were not streamed' (p. 248).

If drama was regarded as a means of challenging dominant structures for the organisation of learning, it also provided opportunities to question the established hierarchies of the English curriculum. Plato's *Phaedrus* had famously privileged the spoken over the written word, fearing that the latter modality would lead to an enfeeblement of the powers of memory and a tendency to authoritarian, monologic discourse; but the English specialists of the period took a different approach to the argument against the dominance of writing. What brought them in on Plato's side (albeit with some *caveats* that will be explored later) was the issue of access. Again, improvisation is regarded as the key. *The Bullock Report* argues that it can 'bring out unsuspected resources in children whose work in written English may not be promising'. One of the most significant of these 'resources', the report adds, in an echo of Finlay-Johnson's and Slade's comments on the language of the home, is 'the inexhaustible fund of grammatical forms and idioms available to children from a very early age' manifest in 'the creativity of speech' (DES, 1975, pp. 159, 158). By enabling what Holbrook calls 'the rejected' to articulate their own life experiences in their own spoken language through the medium of improvisation, drama can help children circumvent the barriers to learning erected by the dominance in schools of the written word and give the 'rejected' a sense that their words and their lives are, as the *Newsom Report* expressed it, 'worth putting into language'.

'The teachers of English', the authors of *The Newsom Report* assert, 'tend to think of their subject from three different but related points of view: as a medium of communication, as a means of creative expression, and as a literature embodying the vision of greatness'(DES, 1963, p. 152). In the case of this third, literary element, no less than for 'communication' and 'creative expression', drama was perceived as a force for access and democratisation, particularly in the case of that most formidable of canonical icons, Shakespeare. Although Caldwell Cook is not mentioned by name, his spirit can be clearly detected behind this 1927 quotation from Aldous Huxley, cited approvingly by Whitehead:

> Shakespeare did not write his plays to be read, with notes, by children sitting at desks; he wrote them to be acted. Children who have read the plays dramatically, who have lived through them with their whole imaginative being, acquire an understanding of Shakespeare, a feeling for the poetry, denied to those who have ploughed through them in class and passed, even with honours, an examination in the notes.
>
> (In Whitehead, 1966, p. 133)

Whitehead's commitment to that principle of active textual engagement advocated by Caldwell Cook, Finlay-Johnson and Hourd and endorsed in the quotation above by Huxley is shared by the other English specialists considered here. For them, drama provides a means of challenging the idea that the reading of literature needs to be just another of those 'abstract' and 'private' activities criticised by Dixon. As the authors of the *Newsom Report* put it, 'a play is not just the words in the book but much more besides' (1963, p. 157). 'Improvisation', *The Bullock Report* asserts, 'can provide a physical context for the printed word to come to life' (DES, 1975, p. 157) and it cites as an example the moment in Act One Scene Two of Shakespeare's *Antony and Cleopatra* where Antony informs Enobarbus that his (Antony's) wife is dead:

Antony:	Fulvia is dead.
Enobarbus:	Sir?
Antony:	Fulvia is dead.
Enobarbus:	Fulvia!
Antony:	Dead.

The authors comment: 'On the page these words are unfulfilled, almost meaningless, until the whole relationship and all its implications have been fully experienced by trying them out in a convincing setting – physical, social and emotional' (p. 157).

To interpret this exchange effectively, the reader needs to engage with all the senses and not just the intellect: How are the words said? How are they received? How long are the pauses between the statements? How are the silences to be considered? Where are the actors standing in relation to each other? Do they move about the stage during the exchange? And so on. As this string of questions suggests, a reading of this kind lends itself to active, dialogic and public exchange – *The Bullock Report* implies as much through its use of the phrase 'trying . . . out'. For Whitehead, the role of the teacher here is to stimulate this dialogic, public reading by asking questions of the kind listed above in order to help the students to develop 'a vivid perception of the imagined situation so that the attempt at acting may proceed from the child's own inner experience' (1966, p. 129).

Nor should children be required to hold the words of canonical writers in awe, as if they were some kind of sacred text. Just as Hourd encourages her students to write their own versions of Greek tragedies or to make links between Shakespeare's *Julius Caesar* and their personal war-time experiences, so Britton quotes with approval a 1967 *HMSO* Report into drama teaching, which describes how students were invited to retell the story of *Macbeth* in their own words. Britton asks: 'can it be that they may somehow come nearer in broad outline to Shakespeare's view of the human condition than the scholar does as his eye passes over a page of Shakespeare's words?' (1970, p. 146). Hawkes uses the same play to make the same point, but is even more forthright in his celebration of the children's right to retell Shakespeare in their own speech, even going so far as to compare their interpretation with the work of the Italian *commedia dell'arte*:

> The plays made in this way move far outside the expectations of the original authors: the 'doctor' asks Lady Macbeth 'What's the matter with you, gal?' and Macbeth shoves him off – 'You leave her alone, she's not feelin' too good. She'll be all right in a minute', and then adds, 'If you don't shut up that moanin' I'll come over and belt you.'
>
> (1964, p. 252)

Interpreting canonical texts – particularly those of Shakespeare – as a group rather than as an individual can provide a sense of security (safety in numbers); 'trying out' interpretations can instil confidence by suggesting that it is all right to make mistakes, to speculate, to consider different readings; assimilating the concerns of the text with the 'child's own inner experience' can help a young person not only to appreciate the transformative power of literature but also to negotiate their relationship with their cultural heritage; engaging with written text through the medium of the senses as well as the intellect can encourage an awareness that mastering the reading process requires far more than the acquisition of a series of word attack strategies.

Positive though their response was, the reception afforded to drama by the English specialists of the period was not unproblematic; and those problems were to have a long-lasting effect upon the relationship between the two subject areas. *The Bullock Report* (DES, 1975, p. 160) concludes its section on drama by posing six questions. They are reproduced in slightly abbreviated form below:

1. Should drama be a separate subject with its own department?
2. Should it be the policy of the drama or English department to encourage teachers in other subjects to use drama in their work?
3. What language resources does drama call upon in individual pupils, according to their ability, background etc.?
4. What areas of language growth are neglected in other kinds of English teaching, and which of these may be regarded as particularly the province of drama?
5. Are there differences of criteria in language work from the points of view of drama specialist and English teacher?
6. What is the role of the teacher in improvised drama, particularly in the development of language?

The fact that such questions needed to be asked at all in a government document published as late as 1975 – 200 years after the publication of *Emile*, almost sixty years after the publication of *The Play Way* and in the decade following the texts by Dixon, Holbrook and Whitehead cited earlier – speaks volumes.

The heart of the problem lies in the first two questions listed above. All the cited specialists take great pains to emphasise that drama is not just some adjunct of English but a subject discipline in its own right whose proper home lies with the arts. Defending drama's place on the curriculum in language of which Hawkes would have approved, the authors of the *Newsom Report* write:

> drama, along with poetry and the other arts, is not a 'frill' which the less able can safely omit or relegate to a minor position on some Friday afternoons. Art is not an expensive substitute for reality. It is through creative arts, including the arts of language, that young people can be helped to come to terms with themselves more surely than by any other route.
>
> (DES, 1963, p. 157)

The Bullock Report appears to question *Newsom*'s positioning of the subject within the linguistic domain by emphasising that 'there are many other sides to drama at least as valuable as the language aspect' and citing as examples 'such activities as movement, dance, mime, and the work which drama prompts in related arts' (DES, 1975, p. 158). Writing eight years earlier, Dixon anticipates Bullock's concern lest drama be too strongly identified with language development by asserting instead the primacy of its aesthetic qualities. Certainly, he concedes, drama can enhance children's engagement with 'register'; but 'this should be subordinated to the symbolic function of drama'. Again, principles of access and democratisation are cited in support of the aesthetic case: 'drama may be, for many deprived children, the most important creative medium, since it demands less verbal explicitness and is inseparable from expressive movement (1967, p. 41).

Clearly, there is some discrepancy here. On the one hand, the English specialists appear to endorse with enthusiasm drama's potential as a learning medium for language development; on the other, they seem just as eager to downplay the importance of that connection. The root of the problem is that, fundamentally, for all their assertions about the artistic integrity of drama, these English specialists are primarily concerned with the subject content and skills of *English*: these are the matters that excite their thinking. They are prepared to explore drama – as that meagre five pages devoted to the subject in *The Bullock Report* indicates – only in so far as it can inform the development of English pedagogy. The authors of *The Bullock Report* tacitly admit as much at the end of their section on drama: 'Some teachers will doubtless feel that our discussion of drama has neglected non-verbal forms of communication and over-emphasised the role of language' (DES, 1975, p. 161).

Instead of suggesting that this might be considered a deficiency and then trying to rectify it by opening up a debate about those 'non-verbal' elements of drama, the importance of which they earlier acknowledged, the authors close down the discussion and wave off any suggested criticism:

> We acknowledge the value and high quality of much of this [non-verbal] work, but it is our contention that in most schools drama has yet to realise its potential

in helping the child to communicate with others, to express his [sic] own feelings
and thoughts, and to gain confidence in a variety of contexts.

(p. 161)

The authors conclude, defiantly, by asserting that it is the literary and spoken, not the
'non-verbal' elements of drama that merit 'serious study and professional discussion':
'Both in its close relation to literature and in its inherent shaping powers for speech,
drama is a powerful instrument to this end' (p. 161).

An even more glaring example of *The Bullock Report's* ambivalence towards
drama is revealed in its brief attempt to answer the first of its six concluding questions
listed earlier. While noting that 84 per cent of the schools surveyed for the report
teach drama within English and that it comprises an 'essential part' of the latter,
the authors of the report add, revealingly, that many teachers of English lack the
'temperament' to 'handle [sic] improvised drama' (1975, p. 224). The verb 'handle' is
interesting enough, but it is the use of that word 'temperament' that is particularly
curious. Would the report have employed it in any other subject context? Might
a teacher of maths be said to lack the 'temperament' to teach geometry or a teacher
of music to lack the 'temperament' to teach singing? If someone were to apply for an
English post, would it be acceptable for them to excuse themselves from teaching
an 'essential part' of the subject on the grounds that they were temperamentally
unsuited to doing so? How can something be at once regarded as an essential
component of a subject and at the same time not demanded as part of the job
specification for each of that subject's practitioners? With this almost casual aside,
The Bullock Report excuses teachers of English from the need to make a professional
commitment to drama.

One of the most significant pedagogical consequences of the tendency to think
about drama from an English perspective can be seen in the specialists' approach to
progression. Despite their praise of improvisation as a medium for purposeful communication, for lifting the literary text off the page or for aiding the learning of those
who find written forms of literacy particularly challenging, it is hard to avoid the
suspicion that contemporary writers about English pedagogy consider the capacity
to engage with the written (preferably canonical) dramatic text as the pinnacle of
achievement. *The Bullock Report* notes that, amongst the schools in its survey, the
'average weekly time on improvisation at fourteen was less than a third of that at
twelve, and the time for work from a printed text had doubled' (p. 160). Is this development to be applauded or deplored? The authors do not say. As with the question
about who should teach drama, the report is strangely equivocal and lacking in clear
guidance: 'Whatever view is taken of improvised drama by heads of English depart-
ments,' it continues, 'there is too rarely any constructive or detailed discussion of its
place in English teaching' (p. 160).

To privilege engagement with the written dramatic text is to foreground reading,
with its implications of detached criticality, as the means by which progression in
drama can be measured. Britton is less evasive on the matter than the authors of
The Bullock Report:

One might say, then, that what is being manipulated in dramatic play, its medium,
is human behaviour; and at the other end of a continuum, that is the medium in
which the dramatist creates his work of art. In dramatic play as it develops in the

primary school, author, players and audience are one: with the dramatist's stage play, they are three.

(1970, p. 142)

Even Dixon – perhaps the most sympathetic of all to the affective elements of drama – describes progression in terms of an increasingly sophisticated capacity for 'seeing more than one way of *"reading"* [my italics] a situation' – a skill that, he argues, will enable students to engage with the works of 'mature dramatists' (1967, p. 39). Whitehead resorts to a similar reading paradigm, arguing that progression in drama moves from the 'purely creative' to the 'interpretative', and asserting that 'the words of the dramatist's script become the arbiter in all that we do' (1966, p. 134). Had the most important author in the literary canon not been a playwright, would these English specialists have bothered to concern themselves with drama at all? Reading comments like this, it is tempting to think not; and Whitehead compounds that suspicion by taking the progression-through-reading model to another level. In words that would have shaken Finlay-Johnson, Caldwell Cook and Hourd, Whitehead suggests that the language of poetry (he does not mean the poetry of play texts) is too valuable and fragile to be subjected to dramatic interpretation. Hawkes and Britton might approve of children improvising Shakespeare in their own words as a means of affording them access to canonical literature but, when it comes to poetry, Whitehead regards the same strategy almost as if it were a diversionary tactic, designed to protect the inviolability of the text. Citing one of Caldwell Cook's favourites, the ballad *Sir Patrick Spens*, as an example, he observes: 'When dramatising a ballad, we are compelled to let the children leave the text behind and make up their own dialogue, for otherwise no spontaneous life will ever find its way into their acting' (p. 131). To attempt a dramatisation of the poem would be nothing short of 'sacrilegious', for 'how on earth, we may ask, is the ship's foundering in the storm to be represented in the class-room without destroying the tragic mood demanded by it?' (p. 131). There are certain spaces within the English curriculum, it seems, that remain strictly out of bounds to drama.

Whitehead's position might seem particularly extreme; but Britton's and Dixon's models of progression also serve – inadvertently, no doubt – to weaken the integrity of drama by privileging certain of its elements at the expense of others. A movement *from* action and *point mode* absorption *to* observation, detachment and interpretation; *from* the *creation* of texts (oral, gestural, written) *to* the *reception* of texts whether read on the page in a classroom or watched 'live' from a seat in a theatre, suggests that the former must be left behind in order to achieve the latter – and that it is the latter that really count.

A further consequence of this English-centred thinking about drama is that the specialists of the period demonstrate a reluctance to engage with important issues of drama pedagogy. *The Bullock Report* offers several examples of this. As well as that unwillingness to enter into debate about the purpose and place of improvisation in the English curriculum noted earlier, or the decision – despite declaring that there was at the time a serious shortage of specialists willing to teach the subject – to allow English teachers to use 'temperament' as an excuse for not committing to drama teaching, the authors of the report steer away from one of the major pedagogical issues of the period: the tension between what were regarded as the divergent claims of theatre on the one hand and of drama in education on the other. Writing about the situation as it prevailed two decades before the publication of *The Bullock Report*, Bolton observes, in language that hints at the intensity of the conflict: 'Teachers found they were under pressure to take sides. Either one was for the refined expression of the stage or, as it seemed to the "experts", one was for the free expression of children's own colloquial banalities' (1984, p. 22).

The authors of *The Bullock Report* are clearly aware of the issues. They deplore the 'sharp opposition' and 'polarisation of view' between 'theatre' and '"educational", "creative" or "free" drama'. 'The ideal situation', they suggest, is a compromise 'where the two forms of activity are complementary, so that the written word may become the spoken word and the spoken word the written' (DES, 1975, p. 157). How this synthesis is to be achieved through the construction of an integrated, coherent and progressive curriculum, they do not say. The most the authors of the report offer is the hope that drama and English teachers will somehow work together (p. 224).

As might be expected from the emphasis upon the application of a reading paradigm to the question of progression in drama noted earlier, *The Bullock Report* regards 'the spectators' role' as the key determiner in the 'theatre' versus 'educational drama' debate:

> Where the spectators' role becomes dominant in all these activities they can be said to turn into theatre or conscious art form. Where spectators are absent, or where they become so involved that they cease to be spectators, what results is also a powerful form of drama. In the context of education this is sometimes called 'educational', 'creative' or 'free' drama.
>
> (1975, p. 156)

This statement has major pedagogical implications. If drama becomes 'theatre or conscious art form' only when 'the spectators' role becomes dominant', where does that leave absorption, *point-mode* or improvisation in terms of aesthetic value? The authors of the report concede that 'educational' drama is '*also* [my italics] a powerful form' – they do not say that it is *as* powerful. The implication is, therefore – and this point echoes Whitehead's construction of a hierarchy of textual engagement – that the latter is the poor relation of the former.

Britton's overriding concern with language means that he, too, while seeming to employ the terminology of the drama versus theatre debate, in fact directs the argument away from issues crucial to drama pedagogy. Like the authors of *The Bullock Report*, Britton establishes a demarcation between 'participant' and 'spectator'. In the participant role, he writes, 'the stress is upon interpreting the new, ongoing experience in the light of the sum total, the world representation'; while for the spectator, 'the principal function is to work upon the world representation, reorganizing it in the light of experiences *not now engaged in but contemplated* [my italics]' (1970, p. 152). Britton's primary concern is with the ways in which these two roles impact upon language use: 'In the participant role they [adolescents] will discuss, argue, confess, explore, theorize . . .'; In spectator mode, adolescents 'are likely to intensify their improvisations upon "the world as I have known it"' (p. 225). The use of the word 'improvisations' may raise false expectations here. The rest of the quotation suggests that, like Whitehead, Britton has in mind a clear hierarchy of receptive and productive media that are to be placed at the disposal of the spectator. The quotation starts promisingly enough by acknowledging a role for 'day-dreaming'; but it quickly moves on to more orthodox territory. The place allotted in the sentence cited below to the phrase 'dramatic improvisation' is significant; by modifying it with the word 'limitations', Britton, the Vygotskian, seems to assert the primacy of individual contemplation through reading and writing over the communal endeavor of dramatic improvisation:

> in the spectator role they are likely to intensify their improvisations upon 'the world as I have known it', whether in their day-dreaming, or in the reading and writing of poetry and fiction, or (where they have the opportunity) in dramatic improvisation – which has the advantages and limitations of being a concerted undertaking.
>
> (1970, p. 225)

Because issues of drama pedagogy are not their primary concern, the English specialists of the period tend to accept received opinions about the subject with a lack of criticality they would never apply to their own area of interest. Rousseau's and Slade's distrust of too-early exposure to the stage and its traditions finds echoes in *The Bullock Report's* concern lest emerging assessment models for drama place too much emphasis upon the 'history of theatre' (DES, 1975, p. 160). Britton is more forceful:

> There is pretty general agreement . . . that the scripted play made into a performance for an audience of parents and friends is not only the least appropriate form of activity for the primary school but would tend, in fact, to militate against those aspects of dramatic work that are of educational importance at this stage.
>
> (1970, p. 142)

Dixon's observations about the play of young children might also have come straight from Slade: 'it is not designed to communicate to outsiders,' he writes, 'yet the intensity of its participants testifies to its significance for them' (1967, p. 40).

References to play are a particular case in point. The links between drama and the play of young children are regarded as self-evident and unproblematic. Whitehead observes an 'essential continuity' between 'the spontaneous imaginative "play" of early childhood' and 'the "dramatic play", which provides the basic raw material for our drama lessons' (1966, p. 123). Britton shares Whitehead's position, discerning a natural 'movement' in a child's development 'from make-believe play to dramatic *improvisation*' (1970, p. 142). One of the key purposes of drama is to nurture this connection. 'It is worth a thought', the authors of *The Bullock Report* observe, having cited approvingly an instance of six-year-olds 'exercising imagination and intellect, physical co-ordination and social sense' by turning their classroom into 'moon rockets' and 'castles', that 'the higher up the school one goes the less likelihood is there of such open "play" happening again, unless it is in the drama lesson.' By the age of nine, the report notes with regret, 43 per cent of surveyed children have no opportunity for improvised classroom drama (DES, 1975, p. 158).

This largely uncritical acceptance of received orthodoxies encourages the English specialists of the period to favour the neo-Wordsworthian privileging of the child as an expert meaning-maker whose dramatic play the teacher has simply to facilitate and then watch admiringly from the side lines. Britton, for example, quotes more than two pages of improvised dialogue taken from the play about the Great Plague enacted by the ten-year-olds cited earlier; but not once in his commentary does he analyse the children's work in terms of specific drama skills, techniques or potential for development. His comments about the improvisation are couched exclusively in terms of social skill. 'Improvisation of this kind', Britton writes, 'relies upon spontaneity, sensitive interaction and cooperation'. For this reason, he concludes cryptically, 'such work acts as a kind of flux in the daily programme' (1970, p. 149).

There is not much guidance here to help English teachers – particularly those described by the Bullock Report as temperamentally unsuited – to 'read' a drama text of the kind reported on by Britton so that they might know how to intervene in order to enrich their students' engagement either with the subject matter or the aesthetic medium chosen for its articulation. Dixon is no more helpful. He suggests, vaguely, that what is needed is: '*awareness* [my italics] among teachers of English of those moments in a lesson, or in a week's work, when what has been said or read moves naturally out to enactment with movement and gesture' (1967, p. 42).

There seems little point in English teachers having 'an awareness' that something needs to be done if they are not equipped with the knowledge and skills to help their students do it. Dixon admits that English teachers need 'a knowledge of teaching method, and a detailed sense of the sequence in drama'. He even goes so far as to sketch the outlines of a potential curriculum 'which moves from the simplest role and schema of events to the more complex, from improvising language and movement to exploring in action the meaning of a script, from being one's own playwright to meeting mature writers (p. 42). But that is as far as he goes. How this curriculum might be taught, progressively and coherently, across the various years of compulsory schooling, Dixon declines to say.

Perhaps the most startling expression of this *laissez-faire* position comes from Hawkes, for whom his 'backward' students' drama is 'a continuance in disciplined forms of children's natural play' and which, quoting Yeats, he positions as a charming '"ceremony of innocence"'. 'Occasionally', Hawkes concedes, 'the work goes flat, at least for the adult watching'. Should this happen, however, the teacher must 'just sit patiently through it and keep faith: he should never break into the play and try to re-arrange and improve: this, I find, does no good' (1964, p. 253).

What today's health and safety inspectors would make of this next bit of advice from Hawkes can only be imagined: 'in class work he [the teacher] should hold on to his seat, even if the noise is alarmingly loud, or a boy has reached the ceiling' (p. 252).

The implications for Whitehead are particularly unfortunate – not surprisingly perhaps, because he is the one who actually quotes Froebel and Slade in his writing about drama. Dutifully, Whitehead declares that 'improvement will not come through conscious application of technique' (1966, p. 129). But handing the curricular initiative to the child at the expense of structured teacher intervention leads on his part to a loss of faith in the power and potential of important modes of dramatic expression. Mime work, for example, should not be attempted with fourteen- and fifteen-year-olds, he writes, because they will find it childish. In fact, anything that pushes the thinking and the imagination of adolescents beyond the limits of naturalism will, Whitehead suggests, be met with rejection as the students 'cloak their inadequacy with a pretence of clowning' (p. 128). The imaginative challenges posed by a medium like physical theatre, for example, would stand little chance of success in Whitehead's classrooms: 'in the secondary school a distracting sense of the ludicrous attends almost all metamorphoses into non-human shape' (p. 128).

It did not have to be like this. By the time these English specialists were attempting to explore the links between drama and their own subject, there was already a substantial body of work available for consultation on issues fundamental to drama pedagogy. Children's play, again, provides a particularly vivid example of how, had they been disposed to do so, English specialists might have refined their thinking about a complex area, rather than contenting themselves with somewhat uncritical assumptions. By the time *The Bullock Report* was published, there existed over a century's worth of scientific studies on the nature and purpose of children's play. A brief reference has already been made earlier in the book to Margaret Lowenfeld's (1890–1973) attempt to consolidate and build upon the work of nineteenth- and early twentieth-century pioneers in the study of play such as Groos, Hall, Bühler and Sully. At this point, however, it would be useful to explore in more detail the major study that she first published in 1935, *Play in Childhood* – not least because an extract from the book dealing particularly with issues pertinent to drama was included in Hodgson's anthology *The Uses of Drama*, which appeared in 1972, three years before the publication of *The Bullock Report*.

Play in Childhood is based on Lowenfeld's observations of 229 young people, aged from one to eighteen years old, who attended her Institute of Child Psychology in London between October 1928 and July 1934. Lowenfeld agrees unequivocally with many of the key principles that have been asserted about play in the book so far: it is a natural human form of expression fundamental to a child's development in terms of imagination, moral awareness, socialisation, cognition and psychic wholeness; it is a preparation for life and a medium of intense intellectual and creative activity – in fact, she cites a quotation from Hall in which the first six years of a child's life are likened to the Bible's account of the first six days of creation. Lowenfeld even goes so far as to assert that the lack of an ability to play 'is not natural and is not an inborn characteristic; it is a neurosis, and should be reckoned as such' (1935, p. 229).

Although Lowenfeld is careful not to 'cross the border-line between play and artistic creation', as she puts it (p. 62), *Play in Childhood*, as Hodgson realised, has a number of important contributions to make to the thinking of practitioners interested in drama pedagogy. For example, Lowenfeld offers a bracing alternative to Hawkes' 'ceremony of innocence'. She quotes Hall's (1907) publication, *Aspects of Child Life and Education*: 'The forces of destruction, aggression, and hostile emotion, which form so powerful an element for good or evil in human character, can display themselves fully in the play of childhood' (In Lowenfeld, 1935, pp. 233–234).

Lowenfeld is not afraid to consider the physicality of children's play, its capacity for violence, the opportunities it affords for exclusion, or for subversion of adult authority. Thus, she writes about the faeces play of very young children or describes how an eight-year-old girl acts out her feelings of resentment against her mother's power by devising a role-play in which their statuses are reversed. Noting that play can be 'used to express certain very deep emotional states not recognised in ordinary life' or therapeutically permit 'a frank expression of aggression in action' (1935, p. 43, p. 227), she recounts an episode of group play as grisly as the episode in which Slade found himself 'eaten in time to . . . music':

> When told there were only ten more minutes, the children decided to end by a final execution, and I.C. [one of the children] brought a stone slab on which to cut off heads. The stone was too heavy to hold, so each in turn had to put his head over a low door and have it sawn off by I.C. and another boy with sticks.
>
> (p. 62)

Lowenfeld draws attention to issues of differentiation in a way that none of the previous writers about drama cited so far have attempted. If they consider the matter at all, they tend to make broad and, by today's standards, very questionable distinctions between the play of boys and girls. Lowenfeld is not immune to this – she writes about 'construction' work for males and 'handcraft' for females (pp. 156–157) – but, building on earlier work by Bühler, she also distinguishes five different roles that children, irrespective of gender, can adopt in their play: *the leader, the follower, the popular child, the protective child and the socially unsuccessful child*. Further – and this is a particularly important point for those who subscribe rather too enthusiastically to the neo-Wordsworthian position – Lowenfeld describes four kinds of children who are inhibited in play: the children who will only play on their own terms; the children who will only perform their own, spontaneous play rather than follow specific forms; the children who cannot initiate or join in with others' play and the shy children who will only join in once they feel comfortable. This is a far cry from Slade's vision of merry children exultantly weaving their archetypal patterns through the playground; and had the drama and English specialists cited so far really engaged with what Lowenfeld is saying here, then thinking about drama pedagogy might have been taken to a richly complex new level to the benefit of students and teachers alike.

Equally helpful from the perspective of differentiation and progression is Lowenfeld's exploration of the various phases and forms of childhood play. While not going as far as Groos (to whom she attributes the suggestion that there are seven major and sixty minor varieties of play), Lowenfeld identifies three broad areas: play that is 'entirely isolated and personal', play that is 'still individual but which creates out of the materials it uses a definite objective play world' and 'playing out with fellow-players themes mutually agreed upon' (1935, p. 201). Within those broad categories can be found *motor play, play with objects, rough-and-tumble, group games, representational games, games of risk, games of chance, games of intellect, games involving running, chasing and capture* and so on. Lowenfeld charts the development of play from birth through to adolescence, noting a movement from play as 'the realisation of experience' to the 'demonstration of phantasy' to 'interior realisation', with social play developing around the ages of four or five and reaching its fullest expression between twelve and fourteen – after which, like Vygotsky, she believes that the play urge is mainly manifested through sports (pp. 230–231). Lowenfeld is not unique, of course, in trying to plot progression and development in play – Rousseau, Froebel and Slade, for example, all attempt a similar task. However, she does bring another voice and perspective to the debate, one informed by scientific observation and one that specialists like Hodgson believed to have a particular contribution to make to drama pedagogy – which is why he chose to include Lowenfeld's work in his anthology in preference to Piaget's 'important' but 'less readable' *Play, Dreams and Imitations in Childhood*. 'By studying the absorbed play of children', Hodgson declares in support of his decision, 'we can appreciate further the functions and purposes of drama, free' he concludes pointedly in a tacit reference to Lowenfeld's scientific credentials, 'from conventions and pseudo-sophisticated associations' (1972, pp. 43, 44).

Hodgson recognised that, for all Lowenfeld's determination not to 'cross the border-line between play and artistic creation', *Play in Childhood* establishes important points of connection with drama. Most significant, perhaps, is the link between play and aesthetic expression. Arguing like Piaget that children possess a 'powerful impulse towards imitation', Lowenfeld insists that 'form' is an essential component of all social play. 'Unless there is a general acceptance of form of some kind', she writes, 'no type of social game, except rough and tumble movements and unorganised group games, can come into being'. Children's interest in form is connected to their love of ritual, melody, rhythm and rhyme; and, as their social play develops, they move inexorably towards modes of expression that lend themselves to theatre, whether it be the 'satirical forms' of 'environmental play' (1935, pp. 133, 172, 145) or buffoonery, clowning and mimicry.

Advice on pedagogy was not only available from child psychologists like Lowenfeld. Established contemporary practitioners of drama also offered potentially fruitful points of connection. The most famous of these, perhaps, is Peter Slade's colleague, Brian Way (1923–2006), whose *Development Through Drama* appeared in 1967, the same year as *Growth Through English*. The shared publication year is significant; for Way's vision of drama endorses completely the democratic impulse and commitment to a 'personal growth' model of education espoused by Dixon and many of the contributors to the Dartmouth Seminar. Arguing that 'there is not a child born anywhere in the world, in any physical or intellectual circumstances or conditions, who cannot do drama' (1967, p. 3), Way, like Slade thirteen years earlier, chooses a sequence of active verbs to declare that the aim of his book is 'helping *the natural, organic development of each individual* [original italics], exploring, discovering and mastering his [sic] own resources, and attaining a sensitive, confident relationship with his environment' (p. 268).

Recalling the development of English pedagogy during this period, Jeffcoate describes 'the introduction of exploratory talk and collaborative group work' into the classroom under the direction of such leading figures as James Britton, Douglas Barnes, Harold Rosen and Andrew Wilkinson as being of 'historical importance' (1992, p. 79). One of the most significant contributions Way might have made to the thinking of his English counterparts was through his championing of the value of talk at an ethical, pedagogical and practical level. The whole of Chapter Six of *Development Through Drama* (almost forty pages of text) is devoted to the subject.

Just how close their thinking on this subject was can be seen by comparing Way's and Britton's comments on the ethical value of collaborative talk. Influenced, like Marjorie Hourd, by Martin Buber, Britton quotes the philosopher as saying: 'Experience comes to man "as I" but it is by experience "as we" that he builds the common world in which he lives' (1970, p. 19). For Britton, talk – and its often neglected but crucial counterpart, listening – are the prime means by which this move from 'I' to 'we' can be achieved:

> Young children, in their egocentrism, have to learn to cooperate and they have to learn the language of cooperation; if talking is to assist cooperative doing, it must

move out of egocentrism towards reciprocity, and success in a joint undertaking is a built-in incentive.

(p. 138)

Way believes that one of the fundamental ethical aims of drama is to facilitate what Britton calls the 'move out of egocentrism towards reciprocity' and that talk is a powerful medium for achieving this goal. So central is this belief to Way's thinking that he uses linguistic imagery to construct a binary opposition between the two states, contrasting what he terms the 'unintended bilingualism' of the former with the 'fully appreciated multilingualism' of the latter. 'Unintended bilingualism' arises, Way writes, 'from the attempt to impose one type of speech on a group of people whose speech root is different' and thus represents the triumph of egocentric assertion. On the other hand, though it develops from a 'deep root of confidence' in one's own voice and home language (for, like his English counterparts, Way believes strongly in nurturing the 'speech music of the family'), 'fully appreciated multilingualism' offers 'the opportunity to realise quite dispassionately and fearlessly the existence of many other ways of speaking' (1967, pp. 122, 120, 122). From this toleration and even celebration of what Bakhtin might call 'heteroglossia' or 'multispeechedness' (Dentith, 1995, p. 35) come two key *desiderata* of drama: the ability to engage imaginatively with the thoughts, feelings and language of other people and the confidence to negotiate one's sense of identity within a wider cultural context. As Way puts it, talk in drama provides opportunities 'to be people other than oneself – to be the people who speak in those other ways' and, by developing this 'real sensitivity to other people', one learns how to operate efficiently the language registers encountered within a particular culture. 'How is this to be achieved?' Way asks. The answer, he believes, is clear: 'There is only one way, and that is through abundant and infinitely patient opportunities to practice [sic] speaking always within an uncritical framework. Drama will provide, in many varied ways, the opportunities for practice' (1967, p. 122).

As well as providing ethical support for a modality of language that, at the time, had still to establish its academic credentials in the curriculum, Way offers pedagogical service to the supporters of classroom talk by attempting not only to map but also to extend its conceptual territory. Almost thirty years before The *New London Group* reconfigured language use to include 'Visual', 'Audio', 'Gestural' and 'Spatial' systems of 'Design' (1996, p. 78), *Development Through Drama* argues that, since 'sound' and 'movement' are both dependent upon 'breath, the basic essential of all life', they must be considered as indivisible – one cannot be explored without reference to the other. The section of the book devoted to *Movement and Speech* sketches out a curriculum agenda that includes the intensely physical (an exploration of breathing as well as of 'external' and 'internal' sounds) – but also argues that 'movement and speech' can 'enrich imagination', develop the 'fully conscious' sensitivity necessary for 'emotional control' and, by effecting 'the liberation and mastery of the physical self through the intuitive development of movement', enhance 'social communication' (1967, p. 149).

On a practical level, too, Way has much to offer English specialists interested in exploring possible connections between drama and their own subject area. Highly aware of the dangers of leaving students (and inexperienced teachers) to 'swim in the limbo of self-experience without assistance' (p. 26) he declares from the start that *Development Through Drama* is 'concerned with practical matters – the "what" to do rather than the "why"' (p. 2). More than any other specialist discussed so far, Way provides such detailed descriptions of drama exercises, improvisations and extended role plays that it would still be possible today for a teacher to deliver a lesson or sequence of lessons from the instructions provided in the book. In the section on *Speaking*, for example, Way offers forty scenarios for improvised dialogue (supported by two and a half pages more of 'further developments') which, with a little updating, could still be employed to good effect in an English classroom focused on the language of persuasion and argument. As the fact that Chapter Nine of *Development Through Drama* is entitled *Fighting and Violence* might indicate, Way's suggestions for activities are all the more convincing because he writes with the authority of someone who understands that, in a real secondary school classroom (he is particularly interested in the ways in which adolescents respond to drama) 'there may be aggressive refusals to cooperate'; and, again, he provides a range of practical solutions to anticipated problems, whether it be the banging of cymbals or a small drum to call the class to attention, or the use of slow motion to focus a fight-scene, or the provision of a script that a teacher might use to win round those who wish to make 'little or no positive contribution' (p. 70). This is a far cry from Hawkes' injunction that the teacher should 'hold on to his seat' no matter what is happening in the classroom.

Perhaps the most important practical point to consider from an English teacher's perspective is the fact that so many of Way's suggested activities and strategies draw upon approaches, concepts and material central to an English curriculum. Like Britton, who quotes approvingly Barbara Hardy's famous observation that 'narrative is "a primary act of mind transferred from art to life"' (1970, p. 153), Way is particularly concerned with narrative, both as a medium for stimulating and articulating drama, and as a means of responding to the world which is of itself worthy of exploration and deconstruction. Arguing that a 'story session is the most comfortable way of easing into the beginnings of drama' (1967, p. 28), he opens Chapter Three of *Development Through Drama*, for example, with a Slade-like story-script designed for a teacher to enact while the attendant class of primary school children perform a carefully documented list of sounds that accompany the text like a series of stage directions. Elsewhere, the adding of a 'particular "if" circumstance' to a sound encourages progression by inviting the students to enter a world of the imagination and to create narratives of their own: 'What would happen *if* [original italics] the clock suddenly stopped and time stood still?' (p. 45). Way is also concerned with the possibilities presented by narrative as a formal, aesthetic device. Thus, he describes how what he calls 'climax' and 'de-climax' can be employed to enrich and shape a story by adding tension, release and contrast or by encouraging mood and atmosphere. An appreciation of 'climax' and 'de-climax' can help students learn how to make powerful narrative choices and to think about the consequences those choices bring: an avalanche approaches a group of climbers; will the story climax with their annihilation – or will the avalanche pass them by, giving them a second chance at life? (pp. 214–219). Elsewhere, Way encourages students to think about narrative structure by inviting them to create a story from an opening or, as a more intriguing alternative, from the final sentence. He comments: 'The suggestions of an opening or ending line, or both, help gradually with the factor of form in a story, working towards a fuller feeling for beginning, middle and end' (p. 53).

Way offers fascinating opportunities for focused work on language structure and grammar. He describes how encouraging students (of all ages) to make up their own 'scribble talk or jabber talk', as he calls it, can help release them from the pressures imposed by 'the intellectual use of language' and allow them to concentrate instead on syntactical patterns as well as on the 'the emotional sound values' conveyed by consonants and vowels (p. 139). On a lexical level, too, Way suggests activities for exploring how adjectives and adverbs can modify nouns and thus shift the focus of an entire sentence, as in the example below:

> A sad, old man gets into a boat and sails out to sea.
> A man gets into a rudderless boat and goes out to sea.
> A man gets into a boat and goes out into an ominously calm sea.
>
> (192)

Perhaps most innovative of all from an English perspective is Way's enthusiasm for media conventions and strategies. Whereas *The Bullock Report's* chapter on 'Technological Aids and Broadcasting' was to position young people largely as consumers of the media, *Development through Drama*, published almost a decade earlier, advocates the same active, productive approach observed above in Way's engagement with language. Arguing that students must learn to *look* [my italics] 'with the selectivity of the lens of a sensitive camera' (p. 59), he devotes a section of the book's chapter on *Improvisation* to an exploration of potential links between drama and film – considering, for example, how a photographic image might afford the starting point for improvisation, or a freeze frame might be 'shot' from different camera angles; or thinking about how a musical score might enhance mood and atmosphere. Way is not simply concerned with harnessing media techniques and conventions to the service of drama. He is also interested in engaging with the media as subjects for dramatic scrutiny in their own right. Hailing film's potential to appeal to 'what is of dynamic interest in the youngsters' own personal lives rather than with the academic subjects of school' (p. 229), for example, Way notes, in a detailed description of a potential documentary film topic entitled *Our School*, the importance of including the drama taking place behind as well as in front of the camera.

Exciting though these potential links with English pedagogy are, they remain implicit. 'As this is not a book on film-making', Way writes in reference to the *Our School* documentary, 'there is no purpose in continuing with the details of developing the film' (p. 233). He might have made the same point about his language as well as his media work. In both cases, he declines to tease out in detail the subject-specific implications of the exercises he describes. Thus, he concludes an account of a documentary-style activity in which each student uses their hands as a 'camera viewfinder, taking shots from many different angles', with the vague suggestion that 'In pairs or small groups, they [the students] then discuss the kind of shots they have taken' (p. 152). Again, when noting the semantic ambiguities of the homophones *key* and *quay*, or the different cultural and grammatical resonances of the word *ring*, he closes down the discussion by noting merely: 'The story [resulting from this stimulus material] was amusing and inventive, and there was great enjoyment at this deliberate play on words' (p. 52). What Way regards as concluding remarks would be viewed as lesson starting-points for the teacher of media or language.

To review the state of the relationship between English and drama by the time of *The Bullock Report* is to feel a sense of excitement and at the same time of frustration. The excitement stems from the fact that, in the wake of the Dartmouth Seminar, English pedagogy was starting to adopt some of the most cherished principles of drama: the privileging of the learner as an active constructor of meanings and a source of authority; the consequent repositioning of the teacher as a facilitator rather than an instructor; the importance of experience, of activity and of process talk; the interrogation of canonical literary texts; the reconfiguring of the spaces in which learning might occur. The concomitant sense of frustration is caused by the seeming reluctance of practitioners from either discipline to engage with each other's pedagogy on more than superficial terms. As a result, the key questions about the relationship between English and drama posed by *The Bullock Report* remained only partially answered.

Chapter 6

Entering the secret garden

An end to romantic child centredness?

In 1973, an oil crisis and stock market crash sent the economies of the West heading towards recession. Three years into the economic down-turn and not long after the publication of *The Bullock Report*, the then Prime Minister of the United Kingdom, James Callaghan, delivered a speech at Ruskin College Oxford, which was to signal a profound shift in educational policy. The reverberations of that speech are still being felt today.

Casting a critical eye on 'informal instruction' in general and the dearth of science and engineering graduates particularly, Callaghan identified a 'need to improve relations between industry and education', declared himself in favour of a 'proper national standard of performance' and demanded that those who paid for the nation's schooling through their taxes be granted access to what he perceived to be the closed – and humanities-biased – world of the curriculum: 'I take it that no one claims exclusive rights in this field. Public interest is strong and legitimate and will be satisfied. We spend £6bn a year on education, so there will be discussion' (*Guardian* UK, 2001).

Drama practitioners were not unwilling to engage in that 'discussion' – even on the terms set out in the Ruskin College speech. Writing at the start of the decade that was to end with the establishment of Callaghan's anticipated National Curriculum, Gavin Bolton, for example, attempted to distance drama from what he called 'Romantic child-centredness' by dismissing Peter Slade's influential pedagogy as 'spontaneous doing' and suggesting that his cherished principle of 'absorption' was a solipsistic example of 'individualisation' (1984, pp. 31, 34, 45). Bolton's account of the kind of 'Child Drama' he associates with Slade might have been precisely what Callaghan had in mind when he expressed unease about 'informal instruction': 'The activity of Child Drama appeared to be without content and without form and the drama lesson without structure apart from a loose sequence of relaxing and releasing activity followed by unfettered dramatic playing (1984, p. 34).

Sensing the way the educational wind was blowing, Bolton sought to stake a claim for drama at the centre of the school curriculum – not by imposing 'fetters', exactly – but by linking it to the disciplines and parameters characteristic of all intensely social enterprises. 'Drama is not about self-expression', he states baldly, in a clear rebuke to Slade. On the contrary, it is 'a group's expression, concerned with celebrating what people share, what man has in common with man [sic]' (p. 45).

Bolton found a powerful and persuasive ally in his colleague, Dorothy Heathcote (1926–2011). She shared his desire to redeem drama from the charge of 'individualisation'. Bolton's criticism of the navel-gazing implicit in the '"go-into-groups-discuss-an-important-issue-and-find-a-dramatic-statement-for-us-to-discuss" sequence' of drama (1984, p. 73) finds an echo in a comment Heathcote made two years earlier and that Bolton quotes approvingly in his 1984 publication. Heathcote complains that: 'A sort of messy, mucky drama has been going on for years, about unselectivity and conglomeration: "Let them have the experience, all of them, every one of them, every minute of every time!"' (in Bolton, 1984, p. 54).

Not afraid to use the language associated with Callaghan's brave new world of educational accountability – words like 'enterprise base', 'client' and 'problem' (Heathcote and Bolton, 1995, pp. 169, 109) appear in their shared writing – Heathcote and Bolton assert that they 'cannot think of a subject that cannot or should not be tackled through drama' (p. 84). As Bolton had argued a decade earlier, drama has a unique 'usefulness as a means of teaching about life . . . particularly at a level of values, issues and implications' because it creates 'an opportunity for coming to know something from the inside, a subjective-objective approach to the material'. 'Well-constructed drama', Bolton continues, 'can make connections so that new things are understood' (1984, pp. 161, 153, 186). If this sounds very similar to the pedagogy practised by Harriet Finlay-Johnson seventy years earlier, Bolton is not unaware of the connection; in fact, he suggests elsewhere in the same book (p. 52) that Johnson's work anticipates Heathcote's practice. However, the quotation continues by highlighting a particularly significant difference, the importance of which Bolton emphasises through the use of italics: '*[Drama]can provide its own built-in frame or lens. It is in this that any argument for seeing drama at the centre of the curriculum must rest*' (p. 186).

The 'frame' that Bolton attributes to Heathcote – and that has become her most enduring legacy – is that of *the mantle of the expert*. Although designed to operate within the new educational dispensation of accountability and economic utility, *the mantle of the expert* draws upon long-established principles of drama peda-gogy. It is somewhat ironic, given Bolton's criticism of 'Romantic child-centredness', that it is predicated upon a model of experiential learning that might have been taken straight from the pages of Rousseau's *Emile*:

> There is a vested interest in checking what *I* can see if the sun is in *my* eyes; how *my* papers will curl if left in direct sunshine; how *my* quill will roll away in dark corners if work benches slope too much.
>
> (p. 68)

If anything, the *mantle of the expert* concept offers an extreme assertion of the principle that it is the child, as active meaning-maker and 'center [sic] for all knowl-edge' (Heathcote and Bolton, 1995, p. 32) who initiates, shapes and gives coherence to learning. Brian Way had been reluctant to place drama 'within the domain of English' because he feared that a focus upon theatre as literature would relegate drama 'to an alternative activity useful only for those who are unable to read fluently' (1967, p. 10); but the *mantle of the expert* concept issues an exhilarating cognitive and imaginative challenge to the argument that drama is some kind of intellectual consolation prize. By providing the learner with 'an "as if" mental set to activate, sustain or intensify . . . engagement' (Bolton, 1984, p. 56); by creating what Boal calls a 'here-and-now' in which 'everything is possible' (1995, p. 20), drama, as mediated through *the mantle of the expert*, can offer young learners a means of engaging with the world of knowledge, not in deficit mode, but from a high status position of expertise.

Thus, in one of the detailed examples provided by Heathcote and Bolton (1995), a group of young learners construct an 'as if' world centred upon life in a medieval monastery. Working in role as monks, they are positioned as authority figures: healers, scribes, builders, architects – roles that, outside the frame of the 'as if' world in which 'everything is possible', they could not hope to experience without years of apprenticeship and study or – equally significant – without privileged access to cultural capital. 'The major learning process for the students', Heathcote and Bolton argue however, 'is that of earning the right to handle more and more complex decisions . . . because they are gaining sufficient expertise to make real decisions' (p. 189). For the 'monks' to make 'real decisions', they need to undertake focused research into a wide range of curriculum areas, including history, language use, physics, biology and religious studies. What medicines or prayers might best help a monk with a broken leg? How should the *scriptorium* be constructed so that it has optimal access to light? What inks will best serve the parchment for a newly commissioned manuscript?

The concept of *the mantle of the expert* is one that is particularly attractive to English teachers, for whom the idea that children come to school with considerable expertise – in at least one language and often several more – is (or should be) a given. There are close links, too, between *mantle of the expert* work and reading. As Wilhelm (2002) puts it:

> The point of all reading, and of all learning activity, is to change our understandings and, as a result, our ways of thinking and being in the world. The goal of studying particular subjects is to understand a topic the way experts in that field understand it.

> (p. 98)

The received wisdom about setting cognitive challenges in the classroom is that one should aim high and then differentiate downwards; but how empowering would it be to take that idea one step further as Wilhelm suggests and approach all aspects of the English curriculum by creating an 'as if' world that invites the students to work in role as experts? A coven of present-day *white witches* are asked to interpret the opening scene of *Macbeth*; a group of war veterans share their responses to Michael Morpurgo's novel and play *Private Peaceful*; a team of researchers into linguistics presents a conference paper on early language acquisition.

Equally persuasive is the status afforded, when working with *the mantle of the expert*, to the power of words. Writing in the same period as Bolton and Heathcote, Peter Medway complains that 'Language in schools, it seems, has always, since antiquity, been divorced from action' (Medway, 1989, p. 30). This is not the case in the 'as if' world of Bolton and Heathcote's medieval monastery. Here, writing, in the form of letters and books, is a felt presence that impacts upon the role-play by issuing challenges, provoking debate and demanding decisions. Above all, a rich variety of spoken language registers are brought, literally, into play: how should a monk address an abbot? What lexis is required to discuss the creation of an illuminated manuscript? What is an appropriate healing prayer to say for the sick? Within the parameters of the 'as if' world, these language registers are invested with what Medway would describe as 'perlocutionary' (p. 28) purposes and consequences.

If there is much in Bolton and Heathcote's practice here that links closely with key principles of drama pedagogy already explored in the book, their account of the teacher's role differs significantly from what has gone before. Closer to Vygotsky than to Wordsworth, Bolton and Heathcote share the former's commitment, not only to socially situated, co-operative learning, but also to working within the zone of proximal development: 'in the presence of an empowering adult', they write, 'a child can reach beyond his [sic] own capacity in carrying out a task' (Heathcote and Bolton, 1995, p. 35). Way had already done much to challenge the Romantic legacy of Slade and his predecessors, which positioned the teacher, in Bolton's words, as a 'loving ally' confined to the role of an onlooker whose task was simply to assist in 'the natural expression of his pupils' (Bolton, 1984, p. 34). Way's detailed account of drama exercises and role-plays also marks a sustained attempt to offer practical, informed guidance to classroom teachers. In Way's practice, however, the teacher remains *outside* the drama, providing instructions for others to implement; and this, for Bolton, means that it falls short much as Slade's visualisation exercises do: they undermine the learners' autonomy by positioning them as responders to and interpreters of others' visions rather than engaging in the moment with their own creativity and imagination.

Bolton and Heathcote propose instead that the teacher *enters* the drama, working in role alongside the learners. Teacher in role work can serve several powerful functions. It can initiate the drama by signalling the move into the 'as if' world (for example, when Dorothy Heathcote begins her work with a group of learners by asking them: 'Did you get the message?'; (Bolton, 1984, p. 111). A teacher in role bearing a letter of request from the bishop to the monks of Durham has the opportunity to shape the aesthetics of the drama by influencing the pace and tension of the situation. The contents of the letter can challenge existing thinking and can invite a new perspective. Working in role as the abbot of the monastery, the teacher can consult his or her expert scribes, architects, builders and nurses and thus assess and celebrate their learning.

This move by the teacher into the previously private creative space of the child – reminiscent of Callaghan's entrance into the supposedly enclosed world of the curriculum – raises a number of issues. On what terms, for example, is the teacher to enter the learner's space? Holding firmly to the principle that learning should be initiated by the child, the introduction to Heathcote and Bolton's (1995) publication declares on the one hand that the teacher needs to be '*admitted* [my italics] as a member of the learning community' – the implication being that the learners have the right to deny access should they wish. On the other hand, the same sentence continues by declaring that the teacher is actually a key member of that community – one whose 'commitment and courage, skills and understanding, are necessary to drive the experience forward' (1995, p. ix). This is a far cry from Hawkes' suggestion that the teacher should simply 'hold on to his seat' while the children do whatever they feel they have to do around him; and it is a far cry, too, from the vague injunctions that passed for practical classroom advice in so many of the writings explored earlier in the book.

In order to 'drive the experience forward', teachers are now expected to deploy a formidable array of general and drama-specific pedagogic skills. They need to know how to initiate the drama and at what level to pitch it; they need to be able to work in a series of different roles, some of which are low status (the students always remain in a high status role) and are therefore particularly challenging in terms of management and commitment; they need to be able to move seamlessly between the 'as if' world of the drama and the actual world of the classroom, encouraging their students not only to participate in the fiction but also to reflect upon it. They need to be able to shape the drama aesthetically, knowing when to move it forward or backwards in time, when to focus in on a particularly significant moment, when to pull back, when to inject tension, when to alter the rhythm or pace, when a technique like *tableaux* or *split-brain* or the introduction of a particular ritual might enrich the work in hand. Both within and outside the drama, teachers need to be able to deploy their knowledge across a range of subject areas so that – to continue Heathcote and Bolton's *driving* metaphor – one hand simultaneously guides a *rein* called *drama* and the other a *rein* called *physics* or *history*. In the medieval monastery role-play, for example, the letter from the bishop is written by the teacher with the dual intention of posing a new challenge within the 'as if' world *and*, outside of it, inviting research into the physics of light or the chemistry of papermaking.

The teacher's task is made more complicated because – true to the long-established principle that the drama teacher must eschew the power and status resources associated with the traditional, dais-dominated classroom – Bolton insists that drama will only work effectively as a pedagogical tool if the participant 'does not see himself as learning', so immersed is he in the 'as if' world. It is important, however, that 'the teacher sees himself as teaching' (1984, p. 157). The task is made more complicated still by Heathcote and Bolton's ambivalent attitude towards child learners. On the one hand, children are to be invested with power: they set the learning agenda and decide whether to admit the teacher into their 'learning community'. On the other hand – and this marks another decisive move away from the *transcendental* account of childhood that appealed so strongly to earlier practitioners – they are seen as vulnerable, uncertain, perhaps not even disposed, as Slade had put it, to 'go to the land [of Child Drama] with the help of an understanding adult'. In Bolton's telling phrase, the drama teacher needs to 'protect' the participants '*into*' emotion' (1984, p. 128). What children need protecting from is not only a reluctance, particularly when afflicted with the self-consciousness of adolescence, to enter into the 'as if' world at all, or from the peer pressures inherent in social learning – for Heathcote and Bolton are both aware that play is not unproblematic and that 'one student's therapeutic indulgence may overstep the threshold of another's vulnerability' (1995, p. 84). Beyond this – and here the teacher's dilemma becomes even more acute – the children may need protecting from their own learning choices. If the subject that they want to explore is deemed to be too challenging for them to cope with, there is a danger that they will either 'retreat into glibness' or be exposed to 'distress' (1995, p. 84).

Heathcote and Bolton's metaphor of the teacher as someone who *drives* the learning seems too forceful, especially as Bolton himself argues that the 'power' of drama lies in the fact that it 'is not itself direct' (1984, p. 51). It would not be too strong to suggest that, in Heathcote and Bolton's model of practice, the teacher coaxes and persuades students into the 'as if' world through an almost guileful application of pedagogic craft. The language of this classroom is elusive and elliptical: direct enquiries from the learners are deflected in the way that the Christ of Luke's Gospel in the

New Testament responds to the question: 'Who is my neighbour?' by telling the story of the Good Samaritan. For example, when invited to explore the subject of piracy, Dorothy Heathcote shifts the context from historical to personal and thus 'disturbs' the enquirers 'into learning' (Heathcote and Bolton, 1995, p. 189) by replying: "'I wonder why you keep going to sea?'" (Bolton, 1984, p. 54). As in Christ's parables or in *Zen* or *Sufi* stories, figurative language plays an important role: students concerned to construct a drama about the search for a cancer cure are encouraged to tell a story about a grove in which the plants wilt and do not recover – thus encountering the bleakness at the heart of that narrative through a '"prismatic" angling of knowledge' (Heathcote and Bolton, 1995, p. 189) effected by the protective, distancing power of metaphor.

The crafted care that is invested in the sophisticated rhetoric of what amounts to a teacher's script can be seen in Bolton's analysis of the words Heathcote uses to initiate a *mantle of the expert* exploration of the relationship between science, medicine, politics and finance set in the United States. Heathcote's words are in italics:

> *They say* [vague, but valuing the choice of topic] *scientists* [introducing the focus/frame, which will be taken up firmly in the next few seconds] *try to find out* [setting the process, not the outcome] *what makes people ill* [the subject of the trying] *get their money* [things like scientists have to be paid for – mantle of the expert is always realistic] *from the government* [scientists in United States are interesting to governments] *in Washington* [the highest level of government] *and the President signs the checks* [the very highest person bestows, authorizes, and *knows about* such projects].
>
> (p. 89)

In terms of dramatic techniques, perhaps one of the most significant strategies introduced by Bolton in order to 'protect' participants into 'emotion' is his refinement of Slade's concept of *projected* play (by no means all of the earlier practitioner's ideas were to be discounted). Contrasting it with *personal play* – which is 'to do with the inner Self and personal mastery' – Slade argues that *projected play* is concerned with 'outward material things and their organisation' (Slade, 1954, p. 67). Bolton focuses upon the connotations of distance in Slade's definition, seeing in it an opportunity to offer reluctant participants incrementally challenging possibilities for engagement below the level of direct participation. Thus, a student might move from the 'passive projected activity' (Bolton, 1984, p. 131) of drawing a map of the 'as if' world or of observing teacher and colleagues working in role, for example, to something demanding more active engagement – such as questioning an empty chair that is representing a role that the participants in the drama might find too difficult to play.

To create opportunities for all students to enter the 'as if' world – from the most extrovert and self-confident of children to those reluctant players identified by Lowenfeld – requires considerable skills of differentiation and persuasion: how might the opening of a door in role indicate an invitation for passively projected players to cross the literal and metaphorical threshold into active engagement? What subtly different role-play challenges are afforded by the following contrasting statements issued by a teacher in role: 'My men have asked me to say this to you' or 'My men have something to say to you'? (1984, p. 136).

Bolton and Heathcote are aware that, by staking a claim for drama as a medium for learning across the curriculum, they run the risk of undermining its status as an art form. Is drama to be reduced to a series of techniques – such as *hot-seating* and *split brain* – which can be used arbitrarily by non-specialists whose primary aim is to teach an aspect of physics or history and for whom the drama is no more than a means to that end? Bolton was not so enamoured of the kind of utilitarian educational agenda presaged by Callaghan's Ruskin Speech that he did not fear it might 'eradicate' (1984, p. 146) the aesthetic dimension from the curriculum. To counter this threat, Bolton and Heathcote broke with a tradition reaching back through Way and Slade to Rousseau by highlighting the similarities between drama in education and the art forms of the theatre. Writing in the introduction to Heathcote and Bolton's 1995 publication, Cecily O'Neill observes that the 'purpose' of *mantle of the expert work* is 'the same as any effective theatre event'. Fundamentally, both operate 'within a powerful imagined context, created through the inner dramatic rules of time, space, role and situation' (1995, p. vii). Heathcote defines these 'rules' – or 'operant laws' of 'theatre expression', as she calls them – as *darkness* and *light*, *sound* and *silence* and *stillness* (1995, p. 195).

How might these 'operant laws' be applied in practice? Take as an example the moment in the medieval monastery role-play where the teacher in role presents the monks with a letter from the bishop requesting that they create a new manuscript. If the main purpose of that action is to initiate a learning activity involving the chemistry of paper and ink making, or even to stimulate a debate about medieval monks' adherence to the rule of obedience, one can imagine that the desired pedagogic effect could have been achieved just as easily by the teacher (either in or even out of role) saying to the students (either in or out of role): 'Here is a letter from the bishop, containing certain instructions. What are the monks going to do about it?' Alternatively, the same action could be performed, literally, according to Heathcote's 'operant laws'. The students in role as monks might be sitting expectantly in a darkened space. The teacher in role as messenger or even bishop might enter with a lit candle angled so that the light falls upon the letter. The teacher might stand completely still and in silence for a minute – and then, slowly, extend an arm and break the silence with the words 'Take this' (which may themselves be uttered loudly and clearly like an order or whispered like a secret message).

'Both dramatic playing and performance', Bolton writes, 'use dramatic metaphors, abstractions which immediately qualify the kind, intensity and degree of emotional response' (1984, p. 118). If the teacher had not crafted the delivery of the letter aesthetically by using the dramatic metaphors of candle-light, darkness, stillness and sound, the students might well have engaged in their follow-up work on papermaking or the moral implications of obedience. However, as Bolton observes, drawing upon the ludic connection between *mantle of the expert* work and theatre:

> Unless such a discussion in role is backed by real concern about the outcome, there will be no game. It will be no nearer drama than a debate – although the participants and their teacher may deceive themselves quite happily.
>
> (1984, p. 90)

One aim of such aesthetic crafting is that it should intensify the students' investment in the learning by moving them so much that they feel deeply and personally committed to it. Bolton quotes Margaret Sutherland: 'we live an imagined situation because it affects us emotionally' (1971, p. 5). There is a second aim. Through the aesthetic crafting of dramatic metaphor, the teacher in role as letter-bearer represents not only that particular letter-bearer in that particular imagined event but also *all* messengers. The letter represents those specific instructions but also *all* commands. The students in role as monks stand for those specific monks but also for *all* who have ever had to decide whether or not to obey the instructions of authority. For Bolton and Heathcote, it is this ability to find the universal (or 'abstraction', as Bolton calls it) within the particular (or 'crystallisation') – to 'expose the inner meanings of an event, to indicate universal implications' – (Bolton, 1984, p. 145) which, ultimately, elevates *mantle of the expert* work to the aesthetic realm.

For Bolton and Heathcote, therefore, aesthetic meaning is constructed from intense, informed observation. It is 'a special quality of attention in the creator or observer' (Bolton, 1984, p. 144). But who is the 'creator' and who is the 'observer' in the letter-exchange incident from the medieval monastery role-play? Although Bolton and Heathcote attempt to seek some accommodation between *the mantle of the expert* and theatre, they take considerable pains to emphasise the differences between the two. One of the most important of these – and here they are in agreement with Rousseau, Slade and Way – is that, as Heathcote puts it: 'Unlike actors, students have not given others "permission to stare"' (Heathcote and Bolton, 1995, p. 185). Likening the distinction between experiencing drama in *point mode* and performing for an audience to the difference between verb and adjective, *being* and *describing*, Bolton argues that an actor wishing to convey, for example, the emotion of regret to an audience, needs to be able to see him or herself as an object, as it were – 'to know how my regretting might appear' (Bolton, 1984, p. 114). If the children playing the monks in the medieval role-play are not to think of themselves as actors who have given 'permission to stare' – if they are to observe the aesthetically crafted intervention of the teacher in role but not craft an aesthetic response of their own – are they to be positioned as observers, but never creators, of art?

In order to address this issue, Bolton and Heathcote turn to Boal's concept of *metaxis*, which Bolton interprets as 'a heightened state of consciousness that holds two worlds in the mind at the same time' (p. 142). Rather than giving 'permission to stare' to an external audience, the students can grant that permission to themselves and to each other as they engage in role-play. By encouraging students to move in and out of the drama, to act and to reflect upon their actions, Bolton tempers Slade's 'absorption' with 'an enhanced degree of *detachment*' (p. 142). Bolton and Heathcote's strategies for projected playing and the '"prismatic" angling of knowledge' facilitate *metaxis* by making the boundaries between the 'as if' and the real world increasingly porous.

This proposed solution does not resolve the issue, however; for what the students reflect upon is not the aesthetics of *the mantle of the expert* work itself but what that work has helped them to learn about papermaking or the monastic rule of obedience. It is no accident that, in the letter-exchange incident from the medieval monastery role-play, it is the teacher in role whose performance is aesthetically crafted. Children in school may not have given permission to be stared at; but every teacher who stands up to address a classroom audience *has* given that permission and by doing so assumes to some extent the responsibilities of the actor. For Bolton and

Heathcote, *some* is replaced by *considerable*: the actor/teacher working within the conventions of *the mantle of the expert* must be able to invite students 'to join in the encounter' by deploying such aesthetic craft skills as: 'appropriate body attitude, gesture, tone of voice, style of delivery, distance, pitch, choice of vocabulary, deliberate uncertainty or confidence, deliberate vagueness or precision' (Heathcote and Bolton, 1995, p. 174).

'What such teacher talk is doing', Heathcote and Bolton suggest, in a development of the theatre analogy, 'is slightly "raising the curtain," inviting the class to take a peep at the metaphorical stage where fiction can take place' (1995, p. 27). However, the principle that the student must not 'see himself as learning' while the teacher must see himself as teaching, holds particularly true for the aesthetic dimension of *mantle of the expert* work. 'The focus of his [the student's] attention must be on "creating a drama" or "solving a problem"', Bolton writes. The 'aesthetic welfare' of the students remains firmly within the purview of the teacher (1984, pp. 157, 112). The students in role as monks may well have been deeply moved by the aesthetics of the letter-exchange episode; but it is not the teacher's task to deconstruct with them the craft which made that exchange so dramatically powerful.

There is again much for the English teacher to take from these elements of Bolton and Heathcote's practice. That '"prismatic" angling of knowledge' effected through Heathcote's oblique responses to direct questions or through the deployment of dramatic metaphor or through Bolton's strategies for 'projected play' speaks persuasively to teachers concerned to show their students that language can be ambiguous, readings can be pluralistic and that narratives do not have to be constrained within a structural straitjacket of chronological plot sequencing and naturalistic or monologic telling. The scrupulous attention that Heathcote and Bolton devote to the scripting of their in-role work issues a powerful reminder to English teachers about the perlocutionary potential of classroom interactions – how, for example, pronouns might be deployed to challenge the traditional teacher/student power relationship; or conditional verbs might provide a bracing cognitive alternative to the deadening familiarities of initiation and response: '"Suppose that . . . if we could. . . . If people would let us . . . I bet if we tried hard we could . . ."' (Heathcote and Bolton, 1995, p. 26).

Where English teachers might part company with Bolton and Heathcote, however, is on the question of aesthetics. To suggest that 'awareness of aesthetic meanings' (Bolton, 1984, p. 157) should remain within the ambit of the teacher rather than being shared with the students, is to exclude them from engagement with the working processes by which art is crafted and thus to restrict their responses to the affective domain inhabited, for example, by a magician's audience who are excited and amazed by the effects of the sleight-of-hand but do not understand how it is achieved. English teachers do not work in this way. Their *raison d'être* is, as it were, to initiate their students 'into the mysteries', to draw their attention to the *constructed* nature of language. In the words of the Russian Formalist, Viktor Shklovsky: 'The technique of art is to make objects "unfamiliar", to make forms difficult, to increase the difficulty and length of perception because the process of perception is an aesthetic end in itself and must be prolonged' (In Lemon and Reis, 1965, p. 12).

It is this kind of 'prolonged' scrutiny that the authors of *The Bullock Report* have in mind when, describing how 'improvisation' might illuminate the exchange between Shakespeare's Antony and Enobarbus cited earlier, they comment: 'On the page these words are unfulfilled, almost meaningless, *until the whole relationship and all its implications have been fully experienced* [my italics] by trying them out in a convincing setting – physical, social and emotional' (DES, 1975, p. 157).

To consider the example of the medieval monastery role-play again: English teachers are not only concerned with the letter-exchange as an act of theatre that drives the narrative forward; they want their students to understand *how* the dramatic metaphors achieve their effect.

Other drama practitioners espoused even more enthusiastically than Bolton and Heathcote the change of educational direction signalled by Callaghan's Ruskin College Speech. Writing in 1987, a year before the implementation of the first statutory National Curriculum for England and Wales, Christopher Havell noted that the triumph of accountability represented by the new legislation would place drama teachers 'under more pressure than ever before to defend what they value' (1987, p. 163). Some ten years and several government-initiated curriculum changes later, David Hornbrook argued that continued economic decline and a shift of global power eastwards had only served to intensify that pressure. He quotes with approval the Gulbenkian Foundation's 1982 endorsement of the spirit of the Ruskin College Speech:

> The basic demands from parents and employers are reasonable enough. They are for a) adequate teaching of certain skills, b) continuing improvements in the general standard of educational attainment, c) adequate information to be made available about pupils' actual achievements and personal potential.
>
> (In Hornbrook, 1998, p. 51)

The formidable teams of writers assembled by Hornbrook in 1998 and, a decade earlier, by Peter Abbs (from whose 1987 edited book, *Living Powers*, the Havell quotation is taken), responded to the 'reasonable' demands of 'parents and employers' by intensifying Bolton's critical interrogation of 'Romantic child-centredness'. Few of the established authority figures from the past escape censure. In an oblique reference to Froebel's metaphor of the teacher as gardener, Hornbrook quips that 'non-evaluative, horticultural accounts of teaching and learning are beginning to look distinctly wilted' (1998, p. 12). Havell criticises Finlay-Johnson because she 'stayed at the side of the playground' and Way for 'placing a great emphasis on doing', which was more like a 'continuous preparation for drama' rather than 'drama in its own right' (1987, pp. 173, 171). Slade comes in for particular censure. Havell comments: 'Slade's preoccupation with the child, with *child*-drama, tended to oust both traditional and aesthetic elements' (p. 169). Hornbrook is even more forthright. He accuses Slade of driving a 'wedge' between 'the professional world of the theatre and his freely expressive classroom drama' (1998, p. 53).

That this critical lexis should contain pejorative applications of phrases such as 'side of the playground', 'non-evaluative', 'doing' or '*child*-drama' – and set these in opposition to adjectives like 'traditional' and 'aesthetic' – gives an indication of the direction in which Abbs and Hornbrook and their colleagues wished to steer drama pedagogy. To summarise the shift in grammatical terms that would have dismayed John Dixon: arguing that '*what* [original italics] is produced' has become 'of marginal importance compared with the simple act of production' (Hornbrook, 1998, p. 10), they sought to reinstate drama in education as *noun* rather than *verb*, as *content* rather than *process*. All those cherished principles of absorption, *point-mode*, learning-by-doing and self-expression – the very qualities that, for Dixon, made drama 'the truest form of learning' because it 'puts knowledge and understanding to their test in action' - are subjected to intense moral, historical and ideological challenge. Hornbrook locates his attack on what Bolton had mildly castigated as 'child-centredness' within a global context, describing it as a 'curiously Western way of looking at things', which is symptomatic of a deep cultural malaise: 'the pinched individualism of our narcissistic society' (1998, p. 11). For Abbs, Rousseau's influence upon the 'modern drama lesson' in which 'children without reference to a past are invited to learn through a discovery process something of immediate relevance' (Abbs, 1987a, p. 22), is not to be viewed positively. For him, the concern with self-discovery and living-in-the-moment is a manifestation of what he regards as the pernicious influence of a twentieth-century Modernism that rejects tradition and heritage in favour of a relentless iconoclasm and projection into the future.

Even the givens of classroom practice are challenged. Improvisation, that ubiquitous strategy favoured by *The Bullock Report* on account of its supposed accessibility, is criticised as being 'uniquely undifferentiated', not only in the indiscriminate, seemingly directionless 'go-into-groups' sense that Bolton means but also – and at last a drama practitioner appears to be heeding the lessons learned from Lowenfeld and acknowledging the *differences* between children – because it privileges 'spontaneity and camaraderie' (Hornbrook, 1998, pp. 55, 56) above all other modes of engagement and thus actually threatens to exclude the shy, the introverted or those whose interest in drama does not involve acting. More than this, however, as Kempe, writing in Hornbrook's (1998) publication observes, improvisation's besetting sin is that it 'elbowed out the teaching of theatre skills and dramatic literature' (Hornbrook, 1998, p. 94).

Abbs and Hornbrook sought to check what they considered to be the unrestrained forward momentum of drama as, literally, a 'doing' verb by advocating a countervailing 'dynamic conservationism' that:

> reveals itself as a new concern with the possibilities of tradition, with the possibilities of form and convention, with the need for continuous and developing engagement by the pupil with the artistic medium, with the need for, at the same time, a critical vocabulary, an awareness of the terms of interpretive discourse.
>
> (Abbs, 1987a, p. 9)

This 'conservationism', this shift from verb back to noun, was very much the educational order of the day for the National Curriculum for England and Wales established in 1988. Those charged with defining the content of the core and foundation subjects for that curriculum across ten levels of progression and four 'key stages' were equally concerned with naming-words like 'tradition', 'form', 'convention', 'medium', 'vocabulary' and 'terms' because they spoke to the prevailing, post-Ruskin Speech discourse of standards, subject content, discipline and academic rigour. Although by 1995 drama had failed to gain entry to the charmed circle of the National

Curriculum, Hornbrook refuses to ally himself with those who regarded this omission as an opportunity for drama to be 'left alone to pursue its own idiosyncratic purposes away from the spotlight of publicly understood and nationally audited arrangements' (1998, p. 52). On the contrary, he engages with the National Curriculum on its own terms, proposing, for example, a key stage three curriculum for eleven to fourteen year olds that would be content-rich enough to answer Kempe's concerns about 'theatre skills and dramatic literature'. According to Hornbrook's proposal, eighteen terminally assessed projects divided into six hour-long sessions would range, for the youngest students, from Indian and Medieval Theatre in term one, to Mask and Comedy in term two and Elizabethan and Street Theatre in term three (1998, p. 63).

Abbs is eager to position drama as one of the 'six great members of the aesthetic family' (the others are defined as Art, Dance, Music, Film and Literature), in order to elevate it from the status of cross-curricular learning tool and to prepare for the challenge of the then imminent National Curriculum. He proposes an elegant solution to the noun/verb issue in suggesting that drama shares with the performing arts a conceptual terrain that can be defined by four present participles: 'making', 'presenting', 'responding' and 'evaluating' (Abbs, 1987a, pp. 63, 54). Writing a decade later, Hornbrook endorses this position, though, in order to cement the relationship further, he conflates 'evaluating' with 'responding' (1998, p. 63) to bring the model into alignment with *Drama in Schools*, the Art's Council's 1992 version of a possible National Curriculum designed to ally drama with dance and music.

As the use of present participles suggests, it is not the intention of Abbs and Hornbrook and their colleagues to re-establish the dais in a sedentary, transmissive drama classroom. What they seek is 'an appropriate balance between a knowledge of drama and the mastery of its practices' (Hornbrook, 1998, p. 9). This is where their critique of 'child-centredness' – or, rather, *transcendent* visions of childhood – becomes particularly challenging. 'The word "self-expression"', Abbs writes, has come to 'falsely characterize the quintessential purpose of the aesthetic curriculum' (Abbs, 1987a, p. 44). Hornbrook develops the argument. The mere fact that a child has created a picture or taken part in a mime activity, he suggests, does not of itself afford that picture or that mime 'aesthetic value'. Hornbrook continues: 'Four year old Sophie's pastel scribbles displayed so proudly on the fridge door are valuable not because they are art but because Sophie has produced them' (Hornbrook, 1998, p. 57). Where Bolton and Heathcote would retain aesthetic crafting within the remit of the teacher, Abbs and Hornbrook demand, true to the spirit of the National Curriculum's concern with 'what students should be able to do, know and understand' (p. 52), that it should be made accessible to the learner. 'In the past,' Hornbrook comments, 'answers to students' questions about how they are getting on in drama have sometimes been less than transparent' because, confined to the pedagogic side lines by a Romantic commitment to the sanctity of child creativity, teachers have entertained 'the belief that there really was no body of knowledge and skills that could be identified with their subject' (pp. 14, 55). Such an attitude, Abbs and Hornbrook would argue, is not only patronising to the students; it also plays into the hands of those who suggest that drama in education is nothing more than a series of techniques that any non-specialist can use at random to facilitate the teaching of science or history. If learners are to be given honest answers to their legitimate questions about 'how they are getting on in drama', they need to understand the criteria against which those evaluative judgements are made. Hornbrook continues:

> Students will not simply *intuit* how to light a performance, any more than they are likely to perform well without being taught at least the rudiments of acting or direct without studying the way in which stage pictures are organised.
>
> (p. 56)

It is not only the 'making' element of the drama triumvirate that requires explicit teaching. 'Evaluating', Abbs writes, demands significant content knowledge: an awareness of drama conventions and techniques; an appreciation of the historical context within which the work should be evaluated; a familiarity with the critical and interpretative literature which has mediated that evaluation in the past. At the time of writing, Abbs concludes, 'these areas . . . hardly exist' as far as drama is concerned (Abbs, 1987a, p. 62).

True to the principle that drama in education should encompass more than improvisation and foster other qualities apart from 'spontaneity and camaraderie', Hornbrook's colleague, Christopher McCullough, teases out the subject-specific content that students need to be taught if they are to make, respond and evaluate effectively. This includes words like: 'writing/devising', 'acting/performing', 'light', 'sound' and 'scenography' (McCullough, 1998, p. 172). In other words – and here, too, Abbs and Hornbrook are in tune with National Curriculum thinking of the period – students need to be taught *skills*. Once again, 'Romantic child-centredness' is blamed for introducing 'ways of doing things in drama classrooms from which theatre skills have been exiled' (Hornbrook, 1998, p. 57) by encouraging the idea that artists are born, not made and by privileging what Bolton condemned as 'unfettered dramatic playing'. 'Where creativity is all', Kempe adds, 'it seems that the acquisition of actual craftsmanship becomes a matter more of chance than intention' (Kempe, 1998, p. 94). Hornbrook reaches back into history to find alternative 'ways of doing things in drama classrooms' – and in the analogy of the medieval guild or craft, he locates a model that resonates powerfully and productively with Lave and Wenger's (1991) conception of learning as induction into a socially situated community of expertise.

Hornbrook's *apprenticeship* model of learning offers a potent alternative to Heathcote and Bolton's *mantle of the expert*. Students who are taught the craft of set design, or stage lighting or movement or voice projection develop a real expertise very different from its fictional equivalent created within the boundaries of an '*imagined* context' [original italics] such as a medieval monastery by means of what Heathcote and Bolton termed, perhaps unfortunately, 'the big lie' (1995, p. vii). More important still, however, are the implications of the words 'induction' and 'community'. Where Abbs and Hornbrook and their colleagues really part company from the proponents of 'child-centredness' is in their interpretation of the phrase 'collaborative enterprise'. Like Heathcote and Bolton, they regard it as 'central to drama' (Hornbrook, 1998, p. 60); but their understanding of collaboration is far broader than the creation of some temporary community established for the purpose of learning about science or history through an extended role-play set in a medieval monastery. Hornbrook writes: 'Providing the opportunity for pupils to practise the craft at levels commensurate with their age and ability is part of their induction into membership of the culture' (p. 60).

The 'culture' Hornbrook has in mind is the whole rich, historical, aesthetic heritage of theatre. It includes the European tradition of Shakespeare and Greek Tragedy, of course; but it reaches out globally, too, embracing 'the highly stylised dream-seeking mime of the Australian Aranda people', for example, or the 'Zauli dancers of the Ivory Coast' (pp. 6, 7). It is not surprising that two of the authorities discussed earlier in this book who actually escape censure from Abbs and his co-writers are Caldwell Cook and Marjorie Hourd – the former because it was felt that he provided his pupils 'with an aesthetic education worthy of the name' by foregrounding 'performance with all due ceremony' (Abbs, 1987a, pp. 52, 58) when inducting them into the theatre of Shakespeare; and the latter because, by encouraging her students to engage with canonical literature, she made accessible to them 'the public resource' [of culture] as 'a personal possession' (Webb, 1987, p. 77).

Conceptualising drama as noun and content rather than verb and action invites a shift in emphasis between Bolton's polarities of 'dramatic playing' ('the intention to be') on the one hand and 'performance mode' ('the *intention to communicate*' [original italics]) on the other (Bolton, 1984, p. 32). Tilting the balance in favour of 'performance mode' signals a renewed focus upon narrative as a medium rather than as a process of interpretation. Where Dixon locates the learning potential of drama in its capacity to put 'knowledge and understanding to their test in action', Hornbrook argues that it is to be found in the 'enactment of stories' (1998, p. 7) and he quotes Martin Esslin's definition of drama as 'narrative made visible, a picture given the power to move in time' (Esslin, 1987, p. 36). If 'performance mode' requires, in Bolton's words, the intention 'to describe to someone the make believe' (Bolton, 1984, p. 32), then in order to be effective, to survive as part of the cultural heritage, the 'make believe' needs to be articulated with skill. One of the most decisive ways in which Abbs and Hornbrook and their colleagues signal a break with their predecessors' long-established mistrust of the theatre is by reasserting the importance of the actor as 'the primary agent' of that 'make-believe' (Hornbrook, 1998, p. 7).

Way had deplored the idea that 'we so often approach the arts as though we were intent on producing professional actors', basing his argument on the democratic principle that this approach sets the bar of attainment too high for all but an elite minority of children with 'natural gift'. For him, 'theatrical conventions' impose 'limitations' to learning in drama (Way, 1967, pp. 119, 3, 6). Bolton and Heathcote are willing to admit learners as actors in the role-play and even to concede that dramatic conventions such as projected play could facilitate learning within the 'as if' world. However, they share Way's concerns about restricted access and elitism and therefore – as their consigning of the responsibility for aesthetic crafting to the teacher suggests – they impose significant constraints upon their students' 'dramatic playing'. Bolton, for example, suggests that concepts such as 'character development' are too artistically demanding for most students to attempt. He does not expect the children engaged in the medieval monastery *mantle of the expert* work, for example, to create and portray complex individual characters as actors in a play or film might, but rather to 'be themselves, functioning in whatever way the situation demands of them'. Playing the role of a monk does not require 'the skill of the performer', Bolton adds. Rather – and again, drama is put to the service of something other than itself – it is *'the skill of bringing oneself to function with a degree of maturity that one's normal "life" role does not demand'* [original italics] (Bolton, 1984, p. 101). The parameters of the role-play are restricted even further by the fact that the self is expected to function in exclusively high status roles requiring expertise. To suggest, as Hornbrook's colleague Kempe does, that dramatic improvisations must accommodate 'a recognition of the conventions of the stage' (Kempe, 1998, p. 92) is to wrest responsibility for aesthetic crafting out of the exclusive control of the teacher and thus to mark another advance of the child into what Callaghan had described in his Ruskin College Speech as the 'secret garden' of the curriculum (*Guardian* UK, 2001).

Privileging the 'intention to communicate' over the 'intention to be' invests renewed authority in the receiver of the 'narrative made visible' – the audience. For Bolton and Heathcote, *metaxis* provides the medium for the learner's aesthetic experience: I reflect, in and out of role as a monk, on the emotional, cognitive and symbolic significance of the bishop's letter delivered in the fictional world of the drama. However, if, as Kempe suggests, the primary question to ask of an improvisation must now become 'How will this happen on stage?' (Kempe, 1998, p. 93) then, as Way feared, the knowledge that 'others are watching what we ourselves are doing' means that 'our concentration is divided between the actual doing and concern for the effect we are having on the watcher' (Way, 1967, p. 14). Kempe does not share Way's reservations about this. For him, a second pressing and entirely legitimate question for the player in the drama to pose is: 'What would the effect be on me if I were to experience this as an audience?' (Kempe, 1998, p. 93). In *The Act of Reading*, Wolfgang Iser cites Virginia Woolf's attempt to identify the enduring qualities of Jane Austen's novels. Woolf concludes that Austen's strength lies in her ability to endow 'scenes which are outwardly trivial' – a game of cards, for example, or a walk along a seaside promenade – 'with the most enduring form of life' (In Iser, 1978, p. 168). Austen achieves this through what Bolton and Heathcote might describe as the '"prismatic" angling of knowledge' – oblique hints in a dialogue or piece of description; things unsaid as well as said. For Iser, the power of Austen's writing is released by means of 'an interaction between the textual signals and the reader's acts of comprehension' (p. 9). 'Communication in literature', he suggests:

> is a process set in motion and regulated not by a given code but by a mutually restrictive and magnifying interaction between the explicit and the implicit, between revelation and concealment. What is concealed spurs the reader into action, but this action is also controlled by what is revealed; the explicit in its turn is transformed when the implicit has been brought to light.
>
> (pp. 168–169)

For Kempe, Iser's account of the 'reconstituting' (p. 169) of significant meanings through the meeting of reader and writer in the text described in the quotation above offers a model for the way in which actors and audience collaborate as performers and spectators to 'revel' – the verb is defiantly celebratory – in 'aesthetic interpretation' (p. 101). Abbs puts it more bluntly: 'no audience – no aesthetic' (Abbs, 1987a, p. 58).

Much as the authors of *The Bullock Report* deplore the 'polarisation of view' between 'theatre' as product and 'educational' drama as process, the sympathies of

English practitioners are strongly drawn to the latter. If the debate has to be couched in terms of personalities, then it is Bolton and Heathcote, rather than Abbs and Hornbrook, who elicit most support. Britton makes this clear when, anticipating by thirty years Hornbrook's description of drama's primary concern as the 'enactment of stories', he quotes approvingly from an article on improvisation written by Dorothy Heathcote that takes the opposite position: 'I must begin by endorsing Dorothy Heathcote's pronouncement: "Drama is *not* stories retold in action. Drama *is* human beings confronted by situations which change them because of what they must face in dealing with those challenges"' (Britton, 1970, p. 145).

The attractions for English practitioners of the drama-as-process approach are many: democratic access – particularly for those who find written forms of literacy difficult – to a wide range of empowering language registers and structures; learning alongside the teacher through discovery rather than learning through transmission from the dais; exploration of one's personal and social identity within a safe fictional context; breaking down of the academic barriers that can place canonical literature beyond popular reach; the acknowledgement that sound, movement and gesture are important components of literacy.

However, as has been noted already – particularly when recalling Whitehead's reservations about dramatising *Sir Patrick Spens* or *The Bullock Report*'s pronouncements upon the increasingly significant role of the spectator as arbitrator of what is or is not theatre – there is also much about Abbs' and Hornbrook's position that appeals to the English practitioner too. Abbs' inclusion of literature as one of the six members of the 'aesthetic family' offers encouragement to those for whom progression is actually marked by a move from self-absorption to something much more distanced: a sense of cultural engagement that is characterised by an increasingly sophisticated capacity for detached contemplation of works of dramatic literature as highly wrought aesthetic objects. In terms of English pedagogy, one of the most important legacies of the privileging of the spectator advocated by Abbs and Hornbrook and their colleagues is the way that it enriches the act of *looking*.

Had Abbs and Hornbrook or their colleagues written the *Drama* section of *The Bullock Report*, it would have been a very different document. The exchange between Antony and Enobarbus from Act One Scene Two of Shakespeare's *Antony and Cleopatra* cited in the report and quoted earlier provides a striking example of just what those differences might have been. As has been noted, the authors of the report consider the extract as an opportunity for personal engagement, for 'trying . . . out' the 'whole relationship and all its implications' until they have been 'fully experienced'. Their approach would have encouraged plentiful opportunities for 'making', 'performing' and 'responding' certainly; but the emphasis would have been on constructing first a personal and then a negotiated group response. Abbs and Hornbrook and their colleagues offer a much more complex, culturally informed interpretation of the three key terms.

McCullough, for example, emphasises the importance of framing a text historically and culturally, arguing that to 'deny history as an informing text is also to contradict the historical processes by which our own individual contexts (race, gender, social class, and so on) influence what things mean to us' (1998, p. 175). What matters from this perspective is the 'iterability' of the drama text – how it is read 'at the historical moment of its reception' and how it demonstrates 'the processes by which culture is made at a specific point in history' (p. 182). Applying such an interpretation of 'trying . . . out' to the extract from *Antony and Cleopatra* from this perspective might invite questions about the play's historical reception – how did audiences respond when it was first performed in the early seventeenth century, perhaps, or just after the release of Mankiewicz's film *Cleopatra* in 1963 or in 2013, at the time of political upheavals in Egypt and economic difficulties in Italy? As Kempe puts it: 'Plays, like myths, develop historically but are encountered in the "now" of the reader or audience' (1998, p. 105).

Equally significant is the way that Abbs and Hornbrook and their colleagues extend chronologically the act of 'responding'. Just as English practitioners might describe a tri-partite model of reading that includes *pre* and *post* activities as well as the actual act of reading itself, so Urian argues that the spectators' role starts long before they take their seats for an actual performance: 'the experience of the play begins from the point when the production is first mentioned and expectations are raised prior to the actual performance . . . it ends with the spectator's memories of the event' (1998, p. 139).

From this perspective, an approach to the *Antony and Cleopatra* extract cited in *The Bullock Report* might begin by inviting students to engage with Julia Kristeva's argument that a text 'is a permutation of texts, an intertextuality. In the space of a single text several *énoncés* from other texts cross and neutralize each other' (1970, p. 12). Before they start to engage with the text itself, what do the students bring to that engagement in terms of knowledge about Shakespeare and his world or about the portrayal of Antony and of Cleopatra in history and in culture? They may be familiar, for example, with *Asterix and Cleopatra*, Goscinny and Uderzo's (1963) comic parody of the Mankiewicz film, or with the video in which the song *Cleopatra* by *Adam and the Ants* is played against a montage of photographic and painted images of her. Similarly, recalling 'the spectator's memories of the event' offers an opportunity to explore the differences between the raw material of a narrative and the way that narrative is crafted and thus to begin to engage with the Russian Formalists Vladimir Propp's and Viktor Shklovsky's concept of *fabula* and *syuzhet*. Three weeks, say, after 'trying . . . out' approaches to the extract from *Antony and Cleopatra*, what moments of interpretation still remain vivid in the students' minds? Which have faded and why? If they were to recount the story now in their own words, how might their version differ from Shakespeare's telling?

As the references to Kristeva and Propp and Shklovsky suggest, the approach to 'making, performing and responding' advocated by Abbs and Hornbrook and their colleagues brings a theoretical formality to the act of looking. One of the qualities that makes theatre and performance such powerful media for learning is their capacity to draw upon *ostension*, which Elam calls 'the most "primitive" form of signification: In order to refer to, indicate or define a given object, one simply picks it up and shows it to the receiver of the message in question' (2002, p. 26).

Ostension has the capacity to bring complex abstract ideas about perception and interpretation vividly to life for students because, to use Elam's terms, one simply 'picks . . . up' those ideas, as it were, and shows them 'to the receiver of the message'. Thus, Heathcote and Bolton's telling of a story about cancer through images of wilting plants *shows* what a dramatic metaphor is, instead of just describing it (1995, p. 189). *Ostension* can enable the exploration of a complex idea from several perspectives. Elam offers as one instance the example of *synecdoche*. The physical building of the theatre is a part that stands for a whole just as in the *Prologue* to Shakespeare's *Henry V*, the 'wooden O' is understood to contain 'the very casques/ That did affright the air at Agincourt' (1993, the *Prologue*, lines 13–14). In another application of the concept, Elam continues, a war tent on stage can stand in for an army – or again, the wielding of a knife can stand in for an act of assassination.

As the physical examples of synecdoche above suggest, 'performances', in the words of Kempe, 'are "polysemic", communicating not just through spoken words alone but via a complex cluster of signs used simultaneously'. Plays, he continues, 'acquire symbolic value by attending to the visual as well as verbal and other aural signifiers' (1998, pp. 96, 104). What Kempe and his colleagues gesture towards in *Living Powers* (Abbs, 1987b) and *On the Subject of Drama* (Hornbrook, 1998) is explored with a forensic thoroughness in Keir Elam's 1980 publication *The Semiotics of Theatre and Drama* (second edition 2002). Elam brings to the attention of an Anglophone audience the work of Eastern European theoreticians of the theatre including members of the early twentieth-century *Prague School* such as Otakar Zich (1879–1934) and Jan Mukařovský (1891–1975) whom he credits with 'radically' developing the 'scientific analysis of theatre and drama' (2002, p. 4). Taking his cue from the Polish academic, Tadeusz Kowzan's (1922–2010) assertion that 'Everything is sign in a theatrical presentation' (Kowzan, 1968, p. 57), Elam examines in detail the Czech and Polish theoreticians' attempts to identify the richly complex patterns of interweaving semiotic systems that contribute to a theatrical performance. 'How many ways of pronouncing the words "I love you"', Kowzan asks, 'can mean passion as well as indifference, irony as well as pity?' And he goes on to describe how:

> Facial mime and gestures of the hand can underline the meaning of words, belie it or give it a particular shade. That is not all. A lot depends on the attitude of the actor's body and his [sic] position in relation to his partners.
>
> (pp. 56–57)

This should be enough to give pause for thought to the authors of *The Bullock Report* who suggested airily that students 'fully experience' the 'whole relationship [between Antony, Enobarbus and presumably Fulvia] and all its implications' (DES, 1975, p. 157). It is not only the spoken lines that can be crafted and reconfigured so flexibly. Drawing upon Kowzan again, Elam demonstrates how, within the framed space of the theatre, conventionally coded channels of communication between 'source' and 'transmitter', 'receiver' and 'destination' (Elam, 2002, p. 31) become malleable and elusive. Who, for example, is the 'source' of the information in a play – the play-wright, the director, the set designer? The principal 'transmitter' of a message might be at one moment an actor – and the next a stage prop or a sound, a lighting effect or even a smell (of a cigarette or of gun smoke, for example). An object like a dagger might symbolise violence and then perform an instrumental function within the play to propel the action forward. The same message can be conveyed through several different channels – by a word, a gesture, a sound or a lighting effect. One director's interpretation of a play text might send out markedly different messages from another's. Elam describes in turn the elaborate coding systems that theoreticians and practitioners have devised to account for what Kowzan calls the 'semiological richness of the art of the spectacle' (Kowzan, 1968, p. 57). As well as Kowzan's thirteen *auditive* and *visual* theatre signs (p. 57), Elam's coverage includes, from the English-speaking world, Scott Burton's (1939–1989) *proxemics* consisting of 'eighty interpersonal situations' (Elam, 2002, p. 60); Ray Birdwhistell's (1918–1994) analysis of sixty examples of 'body motion' or *kinesics* (pp. 62–63) and Richard Pilbrow's four 'functions' and 'properties' of stage lighting (p. 75).

Formal, disciplined *looking* of this kind can penetrate deeply into dramatic texts. Application of the coding systems Elam describes can provide students with powerful analytical tools and with a forensic critical method. Think of the creative challenges posed by inviting a group of students to devise a lighting plot for the witches' scene that opens *Macbeth* according to Pilbrow's criteria of 'selective visibility', 'revelation of form', 'composition', 'mood', 'intensity', 'colour', 'distribution' and 'movement' (Elam, 2002, p. 75). 'The crown on the actor's head is the sign of royalty', Kowzan writes, 'whereas the wrinkles and whiteness of his face, obtained with the help of make-up, and his hesitant gait are all signs of old age' (Kowzan, 1968, p. 57). How might what Kowzan describes as the theatre signs of gesture, movement, make-up, hairstyle and costume interplay with props, décor and lighting to convey the external authority and internal tumult of Claudius when he makes his first appearance in Shakespeare's *Hamlet*? The text, Stanley Fish writes, 'is always a function of interpretation' (1980, p. 342). Negotiating agreement about what these signs might signify, and about how those significations achieve legitimacy, is a powerful means of encouraging that cultural induction that Abbs and Hornbrook regard as such an important principle of dramatic engagement.

There is much to persuade English practitioners here. Commenting upon the radical changes that technology and the media have brought to written literacy, Kress and Bezemer note: 'The *page* is used differently to the way it had been: it now has a different semiotic function. It has become a *site of display* [original italics] with quite specific social and semiotic potentials' (2009, p. 167).

If the (electronic) page and the theatre stage now share, as well as a full rhyme, a common concern for Heathcote's 'operant laws' – the interplay of words and images, movement and stillness, sound and silence – what better way of helping students appreciate the 'social and semiotic potentials' of the former medium than through the *ostended* powers of the latter?

Introducing curriculum rigour in terms of content and critical method not only gives the lie to those who would regard drama as academically 'soft' and inextricably linked to the vagaries of 'self-expression'. It can also, as noted earlier, empower learners with real expertise. If students were to be taught the craft skills of Pilbrow's lighting system, for example, how potent and authoritative would their own work in the medium become – and how authoritatively would English students be able to answer those time-honoured examination questions about the staging of Shakespeare? Choosing this route, however, brings significant consequences for English pedagogy. First, it requires the construction of a coherent and progressive drama curriculum. Second, it implies, in some measure at least, that the dais be returned to the classroom and that the teacher move from co-learner to transmitter of knowledge – a drama-specific knowledge that might lie beyond the ambit of traditional training in English pedagogy. Third – and perhaps most important of all – it threatens to weaken the commitment to democracy, inclusivity and personal growth that makes drama so appealing to English teachers in the first place. If skills are to be taught and applied, then, inevitably, some students will learn to apply those skills more effectively than others. Answers to students' questions about 'how they are getting on in drama', might not always be positive. Subject-specific discourse might empower, but it might also intimidate and exclude. What drama in education might gain in terms of aesthetic crafting, it might lose in terms of 'spontaneity and camaraderie'.

Chapter 7

Daring to speak its name

National curricula and the current state of drama

In 2008, Jonothan Neelands published a briefing paper for student teachers of English in England designed to introduce them to the main issues informing drama pedagogy in contemporary classrooms (Neelands, 2008). What is striking about Neelands' *tour d'horizon* is just how many of the issues from the past that have already been explored in this book – even in its earliest chapters – still demand attention in his paper. Shakespeare's looming presence, for example, features prominently in the work of Caldwell Cook and Finlay-Johnson; but a century later, Neelands still has to explain to the prospective teachers why this particular playwright dominates, uniquely, the 'English model' of drama (p. 1). Forty years on from Dixon's (1967) *Growth Through English* and a decade after the appearance of Hornbrook's (1998) *On the Subject of Drama*, the *noun/verb, process/product* issue is still regarded by Neelands as something about which student teachers need to know and that they can expect to encounter during careers that might last well into the twenty-first century. To give a third example: in 1967, Her Majesty's Inspectors for Schools concluded from their monitoring visits that 'there is no agreement' about the 'real identity' of drama (DES, 1967, p. 2). Forty years later, Neelands feels the need to repeat the observation, noting in contemporary classrooms 'a degree of professional insecurity amongst teachers employed as drama specialists' and 'a long and sometimes fierce contest to define what is legitimate drama in schools' (Neelands, 2008, p. 2). Thinking back even to the very first chapters of this book, it is not too fanciful to detect a faint echo of *transcendent* statements about childhood in Neelands' assertion that, even within a system of compulsory education, 'students cannot be coerced into drama or made to do it. It has to be by choice' (p. 3).

Neelands is not the only contemporary practitioner to re-affirm pedagogic principles with a long established historical heritage. Writing in 2012, John Rainer and Martin Lewis argue the case for drama as a medium of 'authentic learning', using, like Bolton almost thirty years earlier, language of which Rousseau would have approved. Thus the criteria by which they define its 'key characteristics' contain phrases like 'authentic tasks that are of interest to the learner', the importance of 'exploration and enquiry' and 'the world beyond the walls of the classroom' (Rainer and Lewis, 2012, p. 3). Rainer and Lewis are still concerned with the *learning in* or *learning through* drama issue that features in this book's discussion of Finlay-Johnson's work and that was to come to the fore again in relation to the practice of Heathcote. Here, for example, Rainer and Lewis are discussing the use of drama as a medium for the study of history: 'For us, all historical enactment, no matter how far it is based on evidence, is *fiction* – or, at best, fictionalized accounts of real events: it can only be drama *based on* history, not history itself' (p. 9).

The practice of re-affirming and re-visiting is not confined to England. A piece written in 2009 by two Australia-based academics on the relationship between 'virtual worlds' and 'real-life drama in the classroom' (Dunn and O'Toole, 2009, p. 20), shares the Neelands paper's concern to define *process* drama as if its principles and practice still need to be clarified for their intended audience – and this even though one of the authors is based at the University of Melbourne, which for 'well over the past 30 years' (Pascoe and Sallis, 2012, p. 132) has been acknowledged as a 'power-house' famous for its 'excellent pre-service teacher education' (Courtney, 1989, p. 25). In the same collection, Sutton argues the case for the application of lip-syncing technologies to drama in words that practitioners like Hawkes and Holbrook would have appreciated fifty years ago: 'A recurrent feature of . . . lip syncing is seeing some of the most marginalized, insecure young people in school communities given an apparent dramatic [sic] rise in confidence through losing themselves in the moment of syncing' (Sutton, 2009, p. 46).

When turning to contemporary works that deal specifically with the 'close relationship' (Neelands, 2008, p. 1) between English and drama, it is difficult to avoid a sense of exasperation. Another mainly Australia-based study, entitled *Drama and English Teaching* and published in the same year as Neelands' paper, felt it still relevant to repeat the following quotation from Grady, first issued in 2000:

> Learning how to interpret and analyse theatrical events is a critical component in the education of students. . . . However, there is very little available to guide teachers who are struggling. . . . How are teachers supposed to help students become more responsive to theatrical events? What skills do students need in order to openly receive and actively interpret a variety of performance texts?
>
> (In Anderson *et al.*, 2008, p. 10)

It is slightly disheartening to think that questions like these need to be repeated in the twenty-first century, so many years after Kowzan and then Elam explored the complex semiological systems of the theatre – and a decade after Kempe, McCullough, Urian and other contributors to *On the Subject of Drama* addressed precisely these issues.

To cite again examples from England, some of the opening statements made in a 2010 government-sponsored set of drama guidance materials for English teachers would cause the authors of *The Bullock Report* to hang their heads in despair. The following observation might have come straight from the drama section of *A Language for Life*:

> English teachers are skilled and confident at identifying and defining good practice particularly in relation to the teaching and learning of reading and writing, but some are less secure in their understanding of how effective drama can contribute to the development of critical thinking and analytical skills. To ensure that all pupils have full access to opportunities to develop these skills, it is helpful if the department establishes a shared understanding and vision for the role of drama within English.
>
> (DfE, 2010, p. 4)

Perhaps most disturbing of all, after everything that the practitioners reviewed in this book have said through the years about the need for interactive approaches to literature in general and play texts in particular, advisers writing in 2010 still feel the need to say the following:

> Where drama in English is only used to 'present' scripts, improvise ideas or adopt roles to demonstrate different register use, without a layered and developed context and role, then opportunities for improving skills in critical thinking, reading and writing can be missed and shallow rather than deep learning is often observed.
>
> (DfE, 2010, p. 5)

Writing a year later in a special drama-focused edition of *English in Education*, the academic journal of the National Association for the Teaching of English (NATE), the Education Programme Developer for the Royal Shakespeare Company still feels the need to argue a case made a hundred years earlier by Caldwell Cook: 'English teachers should be supported to take risks in trying out active approaches in order to achieve a more dialogic process and a more meaningful relationship with Shakespeare for their students' (Irish, 2011, p. 6). Statements like this are probably not what Abbs hoped for in 1987 when he called for a return to 'dynamic conservationism'.

A hint as to how this state of affairs came about – certainly within the context of England – lies in the title of Neelands' 2008 paper. In an allusion to a famous line from Lord Alfred Douglas' (1894) poem *Two Loves*, he calls it *Drama: The Subject that Dare not Speak its Name*. The catchy title has serious connotations. If English is, to follow the Douglas analogy, the socially acceptable 'love', then why – after a lifetime devoted to advancing its pedagogy and practice – does Neelands believe student teachers need to be warned that drama, by contrast, is the 'love' which is marginalized and deprived of a public voice? The problem, certainly within the English context (Neelands notes that drama is 'included as a discrete subject and as a strand in the Arts in the National Curricula of a growing number of other national education systems' (2008, p. 1) around the world) can be traced back to 1988 and its failure to join art and music as a foundation subject of the statutory National Curriculum.

Her Majesty's Inspectors for Schools worked vigorously to prevent this omission. Mindful perhaps of the incoherence and uncertainty witnessed by their colleagues in 1967 and of the still unanswered questions from *The Bullock Report*, they published in 1989 a twenty-one page A5 document entitled *Drama from 5 to 16* as part of their *Curriculum Matters* series (the fact that the drama document is number seventeen and comes right at the end of the series is not insignificant). The aim of the document was to 'contribute to the continuing debate about the nature of drama in our schools' and thus help educators and politicians reach a 'national agreement about the objectives and content of the school curriculum' (DES, 1989, p. v). 'Agreement' was certainly its watchword. Declaring right at the start that drama in schools 'is a practical artistic subject', it sought to reconcile proponents of both *process* and *product* approaches by devoting sections to 'learning through drama' and 'imagination' on the one hand and 'concepts', 'knowledge and understanding' and 'skills' on the other (DES, 1989, pp. 2, 9, 6, 7, 10). *Drama from 5 to 16* has an admirable brevity that stands in marked contrast to the somewhat over-written, self-absorbed and complex curriculum documents created by the working parties whose subjects did succeed in gaining admission to that first National Curriculum. Had it been granted statutory recognition, students and teachers would have been given a shared set of entitlement statements against which to review progress at ages 7, 11 and 16. They would have had access to a shared metalanguage (albeit a very different one from that proposed by Slade thirty years earlier) with which to discuss the 'elements of learning', including such 'concepts' of drama as *fictions, symbols, character or role, situation and setting, plotting, rules or conventions* and *dialogue*) (DES, 1989, pp. 6–7). Teachers would have been required to acknowledge that 'the study of drama is bound closely to English through language, literature and poetry', certainly; but they would also have been expected to recognise its 'affinities with the media and the other arts, especially music, dance and the visual arts' (DES, 1989, p. 2). Teachers would have been required to develop the knowledge and skills needed to do exactly the opposite of what Hawkes had advised over twenty years earlier – 'intervene in practical work', adopt 'teaching techniques particular to drama' and gauge 'growth in understanding' (DES, 1989, p. 18). Secondary teachers would have been required to liaise with, and build upon the work of, their primary colleagues and to undertake continuous assessment, regarded by Her Majesty's Inspectors as 'essential' (DES, 1989, p. 20).

The consequences of this missed opportunity for drama education have been profound and still exert a potent influence in schools today – certainly in the context of England. Most significantly, English became – and remains – the statutory protector of drama within the National Curriculum, even though the issues raised by *The Bullock Report*'s indulgence towards those teachers who lack the 'temperament' to 'handle improvised drama' had not been addressed by 1989 – and, judging by the statement from 2010 quoted earlier, still remain unresolved. Brian Cox, chairman of the first National Curriculum working party for English, declared himself to be 'very determined that drama activities would play a central role in the English curriculum' (Cox, 1991, p. 86). For all his good intentions, however, Cox, like Bullock before him, views drama through the prism of subject English. To read his account of his working party's thinking about drama in English is to experience Bullock revisited – in fact, the subject is afforded the same number of pages – five – in *Cox on Cox* as in *A Language for Life*. All the arguments from *The Bullock Report* are rehearsed again: the enhancement of language skills and registers; the fostering of teamwork; the exploration of the relationship between the self and the community; the widened definition of reading; the opportunities afforded to those for whom print-bound literacies prove particularly challenging; the potential for interactive engagement with literature.

The members of Cox's working party might have used *Drama from 5 to 16* as a template and, taking their cue from Her Majesty's Inspectors' observation that 'drama is bound closely to English through language, literature and poetry', plotted a coherent pathway for the former through the latter, using perhaps the arts-based *making, performing, responding* configuration for guidance. Instead, the Cox model *stretches* drama across a five-strand, English-based framework consisting of *personal growth*, *cross-curricular* and *adult needs*, *cultural heritage* and *cultural analysis* (Cox, 1991, pp. 21–22). The result is that – to change metaphors again – drama runs like an underground stream through the original English Order, emerging here and there where its presence is deemed useful to the service of the statutory subject. The references to drama in the programmes of study for speaking and listening as recorded in *Cox on Cox* are a case in point. By the age of seven, children are expected to have engaged in 'collaborative', 'exploratory' and 'imaginative' play (the differences between the three forms are not explained) and to have taken part in 'improvised drama' (the Cox working party is very much in favour of *process* drama) (Cox, 1991, p. 185). Then, sometime between the ages of seven and sixteen, they should 'listen and respond to an increasing range . . . of plays', 'work with or devise an increasing range of drama scripts, taking on a variety of dramatic roles' and – and here the emphasis on learning through drama is foregrounded – 'use, and understand the use of, role-play in teaching and learning, *e.g. to explore an aspect of history, a scientific concept or a piece of literature* [Original italics]' (p. 186).

The status of these drama references, already vitiated by the vague, catch-all nature of the wording and the inconsistency of their appearance throughout the programmes of study, is further weakened by the fact that so many of the statements are offered merely as suggested activities. Students working towards level 6 on the National Curriculum's then ten-scale assessment grid, 'might' include 'performance of a play-script for a school production'; drama scripts 'might furnish . . . materials and topics for discussion' for students working towards level seven – but then so might 'responses to the media, pupils' own written work and the use of information technology' (Cox, 1991, p. 188). One can imagine how eagerly those English teachers temperamentally unsuited to 'handle improvised drama' would seize on that conditional verb as a welcome get-out clause. Bizarrely, Cox suggests that, out of this muddle, 'English teachers will be providing experiences for pupils which will help them make an informed choice when considering drama as a subject option' (p. 86)! They will help students make this choice by giving them – revealing phrase – 'the tools of the trade' (p. 89).

The introduction of attainment levels places another pressure upon drama within the English Order by imposing its own assessment logic on what are supposed to be student-centred learning experiences. Thus, the capacity to 'make more extended contributions' to dramatic improvisations, role-play or scripted scenes becomes one of the criteria for access to speaking and listening at level five; being able to perform 'a play-script for a school production' helps gain entry to level six – but, thinking of Hornbrook's criticism of the privileging of 'spontaneity and camaraderie' – presumably only if the student takes part as an actor rather than, say, as a set designer. Drama scripts act as a gateway to level seven – provided the student is able to discuss them. Achievement at the highest level – level ten – means doing more of the same but, in addition – and this is not surprising, given the comments of Britton and other contemporary English practitioners reviewed earlier in the book – also means taking 'effective account of audience and context' (Cox, 1991, p. 189). Cox is as reticent about disclosing whether the audience and context need to be specifically located within drama, as about the precise nature of the 'tools of the trade' that students require in order to make their 'informed choice' about specialisation. None of the subsequent revisions of the original National Curriculum Order for English has succeeded in resolving the tensions and inconsistencies established in the original version.

The decision to place statutory provision for drama in the hands of English teachers raises deeper assessment issues. For all the *New London Group*'s reconfiguration of literacy to include those audio, spatial and visual *tools of design* that comprise the semiotic systems of, for example, 'a well-equipped drama space', Kempe fears that 'even if it were possible to whisk an English class off to the drama studio for some practical experimentation, it is doubtful that many English teachers would feel optimistic about teaching plays in this way'. Far from engaging with 'the polysemic nature of the play in performance', he continues, 'English teachers are obliged to fall back on the codes and practices of literary studies which have tended to privilege . . . literary content' (Kempe, 1998, p. 108). To illustrate his point, Kempe cites J.L. Styan's reference to the famous lines from Act Two Scene Two of *Macbeth*, where Lady Macbeth tries to excuse herself for not killing King Duncan:

> Had he not resembled
> My father as he slept, I had done't

Speculation about 'Lady Macbeth's hidden relationship with her father', Styan argues, is unhelpful because it 'brings us very little closer to the play in question' (in Kempe, 1998, p. 108). It would be understandable if English teachers were to express surprise and perhaps dismay at Styan's argument. Any student who responded to the possibilities suggested by those lines could reasonably be credited for having engaged 'critically and sensitively . . . taking into account alternative approaches and interpretations' and for having demonstrated evidence that they can 'explore and evaluate the ways meanings, ideas and feelings are conveyed through language, structure and form'. By doing so, they would have met the criteria for a top literature grade in an English assessment board's current GCSE examination (AQA, 2008, p. 40).

The problem needs to be considered in the context of Rainer and Lewis's warning against the dangers of *'valuing what is assessed* rather than *assessing what is of value* [original italics]' (Rainer and Lewis, 2012, p. 7). First, assessment procedures that privilege, as English curricula tend to do, written responses to dramatic texts like the plays of Shakespeare encourage what Neelands calls 'a test of reading comprehension rather than a test of students' understanding of Shakespeare's plays in performance' (Neelands, 2008, p. 1). Second, they foreground a certain way of looking that is closely attuned to the conventions of the psychologically 'realistic' novel and to the kind of naturalistic playing that dominates television drama and that may comprise, for a significant number of young people, their primary experience of the art form (Fleming, 1997, p. 4). Lady Macbeth is not a character in a twenty-first century soap opera. *Macbeth* is not a naturalistic play. There are other ways of looking at the world than through the lens of naturalism. What matters here is not how Lady Macbeth might or might not have related to her father but how her words and actions impact on the characters and actions within the play itself in what Manuel memorably describes as the 'ancient dance between reader and words in the act of interpretation' (Manuel, 2008, p. 34). Drama, Fleming argues, is 'an artificial, fictional "construct"'. What makes it powerful as an art form is its 'potential to explore and examine experience in ways which would otherwise be denied to us in real life' (Fleming, 1997, p. 4). Encouraging students to appreciate richer, more diverse ways of looking; helping them to engage ideologically as well as conceptually with all *the tools of design* now at their disposal; breaking the boundaries of conventional 'literary criticism' so that plays are appreciated, in Kempe's words, 'as texts rich in potential for creative interpretation for performers and audience' (Kempe, 1998, p. 108); exploring to the full the implications of Kress and Bezemer's assertion that the *page* has become a *site of display* (2009, p. 171) – these are some of the major challenges that the reception of drama within the statutory protection of the English National Curriculum obliges teachers to confront.

Unfortunately, teachers eager to meet those challenges in the schools of England today will find little official guidance to help them in the investigations of subject English published by the Office for Standards in Education (OFSTED). *English at the Crossroads* – a report based on evidence from 122 primary schools and 120 secondary schools (OFSTED, 2009) – and *Excellence in English* – a more recent case study of twelve schools where pupils are said to make outstanding progress (OFSTED 2011) – are cases in point. Both reports testify to the validity of Neelands' concerns about drama's capacity to be heard above the dominant voice of English. Whenever *English at the Crossroads* and *Excellence in English* mention drama, they do so in glowing terms. In fact, when applied well by effective teachers, drama appears, from their evidence, to be enriching the contemporary English curriculum in all the ways that *The Bullock Report* and the Cox Working Party could have wished. It makes 'a significant difference to . . . pupils' self-confidence and oral abilities' (OFSTED, 2011, p. 52); it brings canonical literature vividly to life ('pupils spoke enthusiastically and well about their reading and also about the drama activities, including performances of Shakespeare, in which they had been involved'); teacher in role activities help GCSE students to make 'excellent use of evidence' and to articulate their arguments 'confidently' (OFSTED, 2009, pp. 20, 16); 'drama games' and 'mimes' where the pupils 'have to identify correct sounds', provide engaging opportunities for phonics work (OFSTED, 2011, p. 38); writing and reading skills are boosted by the interventions of an actor in residence; drama strategies like *conscience alley* help eight-year-olds engage with the issues surrounding bullying. Among 'the common features of English lessons that appealed to them', boys list an 'emphasis on drama in English' (OFSTED, 2011, p. 34). The 'participation' in drama activities involving speaking and listening by students for whom English is an additional language is described by the inspectors as 'striking' (OFSTED, 2009, p. 28). To cap it all, the authors of *Excellence in English* note towards the end of their report that 'Good-quality use of drama was also a feature of several of the most effective schools included in this survey' (OFSTED, 2011, p. 52). Tributes to the efficacy of drama run like a leitmotif through both reports; but there is no consistency or coherence to the references. Drama is mentioned, not as a subject worthy of consideration for itself, but only in terms of what it can to do to further a particular aspect of English pedagogy. There is no reason why reports into a National Curriculum subject that has statutory obligations towards drama should not devote, as a matter of course, a whole section to its provision within schools. What might be even more helpful would be the sub-division of those discrete sections so that each one considered in turn the key questions that *The Bullock Report* posed about the relationship between English and drama and that, almost forty years later, remain largely unanswered.

In countries like England where drama is denied statutory autonomy, practitioners have taken matters into their own hands. Much excellent work has been done. In the United Kingdom, for example, *NATE* has for years engaged in productive dialogue with drama teachers through what is now known as its *Drama and Creativity*

Committee. NATE has a long history, too, of publishing drama guidance material across all four modalities of English and a wealth of resources aimed specifically for English practitioners. As well as the *Drama Packs* series, *NATE* produced, until 2012, a journal called *English, Drama, Media*, which created a forum for discussion and for the dissemination of practical ideas. Like *NATE*, the *English and Media Centre* provides in-service courses and resources in drama, ranging from study guides on canonical authors like Arthur Miller and Shakespeare to material on theatrical genres like *Comedy* and *Tragedy*. Commercial publishers such as Bloomsbury (*Improving Standards in English Through Drama at Key Stage 3 and GCSE*), its imprint Methuen Drama (*Critical Scripts* and *National Theatre Connections*), Heinemann Longman (*Plays for Key Stage 3*) and Oxford University Press (*Playscripts*) – to cite just some examples – provide teachers and their students with access to a range of exciting new plays as well as to dramatised versions of contemporary fictional classics popular in English classrooms. The *Cambridge School Shakespeare* series, like its *Oxford* counterpart, offers an approach to the plays that is far removed from Neelands' feared 'test of reading comprehension'. And these of course are just some of the printed materials: interactive resources to support engagement with drama abound in the form of social networks, blogs, websites, films and software materials.

Writing within a decade of the National Curriculum's implementation, Fleming argued that a number of 'issues' remained 'unresolved' amongst drama practitioners. He continued: 'disagreement centres on whether it is appropriate to focus on the teaching of drama skills and whether a satisfactory account of progression in drama can be provided' (1997, p. 3).

Some practitioners (for example, Clipson-Boyles, 1998) attempted to answer Fleming's questions about focus and progression in drama by engaging with the National Curriculum on its own terms. One of the most striking examples of this approach was produced in 2000 by Kempe and Ashwell, in their publication *Progression in Secondary Drama*. Given that the Foreword is written by David Hornbrook, it is not surprising that the book regards the failure of drama to be included as a statutory subject within the National Curriculum as providing a 'tremendous opportunity to construct a curriculum that is innovative, draws on the teachers' own areas of expertise and reflects the needs of any particular cohort of students' (2000, p. 14). Kempe and Ashwell embrace 'the discourses of the new century's school curriculum' (p. iv) and argue that drama practitioners, even though excluded from the National Curriculum's statutory obligations, should nevertheless accept its constraints: 'Such freedom, however, also carries the weighty responsibility of ensuring that breadth and balance are achieved and that a number of externally imposed requirements are met within the scheme (p. 14).

Kempe and Ashwell construct a programme for drama education that mirrors the then current National Curriculum's model of *strands* (plotted against a *creating* – as opposed to *making* – *performing*, *responding* matrix) and *progression levels* ranging from level one to exceptional performance (beyond level eight). Like Hornbrook before them, they devise a curriculum based on 'units' of work – seven to be completed each year between the ages of eleven and sixteen. Arguing that 'content and form are interwoven in the subject of drama' (p. 28), Kempe and Ashwell explain that a unit 'may focus on a theme, the study of a play, an historical event, a particular style or genre, the exploration of a complex issue, a research project or a combination of these' (p. 34). Thus, students might negotiate their engagement with a *creating* strand entitled 'structuring and notating plays and performances' through the nine levels by working on topics such as *crime and punishment* or classical texts such as *Antigone*, or genres such as *documentary theatre* or technical forms like *sound, lighting, costume and make-up* (pp. 32–33). One of the most remarkable features of Kempe and Ashwell's suggested curriculum model is the way that it takes such detailed account of the pragmatics of National Curriculum teaching. Earlier practitioners like Slade or Hawkes would have been surprised, not only by its insistence that drama, like 'any language . . . can be taught and students can get better at it' (pp. 8–9), but by its use of a policy statement and by its detailed planning, monitoring and assessment systems.

Engaging with the National Curriculum on its terms, *Progression in Secondary Drama* attempts to interweave process and product, form and content into a coherent, progressive and academically challenging curriculum model. It is so detailed and pragmatic that it could be used 'off the peg' by a school department. Kempe and Ashwell's approach has disadvantages, however. Like the Cox model, it can be interrogated and deconstructed. For example, explicit references to *audience* appear at levels three, four and eight of the *working supportively with others in performance* strand – but cannot be found in the statements for levels five, six and seven. The use of puppets is suggested for work at levels one and two of the *realising a range of genres, styles and forms* strand – but even this is just a suggestion and puppetry is not mentioned explicitly again. Participation in a play by Shakespeare becomes one of the criteria for access to level five. And so on. The reference to Shakespeare – that ever recurring, unique because specifically named, author – highlights the second disadvantage. National Curricula are political documents and therefore subject to the will of politicians. What one government deems educationally desirable, another might not. The National Curriculum model that Kempe and Ashwell followed so conscientiously has gone – and so has the *National Literacy Strategy* that they praised for having brought 'a greater awareness of drama forms and processes' in pupils moving from primary to secondary school (2000, p. iv). This is not at all to negate the work undertaken by Kempe and Ashwell over a decade ago; but it does raise the question as to whether – in educational systems that exclude them from statutory recognition – drama practitioners should, reactively, argue a case for admission on the politicians' terms or, remembering that drama and theatre have a long tradition of subversion and non-conformity, proactively assert and advance their own principles. As Thompson observes:

> The application of theatre may fit snugly, or it may grate, it may become an easy complement or a point of friction. An extended use of creative role play in the classroom may be rewarding for the young people, but come into conflict with the tight objectives of a pre-set curriculum.
>
> (1999, p. 10)

Rainer and Lewis have chosen to answer Fleming's questions about focus and progression in drama by selecting the latter option. Kempe and Ashwell are well aware that there is a 'particular tension in the kind of rational planning fostered by the National Curriculum' because learning in the arts 'does not necessarily follow a predictable linear sequence'. However, they are prepared to risk that tension on the basis that 'the development of knowledge, skills and understanding' are 'not simply a matter of chance' and therefore need to be taught (2000, p. 42). Rainer and Lewis, however, regard the subject-discrete National Curriculum as regressive, bearing an 'astounding similarity to the curriculum proposed in England at the turn of the twentieth century' (Rainer and Lewis, 2012, p. 2). For them, its emphasis upon 'the acquisition of high levels of "subject knowledge"', upon linear models of progression, upon modes of assessment that offer starkly evaluative, level-based answers to students' questions about 'how they are getting on' (as Hornbrook puts it) strikes at three core pedagogic principles that characterise 'the best drama teaching': that it should be 'student-centred, process-orientated and participatory' (Lewis and Rainer, 2005, p. 8). If the purpose of taking part in a Shakespeare play is to judge whether or not a particular student has accessed level five of a curriculum, then drama is in danger of ceasing to be 'a safe "no penalty zone" within which students can respond creatively to tasks without fear of failure' (Rainer and Lewis, 2012, p. 5). Issuing a rallying-cry in defence of the 'practical classroom tradition of drama teaching that has evolved to suit the needs of learners over the last 50 years' (Lewis and Rainer, 2005, p. 8) and noting 'a recent resurgence of interest' (Rainer and Lewis, 2012, p. 5) in Dorothy Heathcote's cross-curricular *mantle of the expert* work (see for example Sayers, 2011; Kidd, 2011), Rainer and Lewis argue that the time 'is now right to re-establish drama at the centre of a creative, thematic curriculum' capable of breaking through the subject boundaries established by the 1988 Education Reform Act and replacing them with a 'competence based approach' to learning 'more in tune with the needs of learners in the twenty-first century' (p. 3). In such a model, assessment is seen as 'ipsative' and formative; while a 'normative and linear account of learning' is replaced by a more conceptual, child-centred model of progression predicated on *complexity*, *control*, *depth* and *independence* (Lewis and Rainer, 2005, pp. 16, 13).

Others share Rainer and Lewis's belief that contemporary theories about learning can invest the claims of *process* drama with a new authority and vigour. Drawing upon a 'central tenet of psychodynamic pedagogy', for example, Arnold argues that its effectiveness is 'enhanced by experiences which engage both affect and cognition, preferably in a way which stimulates a dynamic between both'. Considering the context of 'English classes' as an example, she argues that 'the primary focus of drama work may well be on developing an embodied understanding of the way empathetic engagements between participants can influence human dynamics' (2004, p. 273). Similarly, one of the ways in which the *National Literacy Strategy*'s (DfE, 2010) publication *Developing Drama in English* attempts to appeal to teachers is by emphasising drama's potential to develop 'critical thinking skills' and 'deep learning' (pp. 3, 13). Reviewing O'Toole and O'Mara's (2007) four 'paradigms of purpose' for teaching drama (*cognitive/procedural*; *expressive/developmental*; *social/pedagogical*; *functional*), Anderson suggests there are close links here with the 'four dimension of practice' (*intellectual quality*; *connectedness*; *supportive classroom environment*; *working with and valuing difference*) central to the 'productive pedagogies' alternative to 'traditional schooling', which is currently exerting a significant influence upon curricular thinking in Australia (Anderson, 2012, pp. 10, 15).

Although it might seem therefore that entrenched and long-abiding issues still haunt drama in education as it moves further into the twenty-first century, significant positional changes have taken place. Fleming helped to lead the search for answers to his two questions when, in *The Art of Drama Teaching*, he attempted to link *process* and *product* approaches by suggesting ways in which studying the craft of plays from the (mainly Anglophone) heritage of western theatre could enhance students' own work in drama:

> 'Getting better at drama' has partly to do with an increasing skill in being able to take an idea and translate it into dramatic form; that ability is likely to be developed by examining the way dramatists do the same.
>
> (Fleming, 1997, p. 4)

Others have attempted to bridge the supposed divide by arguing that role-play – the driving force behind *process* approaches and, according to Arnold, 'a primary act of mind' (2004, p. 273) – is a shared essential ingredient of both. O'Neill writes:

> the single most powerful dramatic constraint in both theatre and process drama is the kind of concealment and disguise offered by role-playing within the role. It is precisely here that the double nature of theatre is most clearly at work. Playing a role is the means by which the very concept of role itself is investigated.
>
> (O'Neill, 1995, p. 83)

Writing more than a decade later, Neelands endorses this position: 'Imagining oneself as the other, trying to find oneself in the other and in so doing to recognise the other in oneself, is the crucial and irreducible bridge between all forms of drama and theatre work' (2011, p. 2). Viewed from this perspective, Lewis and Rainer argue, role-play 'is clearly a form of acting, and may legitimately be seen alongside other forms of contemporary theatre practice' (2005, p. 6).

There is now a general consensus that skills and conventions need to be taught, whether they are clustered into 'four varieties of dramatic action' (Neelands and Goode, 2000, p. 5); or 'performance skills' and 'knowledge and understanding of theatrical ideas and concepts' (Lewis and Rainer, 2005, p. 10); or 'elements, skills, processes, conventions, forms, styles, history and heritage and drama values' (Pascoe and Sallis, 2012, p. 144). The *making/creating, performing, responding* matrix has been generally accepted – though Lewis and Rainer, drawing upon O'Toole's work on the 'interchangeability of the roles of "actor", "audience" or "director" in different cultures' (2005, p. 7), criticise these categories as being too rigid and impermeable. Nevertheless, as Anderson observes, 'the interdependent relationship between making and appreciating' is generally accepted as lying 'at the centre of effective teaching in the arts' (2012, p. 11).

As it moves through the second decade of the twenty-first century, drama demonstrates an increasing readiness to confront those harsh questions about accountability posed by Callaghan in 1976. Anderson writes: 'we must now articulate for those who control the gates, the purse strings and the curriculum why the arts are needed and what in particular drama education does to support the academic, social and emotional growth of young people' (2012, p. 11).

In comparison with the breezy assertiveness of early advocates like Caldwell Cook and Finlay-Johnson, today's practitioners are more restrained in their arguments. Anderson cites Buckingham's warning – anathema to earlier practitioners – against the tendency 'to romanticize young people', or to take 'a wholly positive view of their critical intelligence and social responsibility'; and he quotes Neelands' suspicions of drama's propensity, 'embedded in the liberal humanist tradition', to indulge in 'hero narratives', which then 'become proof' of its 'efficacy in solving a range of "problems"' (In Anderson, 2012, pp. 9, 11). Kempe, too, is prepared to subject long-established nostrums, including the concept of teacher as 'loving ally', to critical scrutiny:

> What do statements such as 'Drama gives young people the opportunity to express themselves' really mean? Is it always a good thing for people to express themselves? . . . What sort of god-like powers do drama teachers have to make judgements about the 'self', and what might the effects on the 'self' be if their comments were less than complimentary?
>
> (Kempe and Ashwell, 2000, p. 29)

Perhaps surprisingly, this move towards a more level-headed appraisal of what drama can and cannot realistically be expected to achieve has been accompanied by a determination that drama must 'dare to speak its name' – loudly and widely. Neelands raises the global stakes for drama by quoting Martha Nussbaum's assertion that 'the humanities and the arts' have the 'ability to transcend local loyalties' and can thus help the individual 'to approach world problems as a "citizen of the world"' (In Neelands, 2011, p. 3). Hornbrook's (1997) request that practitioners 'begin to relocate drama in the world' (p. 13) chimes contemporaneously with Neelands' call for a 'new trans-cultural paradigm of theatre', which acknowledges 'both the Euro-American performance tradition and other "rich traditions" as well' (1996, p. 24). Lewis and Rainer suggest that the 'theatre anthropology' research of Richard Schechner and Eugenio Barba has helped to 'contextualise the cultural hegemony of Euro-American commercial and art traditions within a wider range of cultural contexts' (2005, p. 6). The potential for the cross-fertilization of ideas afforded by this more-inclusive configuration of drama and theatre has enhanced the possibilities for that 'complex interaction of the global and local characterised by cultural borrowing', which Steger defines as 'glocalization' (2003, p. 75). Developments in 'applied theatre' (Thompson, 1999, p. 9) and 'networked theatre' (Sutton, 2009, p. 42) have served to 'extend the life of the dramatic beyond the boundaries of the physical space in which it may originally, or ultimately, be enacted' and 'beyond the limits of the time allowed in . . . a school timetable' (Cameron, 2009, p. 55), enabling 'geographically dispersed groups of participants to mark out the particulars of their localized experiences and then contextualize these within a universal dramatic framework' (Sutton, 2009, p. 43).

If the voice of drama is speaking more loudly and being heard more widely, it is also, as the quotation from Nussbaum suggests, becoming more politically engaged. When Kempe and Ashwell explore dramatic literature, they are less concerned with its credentials as a member of Abbs' 'aesthetic family' than in the answers it might give to ideological questions about cultural hegemony and the nature of power. 'In whose interests is it', they ask, 'to retain the values and status quo of past and existing cultures?' (2000, p. 29). By offering 'immediate and physical means of getting to grips with texts and textual representation', Neelands argues, drama can help students 'to become more conscious of 'voice' – the ideological interests of the text's producer' (2008, p. 8). Heathcote argued that the 'big shift' in pedagogy 'is to move from holding . . . information and doling it out like charity' (In Cameron and Anderson, 2009, p. 18); for O'Toole, drama can help students realise that literature has to prove its worth to them, rather than they to it. He advises teachers: 'it just starts with asking yourself the question: why should the students read this? What does it have to say to them? If you can't answer that, you shouldn't be using that text' (2008, p. 24).

With so much apparent consensus, it is easy to understand why Anderson should argue that the 'tripartite learning framework often called making, performing and appreciating' has identified 'the understanding of the art form and the making of the art form as central to the learning' and thus rendered 'discussions around process versus product' as 'ultimately useless and fruitless' (2012, p. 14). The debate has not ended, however. The question of who tells their story and how that story should be told still presses. Where is a sense of balance to be found between an oral tradition of story-telling on the one hand and stories told through the medium of the script on the other? Should stories that 'attempt to imitate life in a realistic and detailed fashion' (Kirby, 1987, p. 14) be celebrated for their affirmatory and emancipatory power by communities whose response is offered without judgement or evaluation? Or should so-called 'naturalistic' ways of looking be challenged by artifice? 'Once it is accepted that the normal boundaries of historical time in fiction and non-fiction can be trans-gressed,' Fleming writes, 'the imagination can soar towards the surreal' (1997, p. 76). The impact of digital technology has made these issues more complex, raising new questions about the relationship between audience and participant, about the tensions between physical and virtual space, about new configurations of *fabula* and *syuzhet*. These pressing concerns are as important for English teachers today as for their drama colleagues.

Part 2

Applying theory to practice

Introduction
Working with the practical activities – to the teacher

Part 2 of the book is composed of six activity sequences that are closely linked to the material in Part 1. To emphasise this point, each activity sequence contains a section that makes explicit links to a practitioner or to an issue explored in the first part of the book. Citations are not provided for quotations in Part 2 of the book, unless they are ones that have not been used before. At the end of each activity sequence, there are recommendations for ways in which the ideas might be explored further in the English classroom. These ideas relate to the four modalities of English but include other important areas too, such as media and technology work.

The first activity sequence – *Where Do You Stand?* (Chapter 8) – is intended for use as an in-service activity. Its audience is therefore meant to be teachers; though of course, the fact that it invites participants to take stock of their own ideological and pedagogical position regarding drama means that it might also be useful for older students who are considering studying drama as a subject specialism.

The other five activity sequences are substantial schemes of work for students. They can be used in any order that the teacher feels best. I believe the activity sequences can be adapted to cater for different ages and abilities. Teachers will use their professional judgement about how to shape the activities to suit the specific learning needs of their students. The individual activities within each broader scheme are designed to be followed through sequentially; however, it would be possible to 'dip into' them at various points in the programme if teachers felt that were more appropriate in terms of time and logistics. The activities are informed by the principle that students should come to each session feeling empowered and confident that they have expertise to share. Therefore, a number of the activities assume that opportunities for preliminary research have been provided prior to engaging with the drama itself.

Because this book is designed specifically for English teachers, the activities are tracked against the levels of the writing code (adapted here from Andrews, 2001):

1. Grapho-phonemic
2. Morphological
3. Word
4. Syntactic
5. Sub-textual
6. Textual
7. Contextual

One whole activity sequence is devoted to work between levels 1 and 3.

Similarly, when making explicit references to drama, I have followed Kempe and Ashwell's (2000) classification system by referring to *areas of knowledge, dramatic skills, explorative strategies* and *elements of drama*. When a particular area of knowledge, skill, strategy or element is referenced for the first time in an activity sequence, I indicate this by using italics.

Opportunities for speaking and listening occur so often throughout the practical activities in Part 2 that I have only referred to them explicitly in the sequence that has speaking and listening as its focus. This sequence is called *From Private to Public Space* (Chapter 9).

Some of the activities are addressed to the teacher and some directly to the students. I hope I have made it clear who is being addressed when.

Chapter 8

Where do you stand?

Exploring your own ideological position

Introduction and context

This first set of activities is primarily for teachers. Its purpose is to help you take stock of what you have read in Part 1 of the book and to consider your own ideological position regarding the relationship between English and drama pedagogy. Guidance on English and drama – from *The Bullock Report* (DES, 1975) to *Developing Drama in English* (DfE, 2010) – has emphasised the importance of teachers working together as a team and sharing a vision of the kind of drama curriculum that they feel is right for them and for their students.

Bearing in mind what Neelands said in his 2008 paper about the status of drama in different countries around the world, teachers working in England might be particularly interested to note that the exemplar text below is taken from guidance material for the 2014 Australian arts curriculum, which plans for all students to experience drama as one of five arts subjects until the end of primary school, with the option of specialising in the subject at secondary level.

In terms of the activities that follow, however, it is important that whoever is leading the in-service training session does *not* reveal the context of the statement *until at least the first two* of the *working at contextual level* activities (below) have been completed (see *commentary* for details).

Exemplar text

> In drama, students will explore, depict and celebrate human experience by imagining and representing other people through live enactment. Drama is a collaborative art, combining physical, verbal, visual and aural dimensions. In drama students will experience theatre and develop an understanding of the performer/audience relationship. Learning in drama can be both process and performance. Students will combine the elements of drama to make, present and respond to representations of human situations, characters, behaviour and relationships. They will make drama through dramatic play, role-play and improvisation, structuring the elements into play-building, directing and scriptwriting. In presenting drama they will learn, as actors, to use body and gesture, voice and language, through interpretation and rehearsal processes as well as production and performance. In responding, students will learn about how drama contributes to

personal, social and cultural identity. They will study the diversity of purposes, forms and styles in drama and theatre both contemporary and from other times, places and cultural contexts.

(ACARA, 2011, p. 10)

Questions

• *What historical and theoretical approaches to drama are embedded in this statement?*
• *To what extent does this statement represent your personal views about drama?*
• *Is this statement something your teaching team could work with as your own policy declaration?*

Activities

We could of course simply read the exemplar material and use it as a starting point for discussion; but this section of the book is practice based so I want to suggest that you consider the extract as if it were a 'dynamic, unstable play text' (Irish, 2011, p. 7) and lift it off the page for dramatic interrogation.

Here are a few practical ways in which you might work with this extract at different levels of textual engagement. Activities designed for individuals will also lend themselves to paired or group work, should you feel more comfortable working that way.

Working at contextual level

When Courtney designed a model to indicate the 'plurality of educational drama', he identified three of the figures described in Part 1 of this book as being particularly influential proponents of different informing methodologies: Dewey (*learning by doing*), Caldwell Cook (*learning by dramatic doing*) and Rousseau (*learning through play*) (1989, p. 26).

• Choose one of the figures whose ideas are explored in Part 1 of the book – it could be one of the people Courtney mentions; it might be someone like Hannah More, for example, from an earlier period; it might be someone who makes only a brief appearance, like the 1854 Inspector for Church Schools who commented on the work of Froebel; it might be a modern practitioner.
• Compose and share a brief monologue response to the ACARA statement written from the point of view of your chosen character (or, as a distancing strategy, one prepared by a scholar who has studied your chosen character's theoretical position). Is the monologue written in a neutral tone of voice or is it crafted with rhetorical strategies of persuasion?
• Present the monologues in turn formally to the group or use them as the starting-point for an improvised discussion.
• Now consider the context of the ACARA statement. Thinking from your own point of view as a teacher, rather than as someone assuming a fictional role, how, if at all, has your knowledge of the text's context influenced your response to it?

- Devise a prepared reading of the ACARA statement, deciding together at which points in the text your chosen character might interject with a comment on what they hear. How will the ACARA spokesperson respond?
- A group of scholars representing different theoretical positions engage in a chaired discussion of the ACARA statement.
- The represented characters stand in a circle around the person reading the ACARA statement. As the statement is read, they move closer to or further away from the reader, depending on whether or not they approve of what they hear. Why, when and where do the different characters make their moves?
- Juxtapose a reading of the ACARA statement with an extract from a text that explores similar issues but from a different historical, cultural or genre-based context. A particularly effective choice might be the poem *The Schoolboy* from William Blake's *Songs of Innocence and Experience* or an extract from David Almond's novel *Skellig*, where Mina compares home with school-based education.

Working at word level

- Fleming notes that pauses 'determine the tone' of a text and imply the existence of 'a strong sub-text' (1997, p. 134). Prepare a reading of the ACARA statement: where might the pauses come and why?
- Building on this exercise, invite one person to read the statement aloud; during the reading, the other members of the group repeat words that they regard as particularly significant. What are they and why are they chosen? Do certain words emerge as particularly popular choices? Are there any examples of what Barthes calls 'hinge moments' (1982, p. 266) where the argument takes a decisive turn that might be betrayed by a change of intonation in the reader's voice?
- The ACARA statement contains a large number of verbs. Write each one on a piece of card and distribute these amongst the group. If the group is large, walk around the room and greet each other by saying the verb – *celebrate*, *explore*, *imagining* – and so on. Try to craft your use of the word by experimenting with tone of voice and with gesture. What impression is created by hearing the words individually and by noting which ones seem particularly to lodge in the mind? Alternatively, if the group is small, sit in pairs and, after saying some of the words to each other, discuss what they connote for you and how they might be applied to drama pedagogy.
- Take a sequence of verbs (from the same sentence, perhaps, like *explore*, *depict* and *celebrate*, or from the same grammatical category, like the present participles *imagining*, *representing and combining*). Choose sequences that work particularly well rhythmically (*explore*, *depict* and *celebrate* provide a good example, because of the interplay of short vowels and voiced plosive consonants). Another good sequence to use would be *make*, *present* and *respond* because of its clear links with Abbs' tripartite framework for the arts. Present as a rap, accompanied by clicking fingers or clapping hands. Exercises like this help the mind to retain the words and also provide an opportunity to consider why particular verbs might be linked (as in the *make*, *present* and *respond* sequence).
- Use one of the verbs as the title for a *tableau* that illustrates how that word might be applied in a drama context. Explain your choice – or, better still, get your

audience to explain. Two particularly interesting words to select for this activity would be the first and the last verbs in the statement – *explore* and *study*. Why are they sequenced in this way? How would the tone of the statement be changed if *study* came first and *explore* last?

- Alternatively (or additionally) – run the activity using nouns instead of verbs. Considering either or both provides opportunities to re-examine Dixon's assertion in *Growth Through English* that '"Drama" means doing'.

Commentary

Some of the most important concepts that drama can *ostend* for English practitioners are *context*, *framing* and *point of view*. It is useful, therefore, to engage with these right from the start. Presenting the ACARA statement out of context first, allows us to come at it with fresher eyes. Revealing its provenance *during* the activities helps to highlight the importance of context and to think about how contextual information influences our responses as readers of text. In this particular instance, locating the ACARA statement within its context (see www.acara.edu.au for further information) could invite an interesting discussion about the issues explored in the final chapter of Part 1 of this book, particularly amongst teachers working in countries that take a very different statutory approach to drama.

Looking at the ACARA statement from the perspective of a practitioner described in Part 1 of the book not only encourages us to tease out the connective threads that bind drama pedagogy through the centuries but also demonstrates how frame and point of view can change the way a text is mediated and received. It can also help us to consider the concept of *intertextuality* (Kristeva, 1970). Juxtaposing two very different texts on a similar theme – in this case a twenty-first-century policy statement with an eighteenth-century poem – gestures towards the Russian formalist concept of *ostranenie* or 'making strange' (Elam, 2002, p. 15). Both the statement and the poem share similar, child-centred concerns and communicate them in English; but the words they use are crafted very differently. Comparing the two readings can help us appreciate how ways of making meaning differ between genres and between historical periods. The activity in which listeners move closer to or further from the speaker of the ACARA statement can provide a useful way in to the concept of *textual positioning*.

Questions for reflection

- *How have the activities undertaken in this session informed your response to the ACARA statement?*
- *What is gained and/or lost by exploring text in this way?*
- *What opportunities and challenges does this way of working present in terms of your current practice as an English teacher?*

Opportunities for work in the English classroom

I said that this set of activities is aimed 'primarily' at English teachers. The ACARA statement (or something similar) could be used however as stimulus material for any students who are exploring issues involving education specifically and attitudes to young people in general – be it a newspaper article attacking 'progressive' teaching methods or Mary Shelley's novel *Frankenstein*. It could also be used as a starting-point for drama work in English, helping students to get a sense of key pedagogical issues and a feel for some of the *metalanguage* of drama.

All these activities provide numerous opportunities for engaging with a wide range of spoken language registers – one of the main reasons why the authors of *The Bullock Report* and so many other English practitioners have particularly valued drama. As well as arguing or discussing or critiquing or chanting or declaiming, students who took part in the activities that required them to research some of the historical figures described in Part 1 of the book, or to engage with Blake's poem, would have the chance, amongst much else, to think about how language changes over time. If someone were to speak from the point of view of Caldwell Cook, for example, how might they feel about using his term – *playboys* – to describe students participating in drama? Monologues could be written up; the ACARA statement could be recast as a poem and *The Schoolboy* as an educational manifesto; research could be undertaken into the social conditions experienced by children in the late eighteenth century (working with History colleagues, perhaps) and used for a formal critical study of Blake.

These are just some ideas applied to the four modalities of English. Perhaps the most important point to make is to remember what Neelands said about how drama can provide us with an 'immediate and physical means of getting to grips with texts and textual representation'. Kempe argued that English teachers need to appreciate plays 'as texts rich in potential for creative interpretation'. The activities described in this session have been designed to show that *all* texts – even high-status educational policy statements – can be explored in the way Neelands suggests. That is an ideologically powerful and empowering lesson for students to learn and one that drama is particularly well suited to teach.

Chapter 9

From private to public space

Exploring the art form of drama

Introduction and context

This is a substantial set of activities that could extend to an entire scheme of work. The activities are addressed directly to the students. The discussion points provide opportunities for the whole group to reflect together on the issues raised by the activities. The questions attached to the activities themselves are designed to aid the students' thinking as they work.

You will need to consider whether you are going to tell the students from the start that they are going to share their stories or whether you will only disclose this information at the appropriate point in Activity Sequence 1. If the students are aware from the beginning that they will be sharing, they will have a specific audience in mind from the opening exercise onwards and this will influence the way they think and write about their story. However, 'informed consent' is a most important ethical principle in all teaching.

The activities begin with something that might be conventionally associated with 'English' and end in the 'social art form' (Kempe and Ashwell, 2000, p. 3) of drama. As you work, can you identify a moment where you feel the pedagogy shifts from one subject area to the other? Think, too – especially in Activity Sequence 3 – about the implications for your own knowledge about drama. Might this scheme of work provide opportunities for collaboration with specialist colleagues and with teachers of other curriculum subjects? After all, as noted in Part 1 of the book, Vygotsky said that drama is the 'most syncretic mode of creation' because making, performing and responding to it involve so many of the other arts (see p. 15).

It was noted in Part 1 of this book how Way suggests that a 'story session is the most comfortable way of easing into the beginnings of drama' (see p. 54). Activity Sequence 1 is like a guided workshop on story writing with the workshop leader asking the questions and giving the instructions. Its purpose is threefold: to make the point that we all have stories to tell; to help participants think about where stories come from; and whether the application of frameworks and the use of guiding instructions enhance or impede creativity. The activities in Activity Sequence 1 – particularly the use of the film frame metaphor – draw upon Way's suggestions for using concepts and strategies associated with media education as a means of engaging with drama. It is useful, in this context, to remember what Bolton said about how 'passive projected play' – such as the initial work here with frames and drawings – can help those who, in Hornbrook's words are not so adept at 'camaraderie' and 'spontaneity', to find a way into drama.

Activity Sequence 2 sets about the task of 'easing into the beginnings of drama' by taking the story from a private to a public space. Its purpose is to help participants think about key questions that have run through the whole of the first part of the book: How does the presence of an audience influence the creative act? What are the respective rights of the creator and the audience and how do we reconcile these? What happens when an individual entrusts something they have created to the care of someone else?

Activity Sequence 3 takes the material into communal ownership. It challenges participants to access higher level thinking skills of 'analysing, evaluating, and creating' as well as offering opportunities to engage with some of those 'other major learning domains' described towards the end of Part 1 of the book (see p. 87). For example, the activities in Activity Sequence 3 can be used to assess what Lombardi (2007) calls the 'conative' domain: 'whether a student has the necessary will, desire, commitment, mental energy, and self-determination to actually perform at the highest disciplinary standards' (in Rainer and Lewis, 2012, p. 8). The activities in Activity Sequence 3 are also designed to help participants to appreciate the constraints and opportunities afforded by the intensely social nature of drama and to introduce them to some of the main 'areas of knowledge', 'dramatic skills', 'elements' and 'explorative strategies' (Kempe and Ashwell, 2000, pp. 27–28), which comprise its aesthetic craft. References to key terms are in italics (and in bold where the surrounding text is already italicised). Finally, the activities in Activity Sequence 3 – particularly those associated with *non-naturalistic* representation – offer opportunities to explore the differences between *syuzhet* and *fabula*, distinguished by Bruner as the 'the linear incidents that make the plot' on the one hand and the 'timeless, motionless, underlying theme' on the other (1986, p. 7).

Links with the Part 1 of the book

Review the section where Piaget and Vygotsky provide their contrasting accounts of the role of imaginative play in a child's assimilation and accommodation with its wider host community (see pp. 12–15). Think particularly of the part where Piaget describes a child using a shell to represent a cat walking across a wall as an example of 'subjective generalisation' (see p. 12) and then contrasts this with the 'generalising assimilation' of a spoon being used to indicate the action of pulling. It would be useful to have this section of the book in mind when discussing with the participants the tensions they might have felt when their personal stories were brought to, and then worked upon in, the public domain. It would be helpful at that point, also, to hold as a contrasting thought Vygotsky's observation that in 'dramatic rendering' the 'drive for action, for embodiment, for realization that is present in the very process of imagination here finds complete fulfilment' (see p. 15). Does it? Slade's and Bolton's interpretations of 'personal' and 'projected' play are also worth revisiting in this context (see pp. 35–36, 62). Do their respective accounts help to illuminate the behaviour of your students as they move from the individual and sedentary activities of Activity Sequence 1 to the communal and kinaesthetic work of Activity Sequence 3?

Another significant section is the one where Esslin's and Hornbrook's description of drama as 'narrative made visible' is contrasted with Heathcote's and Britton's assertion that 'Drama is *not* stories retold in action' (see p. 72). How might the activities undertaken in Activity Sequence 3, especially, influence your thinking about these opposing statements? In this context, McCullough's account of the 'iterability' of the dramatic text is important (see p. 72). Giving the participants a particular theatre form to work with in order to shape their presentation obliges them to consider the relationship between contemporary creators and the cultural tradition within which they are working. What constraints and opportunities are afforded by engaging with a particular theatre form? Please think carefully about the forms you advise your students to use. Some of the theatre forms described in Activity Sequence 3 emphasise the strong connections that commentators like Courtney (1989) and Fleming (1997) have noted between drama, ritual and religion. What are the implications of working within (and even against) the perceived conventions of a theatre form that might come from a cultural context very different from the students' own? What issues are raised if that theatre form is linked closely to expressions of religious belief? Finally, attention was drawn in Part 1 of the book to Whitehead's pessimistic assertion that adolescents would find non-naturalistic ways of working in drama too challenging and would respond by trying to 'cloak their inadequacy [sic] with a pretence of clowning' (see p. 50). The activities in Activity Sequence 3 – for example, those that draw upon Way's strategies of *climax* and *de-climax* in relation to the crafting of dramatic tension – provide an opportunity to put that assertion to the test.

Activity Sequence 1: creating and working individually with story

Working at word level

- Close your eyes. Imagine that there is a film playing in your head which allows you to look back at *happy* and/or *amusing* moments from your past. It could be a very recent film or one from many years ago. Let the film play in your mind for a minute.
- At the command *freeze!* pause the film. Study the paused image closely with your eyes still closed.
- Open your eyes. On a sheet of paper, write answers to the following questions, using either one word or a phrase only. At this paused moment in the film:

  o *Where are you?*
  o *What can you see?*
  o *What has just happened?*
  o *What will happen next?*
  o *How do you feel?*

- Imagine that the piece of paper in front of you is a physical copy of the paused frame from the film you have just played in your mind. Using the five words or phrases you have written down as prompts, fill that frame with as much detail about the remembered moment as you can recall. Thinking about your five senses in turn can be helpful here. Use symbols and images to fill the frame. It does not matter whether or not you feel you are able to draw; this is not a test of your draughtsmanship and you do not have to show the resulting picture to anybody else if you do not want to.

Discussion point one

What made you choose your 'film frame' and your five words?

How vividly were you able to recall the details of your story?

Did the guided activities help you develop your ideas? If so, how?

Working at word, syntactical and sentence level

- Look again at the words you wrote down in answer to the five questions. They are most likely lexical rather than grammatical words – though if you have included any of the latter, it would be particularly interesting to reflect on why you have chosen them.
- Organise the five words or phrases into a narrative sequence: are you going to start with your answer to the question *Where are you?* Or maybe you will begin instead with the response you wrote to the question *How do you feel?* Do certain words you have chosen lend themselves to being placed at a particular point in the sequence?
- Using the symbols and drawings you created as further prompts, create five sentences out of your original five written responses. As you compose your text, consider the following questions:

  o *Will all five sentences follow the same pattern?*
  o *Will some be shorter or longer than others?*
  o *Will some begin with an adverb or a verb, for example?*
  o *Will all five be statements or will some be commands and/or questions?*

Activity Sequence 2: bringing a story to a shared space

Working at whole text level

- Familiarise yourself with your story. In a moment, you are going to share it with somebody else.
- Move into pairs. Take it in turns to tell your stories, so that each of you experiences the *roles* of narrator and audience.
- Try to work 'off the page' when you tell your story. If you do not feel comfortable doing this, use your text as a script. Can the words alone convey to the audience the experience you are trying to communicate? Might intonation, pause and gesture make the telling more effective? Why is this?
- When you are the audience for your partner's story, you can use the following three words to request further information at any point during the telling: *action*, *feeling*, *description*. If the word *action* is used, the teller must provide more verbal information about the action that occurred in the story; when *feeling* is used, the teller must say more about the feelings and emotions experienced; when *description* is used, the teller must say more about the setting in which the story takes place. The

interruptions must be used judiciously – at 'hinge' moments, perhaps, or where there seem to be gaps in the narrative. The aim should be to clarify the audience's understanding and to help the teller to craft their story, not to catch them out.

- Move into fours. Each member of the original pair must now tell their partner's (re-crafted) story to the two newcomers. A certain amount of *tension* is introduced to this activity in that the original teller of the story cannot interrupt while their story is being told.

Discussion point two

How did knowing that your story was going to enter a public space affect your feelings about it and the way that you shaped it before sharing it?

Was it helpful to have your partner engage in active listening when you told your story? Were you surprised by any of the calls for elaboration that they made? Did the audience's intervention change the story in any way? How do you feel about this?

How did the fact that you were allowed to intervene in the telling of your partner's story influence the way you listened to it?

How did you feel having to sit and listen while someone else told your story?

What did it feel like when you had to tell your partner's story to other people – especially knowing that the original creator of the story was listening to you too?

Activity Sequence 3: working with the art form of drama

Working at contextual level

- Each group now has oral and written versions of four stories. The members of each group must try to work together to establish what Fish calls an *interpretive community*.
- Each group must use the stories as the raw material for a performance that can be shared with an audience.
- Consider the stories in turn in terms of their dramatic potential. Are there lines and phrases that might be used or reworked as *monologue, dialogue, narrative* or *stage directions* in your performance? You are *not* asked to make evaluative judgements about the stories or to rank them in terms of effectiveness. Each of your comments should be positive: use phrases such as *I enjoyed the part where, I liked the way that you, it was effective when . . .*
- You can either agree on one story to present or – a more challenging cognitive task perhaps – try to create a new story from elements of the original four.
- Whichever option you choose, you need to start by agreeing on a *focus* for the story you are going to present. Does the fact that you were asked originally to tell a positive and/or amusing story make this task easier or harder? If you have chosen the option of creating a new story out of elements of the original four, do you find that all four share common, underlying features?
- It might help to come to agreement about your focus if each member of the group completes the following stem question: *This is a story about . . .* and argues their case with their colleagues until a consensus is reached.

Discussion point three

To work effectively in drama requires particular skills of co-operation and negotiation. Commenting on other people's creative work requires tact and sensitivity. How did you meet these challenges and what have you learned from the experience?

Which of the two story options did you choose to attempt? Did one task seem more challenging than the other? Why was this?

When you reviewed the four stories, did you find that they all shared some common elements or themes?

Did you all provide the same answers in the stem question exercise? What might this tell you about the way that we respond to texts?

Working at contextual level (continued)

- Near the start of Activity Sequence 1, you were invited to imagine a picture frame in which to collect your memories. Now it is time to place your story within a *theatre frame*. You can either choose one as a group or seek the advice of your teacher, who may wish to suggest a specific form for you to work in. *It is important that the choice you make strikes an appropriate balance between challenge and accessibility.*

- The choice of forms is considerable. You might choose established forms from television (for example, *soap operas* and *sitcoms*); from the long established heritage of cinema genres (for example, *silent movies, westerns, film noir, German expressionism*); from historical theatre (for example, *Victorian melodrama, Greek tragedy, medieval mystery plays*); from folk traditions (for example, *guysers* and *mummers* plays); from *agitprop theatre, farce, theatre of the absurd, physical theatre, pantomime* – and so on. And then there is the rich world tradition beyond the western heritage to explore, including – to name just a few examples – *Jatra* from Bengal, *Yokhte Pwe* from Burma, *Khon Mask Theatre* from Thailand.

- Allocate research tasks to each member of your group and find out what you can about the conventions and traditions associated with your chosen form. Report back and share the information you have found. What constraints and opportunities does the form offer? *Khon Theatre*, for example, uses *mime* and *masks*: how would that medium influence your performance? Are some theatre forms just not appropriate for what you plan to do; or do they impose a way of presenting that changes the original focus, style and thrust of your work? To what extent does your chosen form lend itself to *naturalistic* or *non-naturalistic* playing? *Commedia dell'arte*, for example, uses archetypal figures like *Brighella, Pantalone* and *Pulcinella*, and the *Sanskrit drama Naganada* involves non-human protagonists like *Garuda*, king of the birds, and *Shankachuda* the serpent. What kind of *conventions* – for example, *ritual, conscience alley, forum theatre, thought tracking* – might be appropriate or inappropriate for your chosen form?

- Having selected a story and a theatre form with which to present it, you need to think about *when* and *where* the story is to be told. How much leeway does the form allow for experimentation? Can a modern soap opera be played in the style of a *Jacobean Revenge Tragedy*? Or a western be set in a science-fiction dystopia?

Or vice versa? Does changing the time and setting lend the performance a greater sense of *distance* or of *immediacy*?

Discussion point four

Were you surprised by the range and variety of theatre forms that exist around the world?

How many of these have you encountered in English and/or drama lessons or on examination syllabuses? Which ones have you not encountered?

Was it easier to find information about some more than others of the theatre forms allocated for the whole class to research? Why do you think this might be?

How similar to or different from the theatre forms you normally encounter in your cultural life are the ones researched by the whole class?

To what extent do religion and/or ritual appear to have shaped the theatre forms your class has researched?

What are your thoughts about working within a particular dramatic tradition? Is that a liberating or a restricting experience? Is it appropriate to flout the conventions of a particular theatre form?

Working at whole text level

- By reviewing different theatre forms and thinking about how we might experiment with the *contextual significance of time and setting*, we have started to consider ways in which drama can *craft experience aesthetically*.
- We will use examples from *structure*, *mood* and *atmosphere* to explore this further. Think about how you might start your performance. You could use a strictly linear, naturalistic chronological pattern moving from beginning to middle and end. Alternatively, you could disrupt that particular framing pattern by using a series of *non-naturalistic techniques* such as:

  - *Presenting the final moment of the story as a freeze frame and then working backwards to the opening.*
  - *Bookending the opening and the close of the performance with acts of ritual.*
  - *Using music or dance or song to initiate and close the performance.*
  - *Inviting a narrator (one of the characters looking back on past events from some time in the future, perhaps) to tell the story to the audience while other performers act it out in mime or through snatches of dialogue.*
  - *Initiating the performance with actions, or in the middle of an overheard conversation (which may or may not serve to move the story forward.)*
  - *Performing the story as a series of monologues designed to represent **different points of view** and time periods, **juxtaposed** to create a sense of contrast or irony or humour.*

- *Mood* and *atmosphere* can be aesthetically crafted through the careful application of *dramatic tension*. Is the story you are presenting a *mystery*? Does it contain one or more *surprises*? Is there tension in the *relationships* between the various characters portrayed (on and off stage) or between the characters and the time and setting of the piece? Does the story contain a *task* the nature of which invests the whole performance with a sense of tension?

- How will your piece make use of *metaphor* and *symbol*? If all theatre performances can be considered as a part representing a whole (*synecdoche*) – in the way that Shakespeare's 'wooden O' represents the world – what will your performance represent? How will you distinguish between *use of voice*, *gestures*, and *movements* that *set the scene* and those that resonate with symbolic meaning? If you are going to work with *lights*, *make up*, *costume* and *sound*, how might these tell the story at a textual and a sub-textual level? How might you employ *analogy* to articulate difficult experiences, as Heathcote does when she uses the symbolism of plants and flowers to tell a story about cancer?

- How will role be utilised in your performance? Are you trying to create naturalistic *characters* who appear to be invested with a psychologically 'real' hinterland; or is the purpose of your role to convey particular *attitudes*, *beliefs* and *motivations*? If you are using a theatre form that accommodates non-human characters, what opportunities and challenges does this way of working pose? Is it possible for non-animate objects to participate in the same way?

Discussion point five

*How helpful are categories like **areas of knowledge, dramatic skills, elements and explorative strategies** in mapping the work you undertook for the preparation and performance of your piece?*

What differences did you notice in the way you used language, gesture and movement in your preparatory work and in the performance itself?

Where would you place your performance on a continuum between naturalistic and non-naturalistic forms of representation? Was there a particular element, explorative strategy or skill that you found to be particularly effective and/or that particularly challenged your usual way of looking?

Working at contextual level

- Still working in your fours, look again at the first 'thought-collection' exercise you undertook in Activity Sequence 1 and trace together the movement from that original, individual piece of writing to the communal performance that ends the scheme of work. What has been gained and/or lost in that transformative process? How has this experience influenced your thinking about drama?

Opportunities for work in the English classroom

Speaking and listening

This scheme of work presents numerous opportunities for *process* talk across a wide range of registers and audiences. Students can discuss and negotiate in pairs and in small groups; they can describe and explain, summarise and elucidate research findings or make evaluative judgements that may require tact and sensitivity. The *action, description, feeling* exercise requires attentive listening skills that are then tested when the students have to recount their partner's story to a new audience. Attentive listening is required again when research information is shared in Activity Sequence 3.

The performance elements of the scheme of work provide opportunities for *product* talk. As well as in the performances themselves, the students will be able to engage with product talk when they tell their stories to a partner and then relate their partner's story to a new audience. From an English teacher's perspective, it would be particularly interesting to reflect with the students upon the differences in lexis, fluency, intonation and dialogic potential between the process language of everyday communication and the formal, crafted product language of performance. How do scripted and non-scripted forms of language compare in their provision of opportunities for 'dialogic bids' (Irish, 2011, p. 10)? Differences in the way gesture and movement are used in the two modes also provide interesting opportunities for discussion.

Narrative and genre

This scheme of work clearly affords many fruitful opportunities for work on narrative, not least through a consideration of the interplay between *fabula* and *syuzhet* mentioned earlier. 'In putting any particular expression together', Bruner writes, 'one *selects* words and one *combines* them. *How* one selects and combines will depend on the uses to which one wishes to put an utterance' (1986, p. 22).

He quotes Paul Ricoeur's observation that stories are 'models for the redescription of the world' (p. 7). The activities in Activity Sequence 1 lend themselves to an exploration of these statements; and this exploration can be tightly focused in the final exercise from that first section, where the participants have to organise the material from the 'thought collecting exercise' into a carefully selected five-sentence sequence. Listening to a partner retelling the story you have carefully crafted adds another perspective to the comments of Bruner and Ricoeur.

All three parts of the scheme of work are concerned with interpreting and re-interpreting text. Taking a lead from Bruner again, this provides opportunities to explore Iser's distinction between the 'actual' text, which remains 'unchanged', and the 'virtual' text, which 'changes almost moment to moment in the act of reading' (1986, p. 7).

Non-naturalistic modes of representation can present a powerful ideological challenge to conventional 'beginning, middle and end' approaches to the construction of reality. Introducing students to these non-naturalistic modes could really enhance their own writing and also help them to deconstruct the narrative craft of others, be they canonical novelists (see below) or writers of advertising copy.

The activities in Activity Sequence 3 provide opportunities to think about the framing potential of genre. Working in their groups of four, the students have to put a genre frame around their chosen story. Allocating them a particular theatre form through which to present their story raises new issues for them to negotiate: How appropriate is their allocated theatre form to the story they want to tell? Do its conventions oblige them to tell that story in a particular way or from a particular point of view? Is it possible to transgress the boundaries imposed by the genre frame without destroying the integrity of either the genre or the story? Bakhtin argues that 'narrative genres are always enclosed in a solid and unshakable monological framework' (1973, p. 12). What do the students think?

Finally, familiarity with the *areas of knowledge, dramatic skills, elements and explorative strategies* described in this scheme of work will enhance the students' critical vocabulary and help them to engage powerfully with any kind of text they might encounter in the English classroom. Think how an appreciation of, for example, *voice, point of view, juxtapositioning* and *tension* – together with an understanding of non-naturalistic ways of telling – could enhance a reading of the opening paragraph from George Eliot's novel, *Daniel Deronda*:

> Was she beautiful or not beautiful? And what was the secret of form or expression which gave the dynamic quality to her glance? Was the good or the evil genius dominant in those beams? Probably the evil; else why was the effect that of unrest rather than of undisturbed charm? Why was the wish to look again felt as coercion and not as a longing in which the whole being consents?
>
> (1892, p. 1)

Chapter 10

From phoneme to word level

Introduction and context

The activities in this section are not designed to be followed through as one continuous scheme of work. Rather, they should be used at appropriate points in the curriculum as the teacher sees fit. For example, the sections on *onset and rime* (Activity Sequence 7), *phonemes and rhythm* (Activity Sequences 2 and 4) or *compound words* (Activity Sequence 8) might be linked to work on poetry. The activities on *prefixes* and *suffixes* (Activity Sequence 6) might be best placed as part of a series of lessons on spelling. However, the sections do build on each other. For example, the work on *blends and digraphs* (Activity Sequence 5) and *kennings* (Activity Sequence 8) provides opportunities to apply learning accessed in the earlier activity involving rhythm. What matters is that students appreciate the tactile, aural and visual relationships between sounds and the physical marks that represent them (Johnston and Watson, 2007). Secondary students who are still finding aspects of reading or spelling a challenge (for example, *blending* and *segmenting* strategies) might benefit from activities that help them engage with the building blocks of language in a physical, interactive way. They might also appreciate the chance to work in a space that is free of the trappings that they may have come to associate with academic difficulty. Others who feel more confident as readers and writers might find that the activities help them to secure a metalanguage with which to explore their own engagement with the written and spoken word. Presenting the information they have acquired in dramatic form to a young audience just embarking on the journey to print literacy provides a powerful means of securing and consolidating that metalanguage (see Activity Sequence 9: *broadening the context* for details).

From a drama perspective, the students will also have the opportunity to explore a range of areas of knowledge (for example, pantomime in Activity Sequence 9: *broadening the context*); skills (for example, physical theatre in Activity Sequence 7: *onset and rime*); explorative strategies (for example, still or merged images in Activity Sequence 8: *working with compound words*) and elements of drama (for example, movement, rhythm, climax and contrast in Activity Sequence 3: *working with rhythm*).

The students are expected to undertake preliminary research on the key concepts explored in each section before the sequence of work in drama begins. This is in acknowledgement of Dorothy Heathcote's principle of the *mantle of expertise*: students should enter the drama space feeling empowered and with information to share.

The form of address used in the descriptions of the activities varies according to the kind of work being undertaken. Sometimes, the instructions are given to the teacher, sometimes straight to the student participants. The questions in italics offer points for the students to consider as they work. Alternatively, they can provide the structure for a more formal, whole group discussion chaired by the teacher.

Links with Part 1 of the book

The practitioners whose ideas are explored in the first part of the book have taken a consistent line on language work. An abiding principle is that the language that children bring to school from the home must be valued because it is intimately bound into their sense of who they are and because it is the medium through which they construct meanings and communicate with others. This is as true for Caldwell Cook, who condemns a teacher for ridiculing a boy's mispronunciation of *antipodes*, as it is for Brian Way, who deplores what he calls the 'unintended bilingualism', which arises from 'the attempt to impose one type of speech on a group of people whose speech root is different' (see p. 53).

Caldwell Cook and Way are two important sources for the activities described in this section of the book. Caldwell Cook's exploration of non-verbal symbolic systems of communication and Way's advocacy of 'jabber talk' as a means of easing the academic pressure on children's engagement with language have proved influential (see p. 55). Similarly, it would be worth revisiting here Peter Slade's comments about young children's propensity for making symbolic shapes (see p. 36). Both Slade and his colleague Way emphasise the integral links between sound and movement that inform so much of the work described below. The activities that involve engagement with literature – for example, the sections on *kennings* (Activity Sequence 8) or on *creation stories* (Activity Sequence 9) – take as guidance Marjorie Hourd's principle that students should work actively alongside established writers (see p. 19). The starting point for the suggestion that secondary students might devise for a younger audience a theatre performance about language concepts is Harriet Finlay-Johnson's 'strong argument in favour of allowing children to impart knowledge to others' on the grounds that 'they will find the correct terms of expression to convey the necessary intelligence to their hearers' (see p. 19).

Finally, Vygotsky's assertion that the ability to 'combine elements to produce a structure, to combine the old in new ways' is 'the basis of creativity' should be considered here in conjunction with Lombardi's concern about students not getting enough opportunities to access higher order thinking skills (see p. 101). It is hoped that the activities described below demonstrate how drama can provide purposeful opportunities and contexts for the analysing, evaluating and, above all, synthesising, that Vygotsky values so highly.

Activity Sequence 1: start-ups

- The group stands in a circle, ideally in loose fitting clothes to facilitate movement.
- Begin with some loosening exercises such as *stretching tall and crouching small, running on the spot, melting the ice cube* (the body is encased in a slowly thawing

block of ice: as different limbs become free, shake them vigorously to restore circulation until, at last, the whole body is released and moving fluently).

- Breathing exercises next (allow recovery time from the previous exercise). Draw the breath deep into the diaphragm and feel the chest swell. Hold for a certain count and release to the same count. Try to hold and release for a little longer each time.

Activity Sequence 2: working with phonemes

- Start with the consonants. Review in turn the *dentals* (n, d, t), the *fricatives* (f), the *labials* (p, b, v, m, w), the *sibilants* ('soft' c, s, z), *voiceless* (k, 'hard' c, p) and the *voiced* (g, b) *plosives*.
- Students share their research findings about the etymology of the terms. This section should reinforce the point that the physical and the vocal are intimately linked (and acknowledge, incidentally, the debt we owe to Latin for this particular metalanguage). The etymology of *plosive* and *sibilant* is particularly intriguing, especially in a drama context:

  o *dental* from the Latin for *tooth*
  o *fricative* from the Latin for *to rub*
  o *labial* from the Latin for *lip*
  o *plosive* from the Latin for *to drive out by clapping or hissing*
  o *sibilant* from the Latin for *hissing sound*

- Invite the students to vocalise the consonants in turn. As they do so, they should think carefully about the meaning of each of the five terms and how saying a specific consonant requires the breath, lips, mouth and tongue to be used in particular ways.
- Run the same exercise for the vowels, noting the origin of the word in the Latin for *voice*. Again, ask the students to focus on the way they breathe and move lips, mouth and tongue as they vocalise a particular vowel.
- Introduce the difference between *long* and *short* vowel sounds. Increase the space in the circle so that wider movement is possible. Experiment with pronouncing the long and short version of the same vowel. The students should accompany their vocalising of the vowel with a gesture and a movement that seems appropriate to that sound. For example, a *short a* sound might suggest exclamation or surprise; a *long a* sound might suggest puzzlement or enquiry.
- Share some of these examples and explore the reasons why certain sounds suggest a particular interpretation in terms of *gesture, movement and intonation*. Think, too, about how the breath is used in each case.
- Introduce the phonetic pronunciation of the consonants and run the same exercise with one or two examples from each of the five types (*c* is a particularly interesting example to consider).
- Let the students move around the space, experimenting with saying a mix of consonants and vowels from different parts of the body – the forehead, for example, or the back of the throat or the pit of the stomach.
- The students walk around the space, greeting each other with a chosen vowel or consonant sound and its attendant gesture, movement and intonation.
- Back in the circle: share your reflections on this set of exercises.

Activity Sequence 3: working with rhythm

- Introduce the six basic metrical feet of English prosody:

  - *Iambic*: one short followed by one long stress (*da*-**DUM**)
  - *Trochaic*: one long stress followed by one short stress (**DUM**-*da*)
  - *Dactylic*: one long stress followed by two short stresses (**DUM**-*da-da*)
  - *Anapaestic*: two short stresses followed by one long stress (*Da-da*-**DUM**)
  - *Spondaic*: two long stresses (**DUM-DUM**)
  - *Pyrrhic*: two short stresses (*da-da*)

- Students share their preliminary research into the etymology of the six metrical feet:

  - *Iambic* from the Ancient Greek *to put forth*
  - *Trochaic* from the Ancient Greek for *a running spinning foot*
  - *Dactylic* from the Ancient Greek for *a finger* (as in three joints)
  - *Anapaestic* from the Ancient Greek for *to strike back*
  - *Spondaic* from the Ancient Greek for *to make a drinks offering*
  - *Pyrrhic* from the Ancient Greek for *a war dance*

- Invite the students to reflect on why Ancient Greece might have been the linguistic source of these words. Have they noticed that some of the terms (like the Latin words for the consonants and for vowels) are linked to physical actions or parts of the body? Other words – like *Spondaic* and *Pyrrhic*, however, have their origin in a civic activity.
- Move back into a circle and work through the six metrical forms together, clapping out the rhythm of each one. As you do so, consider their respective etymologies and, in the follow-up discussion, share suggestions as to why a particular rhythm might have been associated with its root definition.

Activity Sequence 4: working with phonemes and rhythm

- Divide the students into smaller working groups. Allocate each group one of the six metrical forms. Remind the students about the differences between long and short vowel sounds and between the conventional and phonetic pronunciation of the five consonant types explored earlier (for example, *e* as in *tea* or *get*; *b* as in *bee* or *buh*).
- Each group has to find a phoneme combination that matches their allocated metrical form. For example, a spondaic pattern might be the repeated consonant *TEE-TEE* and a dactylic pattern might be a *long I* followed by two *short I* vowel sounds.
- Using the sound patterns they have decided upon together as the only verbal form of communication, each group prepares and presents a brief choral performance, the title of which is the etymological root definition of their allocated metrical form: for example, *War Dance* or *Strike Back*.
- Students will need to think about which areas of knowledge, dramatic skills, explorative strategies and elements of drama might be most appropriate for their chosen presentation. The Pyrrhic group, for example, might work in the medium

of dance. The Spondaic group's presentation might lend itself to ritual. The Dactylic group might wish to use the strategies and conventions of *physical theatre*.

- While working on their presentations and discussing the performances afterwards, students might consider how they engaged with *gesture*, *movement*, *pace*, *sound*, *rhythm* and *tension*. The following questions might aid reflection:

  o *Was it possible to convey ideas, feelings, mood and atmosphere by using sounds rather than words? What was gained and/or lost?*

  o *How did the rule about only using sounds rather than words influence the way you explored physical and visual forms of communication?*

  o *How did your allocated metrical form influence the decisions you made about gesture, movement, pace, sound, rhythm and tension? Is it possible to convey tension through a spondaic metre? Does the use of a dactylic or anapaestic metrical form necessitate a fast paced delivery or can they be delivered slowly?*

  o *Was it possible to observe differences in the performances whose metrical forms mirror each other (iambic/trochaic; dactylic/anapaestic)?*

Activity Sequence 5: working with blends and digraphs

- Invite the students to share the research they undertook into these terms before the drama lesson as before:

  o a *consonant blend* is a sequence of consonants in which each sound remains distinct (for example, the *b* and *l* sound can clearly be heard as separate elements when combined in the *bl* of *blend*)

  o a *consonant digraph* is a combination of consonants in which both individual sounds merge into a new sound (for example, *s* and *h* unite in *shop* to make *shuh*)

  o a *vowel digraph* occurs where two vowels are required to spell one vowel sound (for example, the *oa* in *coat*)

- In pairs, select either a consonant blend (for example, *bl*, *st*, *pl*) or consonant digraph (for example, *sh*, *ch*, *th*) phoneme combination. Take one of the letters each and, using phonetic pronunciation, set it to an anapaestic rhythm pattern (for example, buh-buh-**BUH**; luh-luh- **LUH** for the consonant blend *bl*). One of the aims of the next exercise is to explore the drama elements of *tension*, *climax* and *contrast*; so the driving, forward-moving rhythm of the anapaest is particularly suitable.

- Spread out around the space. The pairs circle each other, chanting their respective sequences either as a call and response or simultaneously. Experiment with *pace* and with *contrasts* of soft and loud: one suggestion might be to start chanting as quietly as possible and gradually to build up to a climax. At the climax, the two sounds are united and both members of the pair shout together the new sound combination (for example *bl!* or *ch!*) The exercise can be rehearsed so that the sounds and movements operate to a prepared plan and take on a ceremonial and ritualistic quality. Alternatively – and this requires perhaps a different kind of concentration from the participants – the pairs can work spontaneously, relying on aural and visual clues to determine the various moves in the sequence.

- The exercise can be used to explore vowel digraphs as well; but here there is a difference of emphasis in that, at the climax, one of the sounds 'gives way', as it were, to the other. For example, if the chanted phonemes are *long o* and *long a*, the combination sound is *long o* as in *coat*, *coal* or *foal*. This introduces considerations of *status* into the movement activity. As well as reviewing the activity in the follow-up discussion, it would be interesting to reflect upon why the *a* sound gives way to the *o* sound.

Activity Sequence 6: working with morphemes, prefixes and suffixes

- Share the following information:

  o a morpheme is the smallest unit of meaning in language and contains one or more phonemes

  o a morpheme that consists of a single *root word* can stand alone and is therefore known as a *free morpheme* (for example: *mask*)

  o a *bound* morpheme is one that only appears as part of a root word. It is *bound* because it cannot stand alone (for example: ***un** mask*)

  o a bound morpheme may be added to a root word as a *prefix* (***dis**appoint*) or a *suffix* (*disappoint**ment***)

  o a suffix might consist of just one phoneme (*disappointment **s***)

  o words consisting of two free morphemes are called *compound* words (***chair man***)

- The students are to work in small groups. They are given the free morpheme *mask* and asked to consider the connotations of this root word and how they might change when the bound morpheme *un* is added to the root word as a suffix so that it becomes *unmask*. Their task is to devise two tableaux: the first presents the group's response to the word *mask*; the second, their response to the word *unmask*. How do the two tableaux differ and what does this teach us about the power concealed in a bound morpheme? The experience can be intensified if the explorative strategy known as *merged image* is used, whereby the first image gradually morphs into the second: at what exact moment does the bound morpheme reveal its power?

- This activity can be developed to explore the ways in which prefixes and suffixes can alter the meanings of root words. The students need to choose root words that can be extended through the addition of prefixes and suffixes. Root words that can accommodate both (for example: ***dis**appoint**ment***) are particularly effective; but the activity can work well when only a prefix or a suffix is added (for example: ***mal**content*, *content**ment***). Students work in groups of three (if only a suffix or prefix is to be added to a two syllable root word) or in groups of four (if adding both to a two syllable root word). Take *malcontent* as an example. Two members of the group create a tableau to express their interpretation of the root word. This activity departs from the *merged image* strategy in that this time the *constructed frame* is broken by the arrival of an external force: the third member of the group, representing the bound morpheme *mal*. Together, the three group members have to construct a new frame to represent their response to the new word. If the chosen root word takes both a suffix and a prefix, as in *disappointment*, two additional approaches might be explored. The group could run three images – *appoint*, *disappoint*, *disappointment* – together in a fast 'flick-book' frame sequence. Alternatively, four people might work together on this word. The group members stand in a line. The two in the middle mime a response to the word *appoint*. The one at the start of the line on the left (representing the position of the prefix in relation to the root word in a language system that reads from left to right) freezes in a pose that represents a response to the word *disappoint*. The one on the right at the end of the line freezes in a pose that represents a response to the word *disappointment*.

- Work like this can provide an effective means of exploring grammar and tense. *Content* is an interesting example to examine because the grammatical label attached to the root word changes depending on the context in which it is used. If, for example, the bound morpheme suffix *s* is added to the root word, what had appeared to be an abstract noun or possibly an adverb is changed into a common noun. And what happens if, in a dialogue, one character asks another the one-word question: *Content?* As well as exploring grammatical classifications and the use of plurals, the activities described above can also demonstrate how the addition of bound morpheme suffixes like *ing* and *ed* to a root word can indicate changes in tense.

Activity Sequence 7: working with onset and rime

- The preliminary research for this section involves securing the following definitions:
  - ○ *Onset*: the part of the syllable that precedes the vowel of the syllable and consists of a consonant or consonant blend (for example, *S*un)
  - ○ *Rime*: the vowel(s) followed by the remaining consonants in the syllable (for example, *s*UN)

- As well as researching this element of language, students might also collect and share information on the history of Ireland, particularly the period known as *The Troubles* (see next paragraph).

- Activities involving onset and rime are particularly effective for helping students appreciate the dynamic tensions within words. Seamus Heaney's poem *Broagh* (from the 1972 collection *Wintering Out*) provides a particularly powerful example of how attention to onset and rime can enhance appreciation of the power of language. In the poem, Heaney contemplates the name of the township (an Anglicised version of the Irish *bruach abhana*) in his home county of Derry. Focusing on the rime of *Broagh*, the opening vowel evokes a sense of place, the letter *o* reminding him of the mark a heel might make in damp soil. The final *gh* sound of the name, Heaney notes, evokes the power of language to include and exclude: strangers betray the fact that they are outsiders by being unable to pronounce it correctly.

- Share the poem with the students. How might the dramatic skills of *physical theatre* be employed to give a dynamic account of the power and the layered meanings that are contained within that apparently simple place name? Since we are working specifically with a poem by Heaney as an exemplar text, it might be useful to consider the binary oppositions that run through his work: sky god (Hercules) against earth god (Antaeus); coloniser against colonised; reason against emotion; wilderness against city; Celt against Anglo-Saxon; light against dark.

- Some of these tensions are expressed in the onset and rime of *Broagh*. Students should work in groups of six (one person for each letter of the word but with two people working together to represent the consonant blend of the onset *Br* and two people working on *gh*). A decision needs to be made about the vowels at the start of the rime: do they create a digraph, or should they be pronounced separately? What information do we need to help us decide? Heaney himself emphasises the visual and symbolic importance of the letter *o* – should that be more prominently featured than the *a* in a dramatic presentation? Two people work together on the *gh*: again, a decision needs to be made about whether it is a blend or a digraph; and again, students need to think about why that information might be important and where they could locate it. Are there any clues in the Irish version of the name? How is it that such a small place has two names? (The name of Heaney's childhood home, *Mossbawn*, encapsulates the linguistic and cultural divisions of Ireland in that the first part comes from an Old English word *meos*, or *bog*, and the second from the Anglo-Irish *bábhún*, or *enclosure*).

- Read the poem again for the topographical clues it provides: there is a riverbank, a canopy of trees leading to a ford, black, oozing soil, dock leaves and elder trees: what connotations do these images evoke and how might their relationship be represented physically in the interaction between the firm consonants of the onset and the yielding vowels at the start of the rime?

- Heaney's observation that strangers found the *gh* sound which completes the rime difficult to pronounce correctly, alters the frame that we place around the word, so that it changes from being an evocation of place to something which is more politically and culturally charged. The two students representing the *gh* sound need to find some form of physical expression that signifies this shift. The ambiguity of the pronunciation of the sound raises interesting challenges in terms of drama: is the *h* pronounced or not? Is the *g* sound hard or soft? What, literally, is that sound saying in terms of belonging or not belonging and how does it relate to the vowels and consonants that precede it?

Activity Sequence 8: working with compound words

- The preliminary research for this section involves an exploration of two genres of Anglo-Saxon literature: *kennings* (see the first three activities below) and *riddles* (the fourth activity). Anglo-Saxon kennings offer a particularly engaging literary resource for work on compound words, not least for their potential in helping students explore figurative language in general and *metaphor* in particular. Examples include: *bone house* (the body), *battle light* (a sword), *wave floater* (a ship) and *house sun* (a fire that heats a house). Different kennings can represent the same word or concept: *whale road*, *fish home* and *seal bath*, for example, can all mean *the sea*.

- In pairs, reflect on each word in a chosen kenning. Say the words to each other, experimenting with rhythm and intonation. Does *battle light*, for example, have a dactylic rhythm? How might the force of the kenning be altered if it were given an anapaestic rhythm instead? Take one of the kenning words each. Use movement to indicate which word is dominant in the compound by facing each other and having the person who says the dominant word step forward while their partner simultaneously says their word and steps back. Alternatively, *simulate* an 'arm wrestling match': the 'winner' forces (not literally!) the arm of their opponent down on the dominant word.

- Working in groups consisting of two pairs each, choose a kenning and present two tableaux – one that offers a literal and the other a metaphorical interpretation of the compound word. What are the similarities and differences? Track the thinking that took you from one to the other: what ideas might the creators of the kenning have been trying to express? A kenning like *bone house* is particularly interesting to explore in this way, offering opportunities for metaphysical speculation.

- The group divides into sets of five and chooses, or is allocated, a kenning. Each group of five stands in line. The first person in the line represents the first word in the kenning and the last person represents the second word. What are the three moves that take the kenning from *whale*, for example, to *road* or – perhaps more challenging – from *seal* to *bath*?

- Present your interpretation as five brief monologues spoken by each of the five members in sequence. Explain your 'move' but speak in the first person. Craft your monologue in the elliptical style of an Anglo-Saxon riddle – as in these lines 'spoken' by an onion: *I do no harm to anyone unless they cut me first. Then I soon make them cry.* If you want to craft the monologue more intricately, try to use the alliteration that is a hallmark of Anglo-Saxon poetry. Thus, the person speaking as the whale in the given example might say: *I wander the watery wastes.* The second person has to try to 'move' the image closer to its final expression – perhaps by developing the idea suggested by the verb *wander*. They might say: *I am a traveller, trailing the earth* – and so on. Indicate the extent of the imaginative leap made in each of the five moves through the use of *proxemics* (body space). The greater the metaphorical stretch, the larger the physical distance between the five members of the group. Some kennings are more challenging than others. Is it possible to try this activity with the kenning *seal bath* without lapsing into bathos at the end? How has the meaning of the word *bath* changed over time so that it no longer works as effectively as it once did in this particular context?

- The activities described above could be used with the students' own compounds: what might be an effective kenning for *smart phone* or *Twitter*, for example? If grammar is the desired focus, the first two activities could be used to explore how verbs can be used adjectivally as in *swimming pool* or *dining room*. Plenty of comic potential here!

Activity Sequence 9: broadening the context

- The exercises on blends and digraphs, prefixes and suffixes described above could be used as the stimulus material for a theatre project devised by secondary school students to present to primary school children who are encountering the concepts for the first time as they learn to read, especially if the children are working through a programme based on synthetic phonics.

- Models to work from might include Rudyard Kipling's *Just So Stories for Little Children* or the creation stories of Ted Hughes, such as *How the Whale Became* (especially the edition illustrated by Jackie Morris), *The Dreamfighter and other Creation Tales* and *Tales of the Early World*. Alternatively, the University of Georgia in the United States has a fascinating on-line international collection: *Creation Stories from around the World* www.gly.uga.edu/railsback/CS/CSIndex.html

- *How the Digraph Became* or *How the Blend Became* would make an interesting dramatised fairy story, pantomime tale, narrated mime or even a ballet and would pose fascinating dramatic challenges: what costume, mask or make up might the phoneme *b* wear? How would it move? How would the story engage and involve the young audience so that they were gripped by the spectacle and at the same time felt that they gained a clearer understanding of these *ostended* phonetic concepts? In this context, terms like *bound* and *free* morpheme are a gift to the dramatic imagination!

Opportunities for work in the English classroom

Exploring language

The guiding principle informing language work in the English classroom is that it should avoid at all cost what Peter Slade calls 'the bashing-in method' and draw instead upon the kind of active learning strategies advocated by Rousseau, Froebel and Dewey – to name but three of the witnesses from Part 1 of the book who could have been called to testify in support of this approach. Students should feel that linguistic exploration is fascinating in itself and fun to do.

Whether investigating the building blocks of phonology or spelling or lower order reading strategies as so many of the activities described here do, the emphasis should be on undertaking what Rainer and Lewis might call 'authentic' (2012, p. 4) explorations, which give the participants opportunities to speculate and to hypothesise about, for example, the nature of grammatical rules and categories. In Activity Sequence 7: *working with onset and rime*, in which the students have to make decisions about the classification and pronunciation of the *gh* in *Broagh*, for instance, they do so within a purposeful context: the ambiguity and challenge of the task speaks precisely to the symbolic significance of the word and to the central concerns of the poem, which are foregrounded by the uneasy presence of that word. The onset and rime activities described here could be applied, with powerful results, to any word in any kind of text.

If students can discover for themselves how and why a metalanguage operates as it does rather than being told simply to learn the terms by rote, they will not only start to approach potentially complex and abstract ideas with confidence and a sense of expertise, but also absorb an important ideological lesson about questioning and challenging, rather than simply receiving and obeying rules and orders. The activities should help students respect and appreciate the power of language and thus think more carefully about what they say and how they say it. The bound morpheme activity (Activity Sequence 6: *mask/unmask*), for example, demonstrates just how powerful a seemingly negligible prefix can be and reminds us that grammatical, not just lexical, words have an important role to play in spoken and written communication.

Many of the activities provide rich opportunities for research into etymology and the history of language. The derivations of the terms for the six metrical feet described in Activity Sequence 3: *working with rhythm*, for example, are fascinating. They draw attention to Saussure's contention that language is socially constructed and they remind us that if, with the advent of the digital age, the 'page' is becoming a 'site of display' as Kress and Bezemer maintain, then it is only acquiring the characteristics that far older textual media have exhibited for centuries. Words, too, have histories and provenances – some of them harsh and difficult and, as the example of *Broagh* indicates, still contested. It is important for students to learn this.

Working with literature

The activities provide opportunities for engagement with genres from across the spectrum of the literary heritage whether they be Anglo-Saxon kennings or the stories of Ted Hughes. The kennings and riddles activities (Activity Sequence 8) invite the exploration of contemporary expressions of the form: for example, the poem *Bluebottle* by Judith Nicholls (1994). Craig Raine's famous poem *A Martian Sends a Postcard Home* (1979) is another good example. The kennings exercise, again, might provide a way into the work of Metaphysical poets like John Donne, who famously links disparate images such as lovers and the arms of a compass. Advertisers also use this technique, often in very surreal ways; so this would make another interesting area of investigation – while providing, incidentally, an opportunity to take a Russian Formalist approach to literary criticism by comparing the ways that an example of advertising copy might be similar to or different from a poem with which it shares similar rhetorical techniques. Beyond the study of particularly literary genres, of course, the activities provide powerful opportunities to explore some of the core features of poetry itself – particularly *rhythm*, *diction* and *imagery*.

Chapter 11

Working with text
Poetry as an example

Introduction and context

This sequence of activities is designed as an entire scheme of work. It follows a well-established dynamic for textual engagement consisting of *pre-reading*, *reading* and *post-reading* activities. Although poetry is the focus in this instance, the activities – not least those concerned with exploring the 'music' of language – could be used with any literary text. They could also be used with non-fictional texts that employ rhetorical devices to argue or persuade (such as advertising copy, charity leaflets, journalistic opinion pieces, essays) or that use imagery, rhythm and diction to evoke a particular experience, atmosphere or sense of place (travel writing, for example). I have used similar activities to explore the advertising copy on the side of a supermarket rice packet and the description of a journey down the Amazon.

The exemplar text is one of my own poems: *Zip-Wire*. Using one's own material avoids copyright issues – no small matter when it comes to gaining permission to quote poetry! In this case, however, there are pedagogical advantages too. First, I think it is important that English teachers are seen by their students to be practitioners of the arts they purport to teach. Teachers who are writers themselves send out powerful messages about the importance of writing. By practising the same craft we ask the students to practise, we can help to remove the sense of hierarchy and mystique that can bedevil their perception of the writing process. We can share the frustrations, the drafts, the crossings-out – and perhaps the moments of elation too.

So many of the texts that students study in school are enclosed within high-status frames; published in an examination anthology or on an imposing website, perhaps. It is important that students have opportunities for engaging with literature that does not come with a lofty pedigree, that is not stamped with a critical *imprimatur* but that has instead to make its own claims for attention. Students who encounter a poem like *Zip-Wire* do not have to assume that it must be 'good' and authoritative because it has been published. They have more opportunities therefore to make honest critical judgements about it, rather than finding out first what established critics might give them permission to say. Not the least important lesson that students can take from this, perhaps, is the realisation that their teacher's writing is just as open to critical scrutiny as their own. 'In this improvement', Rousseau wrote in *Emile*, 'I shall either go side by side with my pupil, or so little in advance that he will always overtake me easily and sometimes get ahead of me'. Good advice still worth considering by English teachers today. The choice of *Zip-Wire* is also important because it engages with key issues that have informed Part 1 of this book: attitudes towards play; the relationship between spectator and actor; the tensions between spontaneity and that self-consciousness that Way denounced as 'one of the scourges of humanity' (1967, p. 157).

Links with Part I of the book

Louise Rosenblatt famously wrote that 'Literature provides a *living-through*, not simply *knowledge about*' and added that 'the literary experience must be phrased as a *transaction* between the reader and the text' [original italics] (1970, pp. 38, 34–35). The activities described in the following seven sequences describe ways in which students might simultaneously acquire *knowledge about* a literary text (in this case, a poem) while also engaging with it as a resource for *living through* – by bringing their personal stories and experiences to that text and by devising their own, answering creative responses alongside it. Caldwell Cook suggests as much when he declares that his students 'must themselves come forth as poets'. Finlay-Johnson and Hourd also advocate Rosenblatt's principle of *transaction*. Finlay-Johnson, for example, engages her students in a *living through* of Tennyson's *The Charge of the Light Brigade* by inviting them to locate their performance of the text within the dramatic context of the evening roll call that follows the battle. Arguing that 'the final aim of the teaching of poetry appreciation is that the child shall reach a reconciliation of subjective and objective interpretation', Hourd encourages her ten-year-olds to a *transaction* with Homer's *Iliad* when they transpose a scene from the epic poem into a play text set 'on the walls of Troy' (1949, p. 48). In this sense, the activity sequences offer an example of how textual engagement might be structured according to the *making, performing, responding* matrix explored in Part 1 of the book from the sections on Abbs and Hornbrook (Chapter 6) onwards.

Slade's voice can be heard here, too, though he describes the tension between *living through* and *knowledge about* in different terms. He argues that it is the task of adults to help children gain access to what he calls the 'treasure casket of intellectual, emotional and aesthetic joys' (1954, p. 52). Learning that such 'treasures' are for 'sharing', Slade writes, is a 'terrible test' (p. 32), which the young have to undergo if they are to negotiate their sense of identity within the wider social context of the community. Drama can help children to pass Slade's 'test'. As Vygotsky suggests when he cites Sully's account of the sisters playing at being sisters, and as so many practitioners have argued since, drama encourages us to acknowledge the presence of points of view other than our own, to understand how and why rules work and to know why those rules might need to be obeyed or why they might need to be challenged. In cultural terms, drama has a most important role to play in strengthening bonds of identity through the sharing of experiences. I am not suggesting that *Zip-Wire* is a 'treasure casket of intellectual, emotional and aesthetic joys'; but the activity sequences created around that text do offer opportunities for students to experience all three of Slade's 'joys' – irrespective of what they think about the poem – by engaging with the issues, memories and emotions it evokes, by sharing those issues, memories and emotions with other people and by devising creative responses *together*. 'Camaraderie' – to reclaim a word that Hornbrook uses as a term of disparagement – is one of the main 'treasures' in the 'casket'.

Whitehead argues that the 'process of identification' described above 'lies at the heart of all their [children's] intellectual and emotional growth' and that drama is the most powerful medium for encouraging it. In the context of this sequence of activities, therefore, it would be useful to revisit the section in Part 1 of the book where English practitioners of the sixties and seventies – Whitehead himself, Britton, Dixon, Holbrook, the authors of *A Language for Life* – explore the contribution of drama to an English curriculum predicated on a model that Cox was later to define as *adult needs, cross-curricular, cultural heritage, cultural analysis* and *personal growth* (see p. 80). To what extent does the sequence of activities described here meet the concerns of that curricular agenda? Bear in mind, too, the comment from *The Newsom Report* (see p. 39) that 'It is of course within poetry and drama that the use of language goes deepest'. The practitioners named above were concerned with what drama might be able to do for English and therefore paid little more than lip service to its claims as an autonomous subject. Way feared that placing drama 'within the domain of English' might encourage 'teachers of brighter children to look upon theatre and scripts as the correct starting place, relegating drama to an alternative activity useful only for those who are unable to read fluently' (1967, p. 10). Do the activities described in this section address Way's fears? Do they succeed in accommodating the aesthetic and discipline concerns of drama as an autonomous subject in its own right? If not, what issues does this raise and how do we resolve them?

The choice of an exemplar text that explores some of the book's core issues about play and about seeing and being seen recalls Heathcote's comment that, unlike professional actors, children have not given an audience 'permission to stare'. An exploration of *Zip-Wire* provides students with opportunities to engage explicitly with these issues, both in discussion and in the drama activities themselves, particularly when working on the four scenarios in Activity Sequence 5 or the suggestions for *Ritual* in Activity Sequence 6. In this context, it would be useful to revisit the section in Part 1 of the book that discusses Margaret Lowenfeld's account of different kinds of play and the various ways in which children are or are not willing to engage with it (see pp. 50–51). 'Children are only entirely spontaneous in play when they are alone and undisturbed by adult comment' (1935, p. 25), Lowenfeld writes. Consider this statement in the context of the observed play described in *Zip-Wire*. Think here too of Lowenfeld's quotation from Hall: 'The forces of destruction, aggression, and hostile emotion, which form so powerful an element for good or evil in human character, can display themselves fully in the play of childhood.' Compare this with Piaget's assertion that 'the function of play is to protect this universe [of the child's ego] against forced accommodation to ordinary reality'. Vygotsky's and Piaget's comments on the links between play and cognition might be shared with the students, too. Look again at Vygotsky's observation that 'in play activity thought is separated from objects, and action arises from ideas rather than from things'. Compare this with Piaget's assertion that: 'With the projection of . . . "symbolic schemata" on to other objects, the way is clear for the assimilation of any one object to another, since any object can be a make-believe substitute for any other'. Without this cognitive capacity, a zip-wire would remain just a zip-wire.

Exemplar text

Zip-Wire

You took my hand and we
Ran through the playground
Together: a child and a 'senior'
Looking out for the zip-wire.

Suddenly, there we were –
Lining up for your go
Behind older girls.
They were twice your age

And laughed self-consciously
When they saw you watching
As though you had come to tell them
Their time was up.

They piled on the narrow seat
In twos and threes: riding
The delicate line into
Adolescence; arms around
Each other locking tight.

And then they were off and away
Out of the playground.
You stepped to the platform
Ready for your turn.

Activity Sequence 1: first encounters

Working at syntactical level

- Do not let the students see or read the poem yet. Do not tell them what it is called. Divide the poem by punctuation breaks onto individual pieces of card. Do not include the actual punctuation mark itself, just note on the card where the punctuation mark occurs. Do include the capital letters as they appear in the poem. There are eleven punctuation breaks in all. If possible, allocate one punctuation sequence to each member of the group. If the group is too small, some students will have to take two punctuation sequences. If it is too large, think of alternative ways of dividing the sequences (lines 8 to 12, for example, form one punctuation sequence and could be sub-divided into several smaller sections). An alternative approach that works effectively with a poem composed of short line lengths like this one is to divide it into line divisions (see also below).
- Ask the students to familiarise themselves with the words they have been given. Allow them time to move around the space on their own, thinking about the

meaning and significance of these as yet decontextualised words. Ask the students to consider the following questions:

- o   *What might the words denote and connote?*
- o   *Who might say them and in what context?*
- o   *What tone of voice might be used to say the words?*
- o   *What feelings might they express?*
- o   *Who might these words be spoken to and how might that person receive them?*

- Ask the students to walk around the space and to greet each other with their words. They should experiment with different ways of saying them, thinking about the effects created by varying *intonation, projection, pitch, pause,* and *distance from the audience* at the moment of greeting (whispering a phrase into a partner's ear is very different from shouting an effusive greeting from several feet away). The following contexts for saying the words or phrases might prove helpful, though there are plenty of others to choose from as well:

- o   *Sharing a secret*
- o   *Breaking bad news*
- o   *Issuing an order*
- o   *Asking a question*
- o   *Reading a formal statement*
- o   *Telling a joke*

- Does a particular way of saying the words or phrases seem more appropriate to their meaning than others? Why might this be and what clues about the text can we glean from that information?
- Bring the group back together. Ask them to share images or phrases they heard during the greetings exercise: what sticks in the mind? What kind of text might this be? How can we tell? What *theme, mood* or *atmosphere* does this text seem to evoke?

Activity Sequence 2: performing the poem

Working at syntactical level

- The group stands in a circle. Reveal the information that the text is a poem and 'conduct' the students through a reading of it, identifying whose words or phrase is first, whose is second, and so on. The students should try to say their words or phrases without referring to their cards, so that they can free their hands and bodies to add gestures appropriate to the words.
- Give at least two readings in this way so that the group can start to familiarise itself not only with the whole flow of the poem, but also by putting faces to the various speakers of the words and phrases. Now run a third reading, but this time with eyes closed so that the students have to focus on the sounds and rhythms of the words and the particular vocal characteristics of those who are delivering them. All but the student who has responsibility for the opening phrase

will need to listen out carefully for the word or phrase that 'cues' in their own contribution.

- The students open their eyes and are asked to remain standing in a circle. Make sure they are sorted randomly, so that speaker 1 is not next to speaker 2 who is not next to speaker 3, and so on. Their task now is to deliver their word or phrase to the next speaker in the correct chronological sequence. This should mean having to remember where that person is standing in the circle and having to make a journey to get to them. They need to make sure that the time it takes to reach the person to whom they are delivering their lines matches the word or phrase they have to say. Note the contrast between the speaker who has one word to deliver (perhaps to the other side of the circle, perhaps to someone closer at hand) and the speaker who has the longest sequence (in this poem, twenty-six words without a punctuation break). As they walk, they should hold eye contact with the person they are addressing and think about how the way they move across the room might imitate (or *counter point*) the rhythm and meaning of the word or phrase and their *intention* in delivering it.
- Reflect as a group upon this sequence of activities. The following prompt questions might prove helpful:

  o *What kind of punctuation breaks appear to have been used? How do they help to shape the movement and structure of the poem?*
  o *What patterns of rhythm have you noticed and how do these combine with features like alliteration, sibilance and assonance to create the 'music' of the poem?*
  o *What structural features suggest that this text is a poem? What would be gained and/or lost if it were written out in sentences as a piece of narrative prose?*

Working at sub-textual level

- Explain to the group that the poem is composed of five verse sections. Bearing that information in mind, give another communal performance of the poem around the circle. As you listen to it this time, think about where those five verse section divisions might occur. Share your thoughts.
- Invite the students to give the poem a title and to explain their reasons.
- Distribute printed copies of the poem. How do your decisions about the verse divisions, the punctuation marks and your suggested titles for the poem compare with the original?
- Divide the group into five and ask the students to prepare a choral performance of their allocated verse section, which draws upon the points considered in the preceding activities. As they work the students should consider the following questions:

  o *Will the lines be spoken by everybody in the group together or by individuals, or through a mixture of both approaches?*
  o *How might you make use of such devices as **chant** or **echo**?*
  o *How will you negotiate issues of **pitch, dynamics** and **timbre**?*

- Are there certain words in the verse section that have a particular resonance and are open to interpretation at a metaphorical as well as a literal level of meaning?
- Will there be a single narrator, with the other members of the group miming the actions described in the verse section?
- Will you attempt a naturalistic or a non-naturalistic interpretation of your verse section?
- There is no punctuation break between the last line of the second verse section and the first line of the third: how will the two groups manage this transition?
- How will the students working with verse section five bring the poem to its conclusion?

- When the performance is finished, hang a washing line at the back of the drama space and distribute a piece of paper and a clothes peg to each member of the group. Each person writes (or draws as an alternative) the phrase or line in the poem that they feel speaks to them most. Peg the responses on the washing line and invite the group to review them as if looking at pictures in a gallery. Use the mobility of the pegs to cluster together any responses that fall into a particular pattern.
- How do the washing-line responses compare with the group performance of the poem? Are the interpretations similar or has the washing-line exercise revealed new perspectives on the piece?
- Conclude this sequence of activities with a final performance of the poem, altering it if appropriate in the light of the previous discussion.

Activity Sequence 3: exploring imagery

Working at word level

- Focus on the title of the poem. By this stage, the students will have had plenty of opportunities to consider its significance. The group stands in a circle. When the teacher says 'zip-wire', each person must freeze in a gesture that represents their immediate response to the words. Invite different members of the group to explain their response. Use this discussion as the starting point for a sharing of stories about childhood experiences of playgrounds, fairs and amusement parks. Gradually bring the attention of the group back to the image of the zip-wire.
- Introduce the concept of the 'iceberg text': what appears on the surface is only part of a larger, mainly submerged, whole. What does the 'iceberg' of the zip-wire represent? On the 'surface' it is a piece of playground equipment for enjoying a brief adrenaline rush; but what about 'underneath'? This is an opportunity to start to consider the various *perspectives* and *points of view* explored in the poem. Why do the girls piling onto the 'narrow seat' laugh 'self-consciously' when they realise they are being observed by a child half their age? Why does the little child patiently wait her 'turn' instead of joining in the fun of the older girls? In this context, think particularly about the metaphor in the fourth verse section.

- In groups of four or five, *sculpt* the zip-wire. The representation can be a literal one; but a more challenging task would be, in the light of the previous discussion, to sculpt a metaphorical interpretation. If the literal approach is chosen, add a *soundscape* of the kind of noises that would be heard around a zip-wire. If the metaphorical approach is selected, choose an abstract noun as the title for your sculpture.

- Share and discuss the presentations. A way of focusing and adding formality to the discussion would be to run it as a *simulation*. Remind the students of how they were asked to view the washing-line responses in Activity Sequence 2 as if they were visiting an art gallery. Build on that initial experience by inviting them to take it in turns to play the role of Art students who have been given the task of interpreting the sculptures for their colleagues.

- Once all the sculptures have been interpreted, work out of role to share responses: how satisfied are the creators of the sculptures with the interpretations they have heard?

- One of the tensions which inform this poem is that between *movement* and *stillness*. There is the 'iceberg surface' stillness of the zip-wire, the patient little girl and the observing 'senior'. This contrasts with the movement of the adult and child who run eagerly through the playground at the start of the poem and with the horseplay of the older girls as they ride on the wire. Beneath the 'surface' of the 'iceberg', however, there is the metaphorical stillness of the inanimate object, which contrasts with the metaphorical movement of the human beings in the poem, all of whom are negotiating different rites of passage. The little child stands ready to take the place of the older girls who are themselves exchanging the spontaneity of childhood for the self-consciousness of adolescence. The adult in the poem is now old enough to pay 'senior' rates for entrance to the playground.

- Working individually, complete the following sentence stems as if writing from the point of view of the zip-wire. Either single words or phrases can be used:

  o *My name is* (add an abstract noun or noun phrase here)
  o *I see . . .*
  o *I feel . . .*
  o *I want . . .*

- If the focus of this sequence were *point of view* (see below) this writing-stem activity could be repeated for the little child, the older girls and the 'senior'. Choosing the *non-naturalistic* option of the zip-wire itself, however, draws particular attention to the *symbolic function* that it plays in the poem.

- The whole group forms a circle. Each person takes it in turn to read or, better still, perform their monologue. Now go round the circle again, but this time each person reads just their first line. This activity can be repeated for each of the four lines in turn. What similarities and or differences emerge? What *expressions, gestures, movements and intonation* are appropriate for conveying *feelings* as opposed to *wants* or to what is *seen*?

- Powerful work could be achieved by choreographing the statements. The *I see* stem, for example, lends itself particularly to the *explorative strategy* known as *Tell me what you see*. In turn, the members of the group strain to look into – what? The distance? The future? The past? Their inner thoughts and feelings? Would the zip-wire be indifferent to or disturbed and elated by what it could see?

Activity Sequence 4: exploring point of view – a performance-based approach

Working at contextual level

- If the statement-stem activity is repeated for the other people featured in the poem, opportunities arise for more extensive work on the *drama skill* of *monologue* and the *drama element* of *point of view*. This sequence of activities is designated as *contextual level* work because it attempts to develop the human *context* of the poem by exploring the relationships between the different people who appear in it.

- In groups of three (to represent little child, adolescent girls and 'senior', respectively), students should take turns to share with the other two group members the stem-question responses they wrote for the character they have been asked to represent.

- When you have heard all three, prepare a formal dramatic presentation of each of the stem-question responses as a sequence of monologues. *Black out* the performance area and use a *spotlight* (a torch or candle will create a different but equally powerful effect) to illuminate the performer whose turn it is to speak. Simple, hand-held *masks* representing Childhood, Adolescence and Age will add an allegorical dimension to the performance, which could be enhanced further still if the students are given time to research, and inform their performance with, the conventions and stock character-playing associated with *Commedia dell'arte*, for example, or the *medieval mystery plays*. It is important that the masks are hand-held so that they can be kept at a slight distance from the face, thus avoiding restriction of speech.

- The sense of formality can be enhanced further by thinking about *proxemics*. Position the three speakers at different distances from each other, to symbolise the different stages of life they have reached. The 'older girls' are twice the age of the young child; the gap between them will be smaller than that between child, girls and 'senior'.

- Experiment with different *perspectives* and *time-shifts*. Place the person representing the child, with the appropriate mask, in the spotlight. The adolescent now stands behind the child; the 'senior' behind the adolescent. Both hold their respective masks. This time, however, after the person representing the child has delivered their monologue as before, the other two speakers say in turn the lines they wrote for the child in the original sentence-stem activity. Delivering the lines of the child while wearing the mask of the adolescent or the 'senior' adds a poignancy to the performance, which resonates with the poem's sense of transience and its concerns with rites of passage. The 'senior' and the adolescent reach back through time to speak as the children they once were.

Activity Sequence 5: exploring point of view – a *process* approach

Working at contextual level

- A more *process-based* approach to the sentence-stems would be to use the sets of written responses as the stimulus material or *pre-text* for a more spontaneous engagement with the human beings featured in the poem.
- Working in groups of three again, each person is *hot-seated* in role as their allotted character by the other two group members. Their two colleagues can interrupt the prepared monologue with questions for which the person in role has to try to provide spontaneous answers, in role.
- The questions can be pitched at different levels of complexity. For example, if the person playing the adolescent has completed the third stem-sentence with the statement *I feel bewildered*, an obvious follow up question would be *Why?* It might be more thought provoking, however to ask instead: *When did you last not feel bewildered?*
- The teacher might find it useful to let the groups play the hot-seating activity through for a while and then call the whole group together to share their thoughts about the questions asked: which seemed the most effective and why? This discussion could then lead into an exploration of the ways in which *how, who, what, when* and *why* questions can pose different cognitive challenges.
- Moving on to an ideological plane, the students could consider here the status issues implicit in questioning. The following prompts might aid the discussion:

  o *If someone asks you a question, do you have to answer it?*
  o *If different people asked you the same question, would you give the same answer each time?*
  o *How might the question* Where were you last night? *differ when asked by a police officer, a parent or your best friend?*
  o *How might the same question differ if the questioner put the emphasis on different words:* WHERE were you last night? Where WERE you last night? *and so on*

- Back in their groups of three, the students resume the hot-seating activity, drawing on the previous discussion to help each other develop a clearer understanding of the *attitudes, feelings* and *beliefs* that might inform the roles they are representing.
- After all three figures have been hot-seated, the students work together out of role to share their thoughts about how the activity has enhanced their perception of the poem and its themes. What has brought three such different people to the same playground space? What thoughts run through their minds as they watch each other?
- Bring the whole group together and introduce them to William Blake's *The Echoing Green* (1794). Written two centuries ago, the poem explores similar themes to *Zip-Wire* in that it describes elderly people reminiscing about their lost youth as they watch children at play. Like *Zip-Wire*, too, *The Echoing Green* ends by describing a moment of change that can be interpreted literally and metaphorically. As they listen to the reading, ask the students to think about points of comparison

and contrast between the two poems. They might compare the narrative voices, for example, or the different ways in which young and old are portrayed. After the reading, share immediate impressions around the group. Have their attitudes towards the roles they have been working on changed in any way?

- Rearrange the groups (into threes again, if possible) so that all the 'young children', 'adolescents' and 'seniors' now work together. The members of each group share their thoughts about the role with the other two people who have also been working on it.
- In the new groups, improvise the following scenarios:

    Three 'seniors' are sitting together watching the young children they are looking after as they play. What emotions go through their minds as they watch? They fall into conversation: what do they talk about?

    Three adolescent girls approach the zip-wire. They want to have fun with it but are worried about appearing childish: what do they decide to do?

    Three young children approach the zip-wire: what are their thoughts and feelings about it? What does the zip-wire represent in terms of their imaginations? Is their play the unalloyed, spontaneous pleasure depicted in Blake's poem?

    The three adolescent girls and the three young children arrive at the zip-wire at the same time. How do the two groups react? Do they both play on it? If so, does one group go first while the other watches?

- Bring the whole group together. Recall the differences between *fabula* and *syuzhet* explored in *From Private to Public Space*. What might be the most effective order in which to present the four scenarios? Think too about *juxtapositioning*: what effects might be created by contrasting, for example, the scene where the 'seniors' are talking with the scene where the young children are approaching the zip-wire? Might those effects be enhanced if the scenes are intercut so that the *focus* moves backwards and forwards between the two?
- Play the scenes in the negotiated sequence as an example of *rolling theatre* moving, at an agreed signal, from one to the next. The actors for one scenario become the audience for the others.

Activity Sequence 6: working with ritual

Working at textual level

- Rites of passage are often marked by acts of ritual, whether they be coming of age celebrations, ceremonies for school-leavers or funerals.
- The core binary oppositions that inform *Zip-Wire* – youth and age, innocence and experience, spontaneity and self-consciousness – might be expressed in non-naturalistic, ritual form by engaging with an explorative strategy like *Conscience Alley*. The group creates two equal lines, facing inwards. One line represents the 'seniors', the other, the adolescent girls. The two people at the far end of the line represent the young child. They walk slowly down the 'alley' formed by the two lines, from one end to the other. As they walk, the 'seniors' and the adolescents

give the pair words of advice, culled from their own experiences. What do they say and how do they say it? Are they bitter, encouraging, jealous, disdainful? Does the advice from either side of the 'alley' differ or is it similar? Once the couple representing the young child reach the end, they take their places on either side of the 'alley' and the new pair at the bottom walk through. This can be repeated until every pair has had a chance to make the walk. Share your reflections on what you have heard.

- As with Blake's poem, *The Echoing Green*, several of the lines in *Zip-Wire* can be interpreted on a metaphorical as well as a literal level. For example: *arms around/ Each other locking tight; And then they were off and away/Out of the play-ground; You stepped to the platform/Ready for your turn*. Move into groups of four. Thinking back to the washing-line activity in Activity Sequence 2, choose a line or phrase that you feel is particularly evocative. Think about a piece of music that conveys the mood, atmosphere and emotion that the chosen words conjure for you. Explain your choice to the other group members and together come to a decision about which suggestion you feel you can best work with.

- Choreograph a mimed response to your chosen line and perform it to your selected music. If you are working with a song, you may wish to mime to the words as part of your performance.

- Divide the group into five working units, one for each verse section of *Zip-Wire*. Give each group a copy of this poem with *The Echoing Green* printed beside it. Allocate to each group a verse section of *Zip-Wire* and a similar number of sequential lines from Blake's poem. *The Echoing Green* consists of three, ten-line verses so the numerical division cannot be exact. Invite the group to suggest where it might be possible to sub-divide the Blake poem into five sections.

- Having made that decision, allocate a section of *Zip-Wire* and a section of *The Echoing Green* to each of the five groups and ask them to prepare a performance of their respective sections so that one is *intercut* with the other. Are there opportunities for irony? For emphasis? For contrast?

- After the performance, reflect on how this intercutting activity might help to bring a new perspective, not only to the two poems themselves, but also to our understanding of poetry's characteristic qualities. Could *The Echoing Green* be written today? Could *Zip-Wire* have been written in the eighteenth century? How does the intercut version compare with the earlier performances of *Zip-Wire* on its own?

Activity Sequence 7: drafting (a stand-alone activity)

Working at word level

- If you want to try this activity, you need to do so before the students have undertaken any work on the poem. It is therefore an alternative rather than an addition to Activity Sequences 1 and 2.

- Distribute cloze copies of the poem *Zip-Wire* with key words blanked out. In pairs or singly, the students have to think what the missing words might be and fill in the blanks.

- Bring the whole group together and share some answers. Are there spaces where most people seem to have agreed on the same word? Are there some that invited very different interpretations? Share your responses to these questions.

- Give the students the actual words used by the poet. Are there similarities to and/ or differences from their own versions? Which do they prefer and why?
- Students move into pairs. One person represents the author of *Zip-Wire*; the other represents themselves. Improvise a dialogue where you argue over which version of the poem should be submitted for publication.

Opportunities for work in the English classroom

Exploring literature

There is a wealth of literature that engages with the themes of *Zip-Wire*. The tensions between innocence and experience, which are explored extensively by William Blake, also inform a collection like Seamus Heaney's *Death of a Naturalist* as well as Olive Senior's poem *Birdshooting Season* or *A Hymn to Childhood* by Li-Young Lee. Doris Lessing's short story *Through the Tunnel* is concerned with rites of passage as is, to choose an example from classical literature, Book XII of John Milton's epic *Paradise Lost*, which ends with the expulsion of Adam and Eve from Eden. A.A. Milne's *The House at Pooh Corner* concludes with a similar, perhaps even more poignant because child-centred, description of exile and parting.

The darker elements of play are important themes in Graham Greene's short story *The Destructors* and Vernon Scannell's poem *A Case of Murder*. A.E. Housman's poetry is concerned with time and mortality, and Dennis Potter's play *Blue Remembered Hills* – which takes its title from a line of Housman's poetry – explores the ways in which play can lead to horrific consequences, much as Lowenfeld's quotation from Hall suggests. Potter uses adult actors to take the parts of seven-year-old children. It would be interesting to explore the constraints and opportunities provided by this way of working as a follow-up to the mask performance from Activity Sequence 4.

Activity Sequence 7 is designed to draw students' attention to the consoling fact that texts do not suddenly appear, fully formed. The improvisation which concludes that section could lead into an exploration of historical literary collaborations, where one writer has offered advice on another's work. Examples might include Siegfried Sassoon's comments on Wilfred Owen's poem *Anthem for Doomed Youth* or Ezra Pound's amendments to T.S. Eliot's *The Waste Land*. Students could use material from the draft manuscripts as the basis for a dramatisation in which author and advisor argue their respective cases. The relationship between Owen and Sassoon is explored in Stephen MacDonald's play *Not About Heroes*.

Those students who enjoyed writing from the point of view of the zip-wire itself might compare the way they approached the task with the Anglo-Saxon poem *The Dream of the Rood*, which is narrated by the cross on which Christ was crucified. Staying with Anglo-Saxon literature but choosing a lighter note, many riddles, as has been noted in Chapter 10: *From Phoneme to Word Level*, are written from a non-human point of view.

Reading

Baron has argued that 'oral reading' was 'extremely common' in the classical world (2000, pp. 33, 34). The communal readings presented in Activity Sequence 3 re-assert that principle and offer an alternative approach to what is so often an act of solitary engagement – with all the challenges that implies. Van Riel and Fowler allude to some of these challenges when they classify readers into six possible types: *the thrill seeker, the stressed out reader, the avid reader, the self-protective reader, the ambitious reader* and *the indulgent reader* (1996, pp. 14–15). The activities described in the sequences above offer opportunities for students to reflect upon the kind of reader they are and about how context might influence the classifications they choose for themselves. The suggestion that these categories are dependent on context, and subject to tensions and change, offers interesting possibilities for work in drama – a point made by Michael Benton, who describes reading 'as sort of armchair acting' (In Manuel, 2008, p. 38). Appleyard (1991) takes the analogy further by suggesting that readers assume successive roles: *the player, the hero, the thinker* and *the interpreter.* An additional twist to the activities described above would be to invite students to assume one or more of these roles when they read. The same strategy could be applied powerfully to many classroom reading activities. An interesting idea for generating discussion about a text, for example, might be to divide a class into reading groups: each member of the group has to discuss their text in one of the various roles described by Van Riel and Fowler or by Appleyard. For older students, the strategy can be adapted as a way of engaging with critical theory and the history of criticism: what kind of discussion, for example, might a Feminist, Marxist, Post-Structuralist and Leavisite critic hold about the Emily Brontë novel, *Wuthering Heights*?

Questioning

Drama practitioners have stressed the crucially important contribution that questioning makes to their subject (for example: O'Neill and Lambert, 1982; Neelands, 1984; Heathcote and Bolton, 1995). The same point could be made about all learning and teaching – not least, of course, with reference to the English classroom. Unfortunately, as Alexander observes, 'the so-called "recitation script" of closed teacher questions, brief recall answers and minimal feedback' still 'dominates' schools in the United Kingdom and elsewhere. Alexander criticises the supposed alternative – the 'ostensibly heuristic device of mainly open questions' – for actually concealing 'an essentially closed agenda' according to which 'only certain answers were accepted' (2005, pp. 2, 8). As the reference to Lombardi in Chapter 10: *From Phoneme to Word Level* suggests, the practical activities described in Part 2 of this book are designed to encourage the purposeful and authentic use of questioning in order to help students to access, particularly, the higher cognitive domains. Activity Sequence 5 (above) offers a specific opportunity to think about the nature and purpose of questioning. Neelands (1984, pp. 37–39) describes seven types of question that might be used in drama:

- Seeking information
- Containing information
- Provoking research
- Controlling
- Branching
- Seeking opinions
- Encouraging reflection

The hot-seating activities described above in Activity Sequence 5, and the reflection tasks that follow them, could provide a powerful opportunity for students and teachers to explore together the nature and purpose of each of the seven question types described by Neelands. This is more than just a desirable activity; for any teacher really committed to the principles of collaborative learning, it is essential.

Writing

The question-stem statements from Activity Sequence 3 and the performances with masks in Activity Sequence 4 might be written up as poems, just as they are. If the masked performance was presented through the medium of a particular convention, an attempt might be made to write the subsequent poems in a style characteristic of that convention. Alternatively, the question-stem statements could be used as the opening sentences in a piece of personal, reflective prose, written from the point of view of the character selected from the poem. The monologues from Activity Sequence 4 might be scripted and developed in the style of Alan Bennett's *Talking Heads* (adapted for radio or television perhaps); or different monologues could be intercut to create a more dialogic play text. The four scenarios from Activity Sequence 5 could provide the raw material for a series of short stories or for reflective writing in the form of diary entries. An interesting alternative would be to develop them into a series of social networking exchanges such as Tweets or blog entries. Performing two texts in counterpoint as in Activity Sequence 6 offers a useful way into formal, comparative writing as in a conventional critical essay. The questions posed in Activity Sequence 5 provide thought-provoking stimuli for imaginative writing in different genres (think of how interrogation is used in a poem like Roger McGough's *The Identification*). The activity from the same sequence, which shows how the meaning of the same sentence can be altered by placing the emphasis on different words, lends itself to interesting work on syntax and grammar: what is the difference between *WHERE were you last night?* and *Where were YOU last night?*

Chapter 12

Teacher in role
The department store

Introduction and context

Teacher in-role work is the ultimate expression of that reconfiguration of the teacher and student relationship that has been a consistent principle of drama in education from its ideological beginnings in the writings of Rousseau and Froebel to the present day. It requires a strong bond of mutual trust between teachers and students if it is to work and this is why the establishment of what Neelands calls a 'learning contract' (described in Activity Sequence 1) is so important and needs to be negotiated and agreed before any in-role work of this kind is undertaken. The fact that the contract does need to be negotiated and then 'owned' by all the participants – including the teacher – offers the possibility of a truly democratic alternative to traditional power structures in the classroom.

It follows, therefore, that teacher in-role work can, understandably, pose challenges to those teachers who take confidence from feeling that their authority is buttressed by school rules and management hierarchies. In recognition of this concern, the activities described below allocate a high-status role (in this case, that of a morally complex figure not unlike Hamlet's uncle Claudius) to the teacher. This means that she or he has the opportunity to direct and shape the lessons *within* the *as-if* context of the drama rather than having to come out of role to do so. An example occurs when the store owner terminates the press conference in Activity Sequence 3. As confidence and trust grow, teacher (and students) may wish to experiment with different status levels in their role-play. Teachers might, for instance, want to assume a role in which, unlike the store owner in this set of exemplar material, they openly oppose or support the other members of the group. Alternatively, they might take on a role that places them at a status level slightly below that of some or all of the students – perhaps playing the part of an advisor or consultant to a student or students in a superior authority role. Going lower, the teacher in role might play a character who seeks help from the group; and working at a lower status level still, the teacher might play the part of someone who seems to have no power at all – a prisoner or beggar, perhaps, who initiates the drama by addressing the group in a tremulous voice with the question: 'Why have you brought me here?' This latter is a particularly daring gambit to employ because it really does consign to the respondents key decisions about what the context, setting and purpose of the drama are to be. The 'space ship' question (see Activity Sequence 3 and the paragraph below for further details), which might be inappropriate within the context of a scheme of work set in a department store, would be perfectly legitimate within such a decontextualised, open situation. Both teacher and students would have to listen very carefully indeed to the response that question received and apply the principles of the learning contract with the utmost care and mutual trust in order to create from that opening a drama of significance and power.

One of the most important pedagogical benefits of teacher in-role work, therefore, is that it pays so much more than mere lip service to the principles of negotiated and socially constructed meaning-making. Even when the teacher opts for a high-status role rather than the extreme example of low-status play described in the paragraph above, the activity sequences described below provide numerous instances where teacher and students have to reflect together on a learning issue and negotiate a way to take the drama forward. One telling example occurs in Activity Sequence 3, where, as noted earlier, a student in role as a reporter has the opportunity to pose a question that might threaten the integrity of the drama context. Exploring together why something might or might not work in this way requires co-operation and a shared sense of investment in the importance of the work in hand. Possible tensions between what the teacher hopes to teach and what the students wish to learn have to be examined and resolved with a degree of honest dealing, which is probably unequalled in any other classroom context.

The activity sequences below are presented as one extended scheme of work. Teachers could work through the whole set sequentially or focus on particular sequences at different times as appropriate.

Links with Part 1 of the book

There are clear links here with the section on the work of Bolton and Heathcote. Particularly pertinent is their assertion that they 'cannot think of a subject that cannot, or should not be tackled through drama' (see p. 58). Equally relevant is the section in Part 1 of the book that describes how, almost two decades after Bolton and Heathcote issued that statement, Rainer and Lewis note 'a recent resurgence of interest' in their work and declare that the time 'is now right to re-establish drama at the centre of a creative, thematic curriculum' in contrast to what they regard as outmoded, subject-based national curricula of the type currently in operation in England (see p. 86). Interestingly, the ways of working advocated by Bolton and Heathcote or Lewis and Rainer draw upon the same kind of strategies described by Rousseau and Froebel in the earliest sections of Part 1 of this book (see p. 7).

The activity sequences described below certainly offer opportunities for a wide range of cross-curricular activities. As well as numerous opportunities for work in subject English (described at the end of the sequence) students engaging in this scheme of work can explore citizenship, economics, history, moral and social education and politics through what Rainer and Lewis might describe as a 'competence based approach' to learning 'more in tune with the needs of learners in the twenty-first century'. Writing from an Australian perspective, Anderson echoes Rainer and Lewis in suggesting that contemporary drama can offer an alternative to 'traditional schooling'. Look again at the section towards the end of Part 1 of the book (see p. 86) where he argues that O'Toole and O'Mara's 'four paradigms of purpose' for teaching drama – *cognitive/procedural*, *expressive/developmental*, *social/pedagogical*, *functional* – align with the 'four dimensions of practice' – *intellectual quality*, *connectedness, supportive classroom environment, working with and valuing difference* – which he regards as characteristic of the contemporary 'productive pedagogies' model.

As the references to Rainer and Lewis and to Anderson suggest, the final section of Part 1 of the book is also worth revisiting in this context in order to note again its argument that drama in education today has a harder edge than might have been the case when Heathcote and Bolton were first writing; though of course they saw no difficulty in using words like 'enterprise base', 'client' or 'problem'. The opportunities that this scheme of work affords for engagement with citizenship and with economics, gesture towards Anderson's argument that 'we must now articulate for those who control the gates, the purse strings and the curriculum why the arts are needed and what in particular drama education does to support the academic, social and emotional growth of young people'. At the same time, however, it also acknowledges the political and global imperative implied in Neelands' demand that drama help students 'to become more conscious of "voice" – the ideological interests of the text's producer'. There are plenty of opportunities in the activity sequences described below for students, in Martha Nussbaum's phrase, 'to approach world problems as world citizens' – not least if students and teacher bear in mind, throughout, the crucial tension that Bolton identifies between 'abstraction' and 'crystallisation': the capacity to 'expose the inner meanings of an event, to indicate universal implications'.

As well as considering issues regarding teacher in-role work (see 'Introduction and context' above), this sequence of activities also explores Heathcote and Bolton's concept of the *mantle of the expert*. Hughes and Arnold have challenged the term, arguing that 'a danger exists in the implication that this process is a "gift" or "mantle" that is somehow placed on to a student'. They suggest that 'mantle' be replaced by 'enactment' on the grounds that:

> the process, if facilitated to empower, enables the students, individually and as a group, to grow into the role of expert via psychodynamic resources that spring from their latent abilities, which interact with the drama environment and spiral to belief.

(2008, p. 91)

Hughes and Arnold's critique draws attention to some of the key issues regarding *mantle of the expert* work explored in Part 1 of the book. For example, their suggestion that the 'mantle' is 'somehow placed on a student' recalls the tension implicit in Bolton's assertion that drama can only be effective pedagogically if the student 'does not see himself [sic] as learning' but 'the teacher sees himself as teaching'. It was noted in Part 1 of the book that this imbalance of power places significant obligations upon the teacher – in terms of crafting the language with which she or he invites students into the drama; in co-ordinating, to revisit the metaphor used in Part 1 of the book, the 'rein' of drama with the 'rein' of physics or history; in assuming responsibility for the 'aesthetic welfare' of the students. It was noted, too, that some of the obligations appeared to be contradictory: on the one hand, the teacher is to be invited into the 'learning community' of the drama; on the other hand, that same teacher has a duty, as Bolton puts it, to 'protect' the students *into* emotion'. If students are not to see themselves as learning, can they really be involved as equals in the social construction of meanings? If the 'aesthetic welfare' of the students remains in the purview of the teacher, where does that leave the experience of learning *in* as well as *through* drama? What opportunities exist for students who have not given others 'permission to stare' to experience what Bolton describes as *being* and *describing*, working as actor and as spectator? Consider these questions again as you work through the activity sequences: to what extent are they or are they not answered?

Activity Sequence 1: establishing context, focus and setting

Working at contextual level

- Explain to the group that this set of drama activities will *focus* on the following question: *Is there a principle for which you would be prepared to make a considerable sacrifice?* Allow time for reflection, perhaps suggesting some possible lines of thought to help the students think about the kind of answer they might give. Assure them that they do not have to share this information with anyone else – it is personal to them. Invite each member of the group to write their answer on a sheet of paper, seal it in an envelope with their name on and hand it to the teacher for safe keeping. Tell the students that their envelopes will be returned, unopened, at the end of the sequence of lessons and they will be invited to compare their thoughts about the question then with what they have written now. Ask them to keep the question at the back of their minds during the activities that follow.

- Explain that the *setting* for the drama will be an institution where a number of people work together in teams. Choose a *location* and institution that suits you and your students. For the purpose of this exemplar material, the chosen location is a department store.

- As a group, share thoughts, ideas, impressions, experiences of visiting and – if the students are old enough – of working in a department store or some other kind of shop. If possible, organise a group visit to a store and/or shop to meet with staff and patrons.

- Working in groups of four, use the Internet to research and prepare a case study on an established store of your choice. The following questions might be helpful:

  - *How does the store present itself on-line? How does it communicate on-line with its customers? Does it, for example, use social networking media to do this? If so, which ones and how?*
  - *What image is the store trying to convey? What mix of pictures and words does it use to create that impression?*
  - *What contribution does sonic branding play in the creation of the store's image? (Does it have a particular advertising jingle or signature tune, for example?)*
  - *What can you discover about the history of the store? How did it begin and why?*
  - *How is the store organised and funded? What is its economic profile?*
  - *Has the store been in the news recently? If so, what for?*

- Present and share your case study findings to the other members of the group. Were there any common features and issues? Did any significant points of difference emerge from the case studies?
- Ask the group to consider how shops in general and department stores in particular are or have been depicted in media such as television. Why do shops seem to feature so often in soap operas and what function do they serve in that context? Compare documentary programmes about organisations like department stores with their sitcom equivalents. Why do television executives assume that there is an audience for such programmes? An interesting historical case study to consider in this context would be a programme like the 1970s' British sitcom, *Are You Being Served?*

Working at word level

- In your case study groups, draw a Venn diagram on a blank sheet of A3 paper. In the left-hand circle, write as many words or phrases as you can, which you would associate with your store. These might be words and phrases you collected during your research, or that were mentioned during the case study sharing, or that you imagine people who work and shop in such a store might use. In the other circle, do the same for the words and phrases you remember from studying fictional representations of department stores and shops. Can any words be placed in the space where the two circles overlap, indicating that they could be used in both real and fictional institutions?

Working at contextual level

- As a whole group, share your findings and your reflections on the activities described above. Knowing that a fictional department store is going to be the setting for the drama activities, what expectations, observations and ideas might we bring to the drama from these preliminary activities? What openings for focused work on drama *elements* might such a context offer? Where people from different social backgrounds work together in a defined, hierarchical setting, there may, for example, be particular opportunities to explore *tension, status levels, contrasts and use of space.*

Activity Sequence 2: negotiating the learning contract

Working at contextual level

- Explain to the group that they are about to meet the owner of the fictional department store where the drama activities will take place. The *fictional context* is that they are to play the role of reporters from the local radio station who have been invited to hold a preliminary interview with the owner in order to gain material for a feature that will be broadcast to celebrate the centenary of the firm. The setting for the preliminary interview is the office of the store's owner.
- The teacher is to be *hot-seated in role* as the store owner by the reporters. If role-play work of this kind is to be successful, it is most important that a 'learning

contract' is agreed by everybody involved in the activity. Neelands identifies the following elements of this contract: the need for the work to be significant and worth undertaking; the opportunity for participants to build on what they know in order to 'imagine new experiences'; the right for everybody concerned to feel safe, confident and respected; the need 'to establish a different (perhaps) teacher–learner relationship' (1984, pp. 29–31).

- Divide the whole group into four and allocate one element of the learning contract to each of these smaller groups. On a sheet of A3 paper, each group must prepare a series of statements that they regard as essential if their element of the contract is to work. The teacher should also prepare a sheet of A3 with at least one statement for each of the four elements.

- Each group presents and explains its set of statements. The teacher does the same. Once agreement has been reached on the statements (changes may need to be negotiated) they should be placed on a wall in the drama space for the duration of the scheme of work. They thus act as a reference-point, which can be revisited should the drama run into difficulties at any point. As Neelands puts it: 'If the drama isn't working we can turn back to the terms of the contract and see where we're going wrong' (1984, p. 76). Only when the contract has been agreed can the role-play begin.

Activity Sequence 3: a role-play simulation

Working at whole text level

- If time and resources allow, cameras, phones and voice recorders could be used to record the interview between store owner and reporters. Students should use the information they gleaned from their preliminary research work to inform their questions (ideas for work on questioning are included in Activity Sequence 5 of Chapter 11: *Working with Text* (see p. 130) and in the subsequent commentary section).

- What approach to the story will the reporters take? Is this really an opportunity for some free publicity on the part of the store, or will the story be more probing than that? Do the store owner and the reporters have the same agenda?

- Bearing these points in mind, sample different programme selections from your local radio stations. As you do so, consider the following questions:

  o *What is the story and how is it being told?*
  o *Who might be the audience for this story and how do you know?*
  o *Think about the concept of the 'iceberg text' (described in Activity Sequence 3 of Chapter 11: Working with Text, see p. 127): is there another story 'submerged' beneath the one that appears on the 'surface'?*
  o *What strategies do the producers of the radio programme use to engage the listener?*
  o *What are the differences between listening to a story on the radio or Internet and reading about it in a newspaper or magazine, on-line or in hard copy?*

- Ask the students to share their findings and to consider how the information they have gleaned might help them shape the role of reporter in the forthcoming simulation. What attitudes are they going to take? How might the store owner behave during the interview?

- The advantage of locating the hot-seating activity within the formal context of a radio interview is that it provides a clear boundary of demarcation between the real and the *as-if* world of the drama. If the space is set out as for a press conference, students can signal their *movement into role* by taking their seats. A command like *action!* – which is the kind of term that might be used to signify the start of a recording and thus is appropriate for an *as-if* as well as a real-world context – could be used to mark the start of the drama. Similarly, *cut!* could be used to signal the end.

- The details of what the teacher says when hot-seated in role as the store owner will be influenced by the kind of questions the reporters ask. They in turn might agree amongst themselves a broad outline of who might ask what. Alternatively, the tension will be enhanced if they do not share their ideas beforehand but respond to what they hear from their colleagues and from the store owner. In order to advance the drama and to enhance the *context and setting* for the drama, the teacher will need to make sure that a number of points are communicated to the audience (just as in a real interview or press conference). For the purposes of this scheme of work, she or he needs to include the following details:

  o *The store owner is nearing retirement and is proud to have devoted a lifetime to upholding the family heritage by ensuring the survival of this historic business through good times and bad. The family is proud of its century-long relationship with the local community; not only has it provided employment for generations of local people, it has also contributed to local charities and to public works.*

  o *At a time of rising unemployment, the firm wishes to declare its principled commitment to providing local jobs for local people.*

Activity Sequence 4: revisiting the learning contract

Working at whole text level

- For spontaneous hot-seated question-and-answer work of this kind to be successful, everybody involved, in this case reporters and the store owner, must honour the principles agreed in the learning contract. If a reporter were to ask: 'Is it true that a space-ship has just crash-landed outside your department store?' the question would wrench the frame of the drama so violently and require such a radical change of medium and way of playing that it would be impossible to continue the work in its current form. On the other hand, for a reporter to ask: 'Is it true that the firm is in difficulty and is about to close down?' would also be to pose a radical challenge; but this is one that respects the principle of 'significance' and therefore is viable in terms of the established dramatic context. If the latter question were asked, the teacher could work with it without coming out of role by, for example, hotly denying the allegation, protesting that an invited reporter, a guest in the establishment, could behave so rudely on what is meant to be a celebratory occasion. Working in a high-status role such as that of the store owner allows the teacher to bring matters to a close by promptly terminating the interview.

- Out of role, the whole group reflect on what they have learned from the interview. For the drama to continue, there has to be an element of *tension*: if everything the store owner said is true and the company is in fine shape as it heads into its second century, then there is no story. The issue now is how to *focus and frame* that tension. Staying true to the principles of the learning contract, if the reporters want to develop the suggestion that the firm is duplicitous in some way, they have to justify their assertion in terms of the drama context. Here the teacher, working out of role, could lead the questioning of the students, reminding them of what the store owner said. Is it likely that such an established family firm, one that prides itself on its heritage and reputation, one that has forged enduring links with the local community, would risk a century's worth of goodwill lightly? Is it likely that the store owner would wish to see a life-time's effort thrown into jeopardy? Might the reporters have made these allegations maliciously or because they are working to a particular agenda?

- At this point, the drama could move in a number of different directions. It could, for example, explore the tensions beneath the 'iceberg surface' of the reporter's challenging question.

- Thinking about the learning contract again, the teacher needs to find a way of taking the work forward, which honours the students' rights to build on what they know in order to 'imagine new experiences', as Neelands puts it, while at the same time addressing their own pedagogical obligations and intentions. One way to do this might be to suggest to the group that they respond to the reporter's question by focusing not on the interrogator but on the respondent.

Activity Sequence 5: developing context, setting, tension and role

Working at word level

- Place a large paper cut-out of the store owner on the wall of the drama space. Split the group into smaller units of three or four and give each person a notelet, which can be stuck to the larger sheet of paper. On the notelet, each person is to write at least one adjective that, in the light of the interview and the subsequent discussion, they feel describes the store owner. Stick the notelets on the wall and invite the whole group to come up to the cut-out and review what has been written. Invite the students to comment on what they read and to ask the person who wrote the comment to explain their choice. How similar or different are the various statements? What can we learn from this?

- Move back into your groups of three or four. The context now shifts to the department store itself. The store sells a range of goods: electrical, furnishings, clothes and toys. Thinking back to all you have heard about the store, decide together on a name for it. What would be an appropriate logo and motto for the firm? Students can work individually or in small groups on their suggestions, arguing their case in front of the whole group, who then vote to decide which name, logo and motto to choose. If some students do not agree with the final choice, they should take that into account when they come to create a character to play and have to think about that character's attitude towards the firm and its owner (see activities below).

Working at contextual level

- In your groups, select a department to work in. On a large sheet of paper, design the layout of the department and decide who does what.
- Drawing upon all the information you have received so far regarding the store and its owner, prepare a brief *improvisation* that shows the staff at work in their department. How do they get on with each other? What is the age and gender range of the team? Is there a veteran in charge and a new recruit? As part of the brief for the improvisation, you must imagine that the staff have heard, or heard about, the radio interview with their boss. At some stage in the improvisation, they must discuss their response to the broadcast.
- The groups present their improvisations in sequence as a piece of *rolling theatre* (see Activity Sequence 5 of Chapter 11: *Working with Text*, p. 131). As a whole group, reflect upon what you have seen. What seems to be the state of staff morale in the store? Does the account presented by the store owner in the radio broadcast ring true?

Working at whole text level

- Working still within your 'department' groups, split into pairs and take turns at using hot-seating questioning to develop the role you played in the rolling theatre presentation. The following question prompts might help (but if you can think of more thought-provoking alternatives, so much the better):

  o *What is your name?*
  o *How long have you worked at the store?*
  o *Do you enjoy it here?*
  o *How do you get on with the other members of staff?*
  o *Where do you see yourself in five years' time?*
  o *When were you happiest?*
  o *If you won the lottery, what would be the first thing you would do with the money?*
  o *What is your greatest fear?*
  o *If you could save just one item of belongings from a fire, what would it be?*

- When you have completed the hot-seating questions, discuss with your partner the *character* you have started to create. Think about dramatic potential in terms of *motivation* and possible tensions.
- Bearing this information in mind, work individually either with pen and paper or on a computer to devise answers for these questions:

  o *What kind of mobile phone does your character have?*
  o *Does your character own or rent the phone?*
  o *Does the phone have a protective case? If so, what kind of case is it?*
  o *What ring tone is on the phone?*
  o *Does it have a screen-saver? If so, what is it?*
  o *What would be a typical text message sent by your character and who would they send it to?*
  o *Does your character engage in social networking? If so, what media do they use?*

- *If they have a social networking page, what pictures might be on it? What have they signalled as 'likes'? What kinds of events might be on their timeline?*

- Write a blog or diary entry, or a letter or email to a friend, in the style of your character.
- Back in your 'department' groups, present your character to the other members of the group. You can do this by talking about them in the third person or by reading the piece of writing you have composed. Alternatively, communicate the information as a *monologue*: if you are interrupted, try to answer the questions in role.
- Out of role, reflect as a group on how your knowledge about the department team has been changed by this additional information. Write the names of the characters in your department team on a sheet of A3 paper. Using either pins and string or marker pens, plot the connections between the different members of the team: where are the points of connection? Where are the pressure points?
- Each 'department' shares this information with the whole group.

Activity Sequence 6: a meeting convention (spontaneous improvisation)

Working at whole text level

- The store is shut for a training day so the whole staff, unusually, has a chance to meet as a body. Everybody enters the staff canteen for a lunch break. Your entrance through the door is the signal that you are *going into role* as your character. Before you enter, think about the following questions:

  - *How would your character move in the canteen space?*
  - *How do they feel about the training session they have just had?*
  - *What expression is on your character's face? Would it alter depending on whom they encountered as they walked into the canteen?*
  - *Who would your character try to talk to or sit beside in the canteen? Who would they avoid?*

- Once everybody is seated in the canteen, the cleaner enters and asks for silence. This part can be played either by the teacher in role or by a student who has been briefed in private on the information they now have to impart in order to move the drama forward.
- The cleaner announces that, when tidying the store owner's office this morning, they inadvertently touched the computer keyboard so that the screen appeared. The cleaner could not help noticing that the page was open at an email, the title of which read: RE: STORE CLOSURE. Shocked, the cleaner read on to discover that the firm is in dire economic straits and that major redundancies, perhaps even total closure, are imminent.
- When the cleaner has delivered this information, the whole group should *mark the moment* by 'freezing' and reflecting on what this news means for their character. Out of role, the teacher moves amongst the members of the group, indicating

to certain individuals that they should say what they are feeling at this moment and why.

Activity Sequence 7: reflecting in and out of role

Working at contextual level

- Thinking about the elements of the learning contract again, the whole group comes out of role to reflect upon the significance of this news. What issues does it raise? Questions that might arise in the course of the discussion include:

  o *Why might a business that has survived the economic vicissitudes of the past hundred years now find itself in a position where it is no longer able to continue?*

  o *Does a firm that prides itself on its heritage, its sense of family and its commitment to the local community have a particular moral obligation to keep the business operating, even at a financial loss?*

  o *Does the firm have a moral obligation to the staff whom it will have to 'let go'? Should it be a question of 'last in, first out' and should those who have served longest receive particular compensation, irrespective of their home and financial circumstances?*

  o *Should the staff expect the firm to provide them with a steady job for life?*

  o *Should the store owner have kept the information about the parlous financial state of the firm from the staff? Is there any justification for doing so?*

  o *Are there any alternatives to closure?*

- Having had a chance to share their thoughts about these questions, the whole group should now try to apply those reflections to the specific context of the drama through the use of the *explorative strategy* known as *forum theatre*. The group sits in a circle around an enclosed acting space. In role, two of the students enter the acting space and start to improvise a *dialogue* on one of the previously discussed questions. If one of the watching students feels they want to add something to that debate, they enter the acting space in role as their character, signal to the person whom they wish to replace (that person then sits down) and continue the dialogue. As the discussion becomes more heated, the movement into and out of the acting space will become faster with people making interventions several times perhaps in the course of the session.

- Out of role, but still seated in the circle, reflect upon what you have heard. Has your perspective on the six questions discussed earlier changed in any way? Give reasons for your answer.

Activity Sequence 8: exploring time and perspective (non-naturalistic playing)

Working at contextual level

- Students move back into their 'department' groups. Either speaking in role or in the third person as before, explain to the other members of the group why your character really cannot afford to be made redundant. Compare answers and together choose the story that you feel makes the most compelling case.

- Devise a presentation which makes that case as eloquently as you can. You may wish to use one of the following *non-naturalistic* explorative strategies:

  ○ *A slow-motion dream sequence where the chosen character imagines an ideal solution to their current problems or confronts them in the form of a nightmare.*

  ○ *It is five years in the future. Four friends or relations of the chosen character relate the story of what happened to this person after the firm's closure. The story could be narrated formally as a series of monologues. Alternatively, each member of the group could run into the acting space shouting out a key event from the character's subsequent life in the manner of a newspaper seller. Taking turns to be the 'headline' bearer, the other three actors mime an interpretation of the words until all four key events have been presented. How do the four mimes vary in focus, pace and tension? Again, the character's story could be recited as a ballad, perhaps in the style of a poem like Charles Causley's* Timothy Winters.

  ○ *Shift the time frame back to the day when the character began work at the firm. The character talks to three important people in their life: what do they say? How do they view the future? What advice might the three other people give the character?*

  ○ *The members of the group write and perform a script that implies, but does not explicitly reveal, what happened to their chosen character after the firm closed down. How does the use of pauses, facial expression and intonation contribute to the effect?*

Activity Sequence 9: exploring tension, choice and consequences (spontaneous improvisation)

Working at contextual level

- Back to the canteen and the training day. The teacher out of role announces that the store's owner wants to take advantage of the fact that the whole staff are present by holding a crisis meeting with them.
- The teacher exits and re-enters the space in role as the store owner: how do the staff respond? Under questioning, the store owner reluctantly admits that the email is correct and that the firm faces economic collapse. The owner explains that the reason nothing was said beforehand to the staff was because the management team has been working heroically to find suppliers who can produce and deliver the store's merchandise at a cost low enough to make the survival of the business a distinct possibility.
- In role, the students react to the news. They have just witnessed what closure might mean in human terms to themselves and their colleagues. This knowledge should intensify their response.
- At that moment, one of the staff stands up and shouts for silence. (The part should be played by one of the students who has been briefed earlier by the

teacher.) This person has some unpleasant news to share. Information has come to light that the suppliers the firm intends to use rely on sweated labour. Reluctantly, the store owner admits that the news is true but argues that it is the only viable means of averting financial ruin.

- Appealing directly to the staff, the store owner asks them to make a stark decision: either the firm closes down, or they retain their jobs, knowing that other people are being exploited in order to give them financial security. What is it to be? Those who are willing to take the offer are to declare themselves by standing up and following the store owner out of the canteen.
- Out of role, the teacher calls the whole group back together and distributes the sealed envelopes collected in at the start of the scheme of work. The students are invited to read again what they wrote then and to reflect on whether their views have altered during the course of the drama sessions. To what extent do their personal views resemble those of the character they have played? This whole final sequence of reflection is undertaken privately and thoughts and reflections are not shared.

Opportunities for work in the English classroom

Working with character

Part 1 of the book has suggested that many drama practitioners have held an ambivalent attitude towards characterisation: to engage with it effectively, students need the levels of skill and sophistication associated with professional actors. It is enough, the argument runs, that students who have not given others 'permission to stare' should be able to sustain the attitudes, motivations and beliefs associated with a role. Kempe's declared lack of interest in Lady Macbeth's relationship with her father comes to mind again in this context.

Having said that, however, English teachers who are interested in the ways that written language – particularly the language of the novel, short story or biography – can initiate and sustain a detailed investigation of character in terms of appearance, motivation, history, relationships and psychological make up, might well wish to make use of the opportunities this sequence of activities affords for exploring character. By the end of the scheme of work, students will together have created a wealth of characters of different ages and backgrounds who have developed a complex web of relationships with each other. These could be written up in a variety of forms: journals, short stories, play texts, letter exchanges, blog posts – and so on.

It was noted earlier that the role played by the teacher in this sequence of activities bears a resemblance to the morally ambivalent Claudius from Shakespeare's *Hamlet*. The tensions and dilemmas explored throughout the drama are – remembering what Heathcote and Bolton say about finding the universal in the particular – mirrored throughout literature. Arthur Miller's play *The Crucible*, for example, asks the same question that opens Activity Sequence 1: *Is there a principle for which you would be prepared to make a considerable sacrifice?* Again, the Willy Loman of *Death of a Salesman* would recognise, with sickening familiarity, the pressures faced by the department store workers threatened with redundancy.

Working with the media

This activity sequence presents numerous opportunities for media work. Students can investigate the role of journalists, particularly those who are employed in local radio (a fact-finding visit to a nearby station would make a valuable preliminary activity before undertaking Activity Sequence 3). In that role-play simulation itself, students could actually record the interview on camera or on audio. If the necessary software is available, they could edit the material to produce a completed 'package' – how editorially neutral would it be? The research conducted for Activity Sequence 1 offers opportunities to explore the ways in which big businesses try to market themselves to on-line consumers. Activity Sequence 8 offers, as one of its examples of non-naturalistic playing, an unusual take on the language of newspaper headlines.

Activity Sequence 1 explores the medium of television, considering how its portrayal of the same human phenomenon – in this case a department store – might be mediated through different genres and from different points of view. The reference to long-vanished sitcoms offers a reminder that television will soon be a hundred years old and that it therefore has a history that can be explored and interrogated like any other.

Working with technology

Dunn and O'Toole argue that the virtual environments created by technology have given 'all of us a "bigger place to play"' (2009, p. 36). Cameron suggests that 'the embedding of mobile media, particularly mobile phones, in youth cultures around the world' offers 'the greatest opportunities' for 'blending . . . with drama conventions' (2009, p. 59). Technology can be used within the context of the drama itself. In Activity Sequence 5, for example, thinking about how a particular individual might customise their mobile phone or their social networking sites, helps to create a rich sense of character. In Activity Sequence 6, the discovery of an email moves the plot forward and creates a sense of tension. In Activity Sequence 3, mobile phone cameras could be used to intensify the atmosphere and enhance a sense of verisimilitude by recording the meeting with the radio reporters. The evidence collected in this way could then be analysed for textual and sub-textual information.

Technology also provides a medium for developing and/or reflecting upon the drama through the modality of writing. Working in role, the various members of the department store staff might be connected in social networking groups. As the drama progresses, they could send posts, pictures and links to each other, which could in turn advance the plot, enrich the characterisation and the social dynamic and provide new perspectives on what is happening. Would all the characters in the store have the same equal access to technology, either in financial terms or because of varying degrees of technological competence? What happens to those who are 'out of the technological loop' in the drama? What issues does this raise? Working out of role, students could keep on-line journals in the form of blog posts, recording their thoughts about the dilemmas encountered in the drama, or developing, through writing, their exploration of the character they are playing.

Finally, Activity Sequence 1 offers opportunities for students not only to explore the research potential of the Internet but also to think about the ways in which it presents information. In terms of ideology, the case study exercise in this sequence raises questions about whose voices have most power on-line and why. As well as recalling what Neelands says about exposing 'the ideological interests of the text's producer', this activity brings once again to mind Kress and Bezemer's point about the page becoming a *site of display*.

Chapter 13

Working with play texts

Shakespeare as an example

Introduction and context

Given that Shakespeare's presence has loomed over Part 1 of the book from Chapter 3 on Caldwell Cook, Finlay-Johnson and Hourd onwards, it is inevitable that he should make an appearance in the practical section as well. The word 'example' has been added to the title of this series of activity sequences, however, because all the strategies explored here could be applied to any play text, including scripts written by the students themselves. The decision to 'start small' by using a cast list as stimulus material has two purposes: to signal at once that a play text is very different from other genres of writing such as novels and poems (even if, as in this case, it happens to be written in verse). The second purpose is to try to remove some of that sense of 'boredom and dread' (Irish, 2011, p. 11), which, over a century since Caldwell Cook encouraged his 'playboys' to have fun with Shakespeare, still seems to be a too familiar first reaction to the mention of his name. Cast lists rarely feature in Shakespeare examinations so they are less likely to come burdened with academic connotations. At the same time, they offer clear and accessible opportunities for imaginative engagement. What on earth is a 'prophet' – and one who hails from Pontefract in West Yorkshire at that – doing in a play that seems to be filled with royalty and nobles?

'If it's a Shakespeare play', John O'Toole writes, 'whatever you do, don't start by reading it, especially starting at Act I, scene I' (2008, p. 23). That seems good advice. It would be difficult to imagine anybody not feeling intrigued and concerned by the opening of this sequence's exemplar text, which begins with the entrance of Hubert and the executioners at the start of Act Four Scene One of *The Life and Death of King John*. It certainly seemed to work for Finlay-Johnson's primary-school students a century ago; and the reason this particular scene from one of Shakespeare's less frequently performed plays has been chosen is because her response to it raised an important discussion point in Part 1 of the book. More of this in the next section. It should go without saying by now that the activity sequences described below are all concerned with getting students on their feet so that they can engage actively with Shakespeare and realise that, as Irish puts it, he 'wrote to explore questions' (2011, p. 7).

Links with Part 1 of the book

It was noted in Part 1 of the book that when Finlay-Johnson introduced her primary-school students to Act Four Scene One of *The Life and Death of King John* (see p. 23), what fascinated her was the imaginative props they created to represent Hubert's implements of torture (see Activity Sequence 4 below). Finding an aesthetically pleasing solution to that problem of representation seemed enough. In one way, I argued in Part 1, the students who suggested red chalk as a means of representing a glowing instrument of torture could be said to have met Vygotsky's criteria of 'creativity' because they demonstrated the ability to 'combine elements to produce a structure' and 'to combine the old in new ways' (see p. 23). The children need to do more, however, if they are to win that particular plaudit from Vygotsky. Returning to his analogy of the boy who creates a play activity in which a stick represents a horse, he argues that the stick 'becomes a pivot for severing the meaning of horse from a real horse'. What makes this activity so important in terms of cognitive development, Vygotsky suggests, is the idea that when a child calls a stick a horse, 'mentally he sees the object standing behind the word'. That conceptual break-through offers an opportunity to begin to access the powerful thinking tools of metaphor, metonymy and synecdoche. I would suggest that the children who chose red chalk to represent an instrument of torture have not seen 'the object standing behind the word'. They do not appreciate the fact that the 'particular' (as Bolton and Heathcote might say) – the red-hot iron, which Hubert's executioners are preparing in order to blind a child – represents metaphorically the hideous 'universal' of human cruelty. Simply to put on 'black paper masks' as Finlay-Johnson's students do, is not enough. One of the purposes of revisiting this scene a century after Finlay-Johnson is to explore again the relationship between drama and aesthetics; and in this context, it would be useful to re-read the sections of Part 1 of the book that consider respectively the two collections of essays compiled by Abbs (1987) and Hornbrook (1998): *Living Powers* and *On the Subject of Drama* (see pp. 66–70). The activities described below attempt to engage with the same material encountered by Finlay-Johnson's students. Like them, the students addressed in these activity sequences are encouraged to use naturalistic and non-naturalistic strategies to craft aesthetically their explorations of and responses to the text. Unlike Finlay-Johnson's students (but perhaps more like Hourd's), however, they are also encouraged to engage with the 'particular' metaphorical representations of a 'universal' horror. They also attempt to acknowledge those claims of drama as a subject discipline voiced by Kempe and Ashwell and the call to ethical commitment voiced by Neelands. The sections of Part 1 of the book that explore their ideas should also be referenced in the context of this set of activity sequences (see pp. 67–88; 77–88). Finally, the activities described below are an attempt to explore the full implications of what the authors of *A Language for Life* (DES, 1975) meant when they suggested that the exchange between Antony and Enobarbus in Shakespeare's *Antony and Cleopatra* remains 'unfulfilled' until 'the relationship and all its implications have been fully experienced by trying them out in a convincing setting – physical, social and emotional' (see p. 42).

Activity Sequence 1: working with cast lists

Working at sub-textual level

Exemplar text (1)

> *Dramatis Personae*
>
> King John
> Prince Henry, son to the king
> Arthur, Duke of Bretagne, nephew to the king
> The Earl of Pembroke
> The Earl of Essex
> The Earl of Salisbury
> The Lord Bigot
> Hubert de Burgh
> Robert Faulconbridge, Son to Sir Robert Faulconbridge
> Philip the Bastard, his half-brother
> James Gurney, servant to Lady Faulconbridge
> Peter Of Pomfret, a prophet
> Philip, King of France
> Lewis, the Dauphin
> Lymoges, Duke of Austria
> Cardinal Pandulph, the Pope's legate
> Melun, a French Lord
> Chatillon, ambassador from France to King John
> Queen Eleonor, mother to King John
> Constance, mother to Arthur
> Blanche of Spain, niece to King John
> Lady Faulconbridge
> Lords, Citizens of Angiers, Sheriff, Heralds, Officers, Soldiers, Messengers, and other Attendants

- What kind of text is this? How do you know? Read it quickly to establish a general impression of its contents. What might be its *setting* and *time frame*? Share your immediate ideas with the other members of the group.
- Once the group has established that they are looking at a *cast list* for a *play text*, ask them to work either individually or in pairs. How much can they deduce about the play's contents and themes from the textual information in front of them? The following questions might help:

  - *Why is the title to this text in Latin and what do the words mean?*
  - *What is significant about the order in which the characters are listed?*
  - *Into how many semantic fields can you classify the information?*
  - *Why are some named characters provided with a description and others not?*
  - *Are there any differences between the ways that men and women are described in the text?*
  - *Are any of the descriptions unusual or surprising? Do they challenge your first impressions of what the play might be about?*

- *Do any of the words suggest that the play is set in a specific time period?*
- *Given the information presented in the cast list, where do you think the play is set?*

- Invite the group to share their findings and then inform them that the play is called *The Life and Death of King John*. Does this information change their expectations about the play's content and themes? If so, how and why?
- Explain that the play was written by Shakespeare, probably towards the end of the sixteenth century. Give each member of the group an *expectation card* and ask them to write down their immediate response to this information. Has it changed their attitude to the play? If so, how and why?
- Post the expectation card responses as a word wall. Inspect the wall and share various responses, inviting the authors to explain their statements.

Activity Sequence 2: exploring historical context

Working at contextual level

- Inform the group that *The Life and Death of King John first* appeared in print form in the *First Folio* of Shakespeare's plays, published in 1623. Divide the group into smaller research teams and ask them to work on-line to discover what they can about the *First Folio*. The most important pieces of information they should unearth in terms of this set of activities include the following:

Shakespeare never published a manuscript of any of his plays; he worked from drafts known as foul papers *and, because paper was precious and writing time-consuming, distributed sections of the script amongst the actors as appropriate, rather than providing full copies of the text to all.*

The First Folio *was published in 1623, seven years after Shakespeare's death in 1616.*

A network of people was involved in the publication: Shakespeare's actor friends John Heminges and Henry Condell; the publisher William Jaggard and the reputed scribe of the manuscripts, Ralph Crane.

A Flemish artist called Martin Droeshout was commissioned to create a copper engraving of Shakespeare (whom he may never have met) for the title page of the First Folio.

There were no copyright laws in existence when the First Folio *was published: the plays became the property of the person who printed and published them. Selling works that were in effect their livelihood was a significant action for actors.*

Of the original 500 copies of the First Folio, *238 still survive.*

- How far the students wish to take their research into the fascinating history of the *First Folio* will be up to the discretion of the teacher and the interest of the group as a whole. For the purpose of this sequence of activities, the main point is that they should appreciate the various *contextual frames* that can be placed around the cast list and consider how these frames inform their response to the text.

- Divide the group into teams of six and ask them to move into different parts of the drama space. Each group must set up two chairs, one at each end of their allocated space. One chair represents the play text *The Life and Death of King John*. The chair at the other end represents a reader of 1623. On a sheet of paper, the members of each group create their own *dramatis personae* as follows:

William Shakespeare
John Heminges
Henry Condell
William Jaggard
Ralph Crane
Martin Droeshout

- Thinking of the cast list for *The Life and Death of King John* as a model, how are you going to describe the six characters? Will a word of description suffice; or will at least a phrase be needed? Will the description be purely factual – perhaps simply defining each person by occupation – or will it attempt to say something about *personality and motivation*? Is Shakespeare, for example, to be described as 'play-wright' (he was also an actor and a businessman)? Crane was a scribe; but he also saw himself as something of a poet. Heminges was a friend whom Shakespeare remembered in his will; but he was not averse to engaging in litigation against members of his own family – and selling Shakespeare's plays to Jaggard. The activity can be kept simple or it can be made much more complex, depending on how far into the history and the context the students are prepared to go.
- Place each of the six characters at an agreed point between the chair representing the text and the chair representing the reader of 1623. Each character is allowed to make one statement about their relationship to the text and/or the reader: what will they choose to say and why?
- Compare each group's presentations. Did each group place the six characters in the same order and the same distance from the two chairs? What can we learn from this about the way that drama texts in general and published versions of Shakespeare's plays in particular, are *framed*? Is it surprising that no women appear to feature in the story of the publication of the *First Folio*?

Activity Sequence 3: working with stage directions

Working at word level

Exemplar text (2)

Scene 1
Northampton. A room in the castle.
(Hubert, Executioners, Arthur)
Enter Hubert and Executioners.

- Working either individually or in pairs, read the stage directions that precede the dialogue in this extract. Note that, as with the cast list in Activity Sequence 1, the text is framed with a specialist word. Trace the etymology of *scene* back through its linguistic heritage in French and Latin to Ancient Greek. Its first use in a dramatic context in English seems to have occurred fifty or sixty years before Shakespeare wrote this play. What conceptual pathway takes us from *scene* as in *division for a play* to the Ancient Greek for *tent* or *booth giving shade*?

- Bearing in mind again the research undertaken in Activity Sequence 1, think about how the reader is meant to interpret the stage directions. Knowing that Shakespeare never published a manuscript during his lifetime, who is responsible for placing this particular frame around the spoken words? To what extent should we allow the directions to 'direct' our reading of the text that it frames? Compare different editions of Act Four Scene One of *The Life and Death of King John*. Do they all begin with the same stage directions? Share your findings and your reactions to these questions as a whole group.

- Notice the geographical location for the scene. Given the various place names listed in the cast list for the play (see Activity Sequence 1), are you surprised by the setting? Undertake some on-line research into Northampton Castle. How appropriate is it that a pivotal scene from a play about King John should be set here? (Students should discover that the castle was within a day's journey of London and that it was one of King John's favourite locations. He visited it thirty times and established the Royal Treasury there in 1205.) Would it make any difference to the scene if the geographical location was removed and the stage direction simply began: *A room in the castle*? Why are the town and the castle identified, whereas the actual location *within* the castle is left vague? Share your thoughts.

Working at syntactic level

- Given what you have probably been taught about writing in sentences, what do you think about the way the opening stage direction is punctuated?

- In groups of four, use *physical theatre* techniques to communicate the information presented in each line of the opening *stage directions*. Present them as three distinct episodes.

- Thinking of the first line, how will you portray the sequentially narrowing movement from open space (the whole town of Northampton) to the perimeters of the castle and finally to the confines of 'a room'?

- Line two describes people rather than places. What do you notice about the sequence in which they are introduced? Why might the individuals be named but the anonymous group be classified by occupation? Line two offers few of the verbal clues provided by the cast list of the play: how, therefore, are these figures to be portrayed? The word *executioners* gives us something to go on in that we can think about how the noun might be transposed into a verb – but even then, what kind of executioners might they be? The two forenames in the line offer little help: the first is appropriate to the setting of the play because it was popularised by the Normans; the second evokes thoughts of Arthurian legend, perhaps. Reading ahead to line three provides a clue to how line two might be interpreted: the fact that only Hubert and the Executioners 'enter' suggests that they come into the space together. Arthur is probably alone and already present in the room. A dynamic pattern of movement against stillness, activity against passivity, is therefore suggested and this might provide the key to inter-preting line two.

- The verb in line three confirms the sense of movement; but how are Hubert and the Executioners to 'enter'? Do they care if Arthur hears them coming or not? Is he even aware of their presence? Should he be physically present in this presentation?

- Compare presentations. Reflect on the way that the lexis and punctuation of this stage direction explore *dynamics of space, movement and character representation*. How has this drama activity informed your interpretation of the stage direction and the relationship between play text and performance?

Activity Sequence 4: working with script

Working at syntactic level

Exemplar text (3)

> *Hubert*: Heat me these irons hot, and look thou stand
> Within the arras. When I strike my foot
> Upon the bosom of the ground, rush forth
> And bind the boy which you shall find with me
> Fast to the chair. Be heedful. Hence, and watch.

- Having explored the frames around Act Four Scene One of *The Life and Death of King John*, we now encounter the first spoken words. To read these opening lines is to necessitate a reinterpretation of the work undertaken for Activity Sequence 2. Read to yourself the lines spoken here by Hubert: do they confirm or change in any way the perception of him and his *dramatic function* in the play that you had established from the work undertaken in Activity Sequence 2? Share your thoughts with the whole group.

- Find a space in the room where you can work individually. Move around the space, reading Hubert's five lines of verse aloud to yourself. The first time you do this, concentrate exclusively on the *sounds* of the words. Notice, for example, the repetition of *s* sounds and the alliteration of the letter *b*. Come together as a group and share your thoughts. Individuals can demonstrate different interpretations to their colleagues by using the circle as a performance space.

- Repeat the activity, but this time concentrate on the *rhythm* of the lines (see also Activity Sequences 3 and 4 of Chapter 10: *From Phoneme to Word Level* (pp. 113–114)). Once again, move as you say the lines (remember the dynamic suggested by the stage directions). At the end of each line, change direction: how does the line-break work – with or against the punctuation of the sentences Hubert is speaking? Does it surprise you that such wicked activities should be spoken in verse? Say the lines again; but this time, change direction on each punctuation break. Think about the length and significance of the pauses suggested by the commas and full stops in this extract. What further insights have these two different ways of saying the lines offered you? Return to the circle and share as before.

- Move into pairs. Drawing on all the discussions that have taken place in Activity Sequences 2 and 3, share your thoughts about the character of Hubert. The following questions might help to inform your reflections:

    o *Who is 'the boy'?*
    o *Why is he not named?*
    o *What does Hubert intend to do to him and how do we know?*
    o *What do you make of the fact that Hubert personifies the floor as 'the bosom of the ground' and that the bosom is to be struck with his foot?*

Working at word level

- You are going to undertake a final walk-through of the lines and then come together again as a pair to compare your responses. One of you is to focus this time on the verbs that Hubert uses; the other is to focus on the personal and demonstrative pronouns. As you walk through the lines, think of an *action, gesture and intonation* that might make an appropriate accompaniment to the selected words. An interesting and perhaps even more challenging variation to this activity would be to choose an action, gesture or intonation that conveys a very different meaning from that suggested by the word.
- Back in your pairs, perform the lines for your partner and ask her or him to comment on the performance in terms of what it has taught them about your interpretation of Hubert. Has your partner understood what you were trying to convey? Do your interpretations of the character differ in any way? If so, how and why?

Working at sub-textual level

- Call the whole group back together and introduce them to Grice's (1975) four *maxims of conversation: quantity, quality, relation* and *manner*. Note that Grice argues that effective conversation should be relevant, truthful, clear, well informed and to the point.
- Working in your pairs, say Hubert's lines to each other again and measure them against Grice's criteria of effectiveness. Which ones does Hubert seem to meet? His speech is a series of imperatives: each of those commands certainly seems to be to the point, unambiguous and relevant! What about clarity and truthfulness, however? Thinking back to the questions that informed your earlier discussion, focus on the phrase *the boy which you shall find with me*. You will have already discussed the significance of the fact that 'the boy' is not named and reflected on a possible link with the *Arthur* who features in the stage directions but has, as yet, not appeared in the scene. Think now about the verb 'find': how appropriate is it, given the context of the speech in which it is located?

Working at syntactic level

- In your pairs, divide this section of the speech so that the main and relative clauses are re-arranged to read: *Bind fast to the chair* and *The boy which you shall find with me.*

- Is there any context in which the phrase *Bind fast to the chair* could be spoken so that it did not connote an act of violence? Think about the phrase's rhythm in terms of the metrical feet explored in Activity Sequence 3 of Chapter 10: *From Phoneme to Word Level* (pp. 113–114). Does it consist of a spondee followed by an anapaest? What dynamic effect does this rhythm create and how appropriate is it to the dynamic pattern suggested by the stage directions?
- Does the phrase *The boy which you shall find with me* follow a conventional iambic metre? Such a pattern would certainly emphasise the main words in the clause and offer a conventional, even-tempered *counterpoint* to the ferocity of the order that Hubert gives.
- In your pairs, use the techniques of *physical theatre* again to choreograph a dramatised response to the two clauses. Use your performance to emphasise the tension between their very different rhythm patterns and use of short and long vowels.
- Back in the circle, individual pairs can share their interpretations with the whole group. What have these activities added to your sense of engagement with the text?

Activity Sequence 5: working with non-verbal signs

Working at word level

- So far, the activities have focused on written text: a cast list, stage directions, an extract from the script. Now it is time to think about what Kowzan (1968) describes as the *auditive* and *visual* signs through which meanings are made in an acting space.
- A useful way in would be to consider here Elam's reference to Birdwhistell's (1970) concept of *kinesics*, which can be explored in terms of *posture*, *gesture*, *stance* and *movement*.
- Look again at the opening five lines spoken by Hubert. They are addressed to the executioners – however many they may be. They do not say a word in response. In order to communicate with the audience their reactions to Hubert's orders, the actors need to draw upon kinesic skills.
- Move into groups of four and find a performance space. One person will play Hubert and the other three the unspecified number of executioners. As Caldwell Cook noted, one of the reasons that Shakespeare's stage directions are so pithy is because he incorporated them into the lines spoken by his actors. So here: Hubert describes the setting and the props needed for this scene: there is a chair on the 'bosom of the ground' and there is an arras that conceals a space in which the executioners are to hide. There are 'irons' that need to be heated for some unnamed (and thus even more terrifying) purpose and there are ropes (which reinforce the dynamic pattern of movement to constriction). There must be a brazier to heat the 'irons': where is it? Do the executioners carry it in? Is it already in the room, serving the innocent purpose of providing heat and comfort (and thus is about to change radically its symbolic meaning)? Is it concealed behind the arras? (If the latter, the executioners are going to get extremely hot and restive while they watch Hubert at his work – something that will heighten the tension of the ensuing scene.)

Working at sub-textual level

- Now that you have worked so intensively on this extract, switch the *perspective* so that you explore the lines, not from Hubert's point of view, but from that of the executioners. How will they use *posture, gesture, stance and movement* – not only to communicate their response to what Hubert is saying, but also to indicate the relationship between themselves and the objects described in the paragraph above? Do all three executioners react in the same way and at the same time? Do Hubert's different orders provoke different responses? He explains that they are to 'rush forth' at his signal (in the future) but for now are to remain still and watchful. How might this dynamic pattern be interpreted for an audience?
- Bring the whole group back to the circle and share some of the presentations, exploring how focusing on kinesics has informed students' responses to the opening of Act Four Scene One.

Activity Sequence 6: exploring tension and irony

Working at sub-textual level

Exemplar text (4)

> *Executioner*: I hope your warrant will bear out the deed.
> *Hubert*:   Uncleanly scruples! Fear not you. Look to't.

Exeunt Executioners.

> Young lad, come forth; I have to say with you.

Enter Arthur.

> *Arthur*:   Good morrow, Hubert.
> *Hubert*:   Good morrow, little prince.
> *Arthur*:   As little prince, having so great a title
>   To be more prince, as may be. You are sad.
> *Hubert*:   Indeed I have been merrier.
> *Arthur*:   Mercy on me!
>   Methinks nobody should be sad but I.
>   Yet I remember, when I was in France,
>   Young gentlemen would be as sad as night,
>   Only for wantonness. By my christendom,
>   So I were out of prison and kept sheep,
>   I should be as merry as the day is long;
>   And so I would be here, but that I doubt
>   My uncle practices more harm to me.
>   He is afraid of me and I of him.
>   Is it my fault that I was Geoffrey's son?
>   No indeed is't not; and I would to heaven
>   I were your son, so you would love me, Hubert.

Hubert:	*Aside.*

> If I talk to him, with his innocent prate
> He will awake my mercy, which lies dead;
> Therefore I will be sudden, and dispatch.

- Explain the context of this extract. It contains the next twenty-four lines of dialogue in Act Four Scene One. The 'uncle' to whom Arthur refers is King John and 'Geoffrey' is the king's late brother. John is afraid of Arthur because he fears he might take the throne from him. Arthur, in his turn, fears – rightly – that John intends to murder him as a potential rival.

- Share with the group Fleming's observation that 'In the broadest sense of the term, some form of irony is central to all drama in that meaning is invariably at a deeper level than its surface manifestation' (1997, p. 81). Fleming's words are particularly apt with regard to this extract from Act Four Scene One. The exchange between Hubert and Arthur is deeply ironic: the 'surface manifestations' of the former cannot be interpreted accurately by the latter, no matter how anxiously he attempts to decipher words, looks and gestures. The emphasis upon sight and deception is compounded by the fact that there are three audiences watching this scene: the audience separated from the actors by the *fourth wall* of the performance space and two audiences within the play itself – the executioners concealed behind the arras and the Hubert who pretends in front of Arthur but reveals his true feelings in an aside to the audience beyond the fourth wall, though not to the audience of executioners.

Working at syntactical level

- Move into groups of four and find a space to work in. Select four lines from the extract that really highlight the ironic contrast between 'surface manifestation' and 'deeper level'. Hubert's *Good morrow, little prince* is a good example. Prepare a *thought-tracking* presentation of the lines. Move into pairs. One pair represents Hubert and his real thoughts; the other, Arthur and his. In the performance, Hubert's actual line will be followed immediately by his real thoughts – and so on. Thinking again of posture, gesture, stance and movement, show how both characters deliver their lines and how they react to what is said to them.

- Once the groups have had an opportunity to rehearse their work, bring them back together in a circle and ask them to think again about these lines spoken by Hubert at the beginning of the scene:

> When I strike my foot
> Upon the bosom of the ground, rush forth
> And bind the boy which you shall find with me
> Fast to the chair.

- The image of the striking foot does not only serve to draw attention to Hubert's propensity for violence; it also adds an even more heightened sense of tension to the exchange with Arthur. The audience beyond the fourth wall probably by now guesses what the audience behind the arras definitely knows: when Hubert stamps his foot, catastrophic violence will be unleashed on Arthur.

- Ask the performance groups to take this information back with them into rehearsal. How might they use kinesic sign systems to make the audience aware of just how significant that seemingly casual physical gesture is? Is it possible to choreograph the movements of the actors so that attention is directed towards and away from Hubert's foot in a manner that now enhances, now decreases the tension of the scene?
- Share the performances and consider how *aural and visual sign systems* contribute to our capacity to 'read' text in its widest sense.

Activity Sequence 7: thinking about overall design concepts

Working at contextual level

- Look again at the opening stage direction of Act Four Scene One: *Northampton. A room in the castle.* Earlier activity sequences have explored the ways in which that brief statement establishes a dynamic pattern that moves inwards – literally, when Hubert and the executioners 'enter', and metaphorically as they prepare to violate Arthur's private space. Thinking again about what might lie beneath the 'surface' of this 'iceberg text' (see Activity Sequence 3 of Chapter 11: *Working with Text*, p. 127), consider what other connotations are evoked by the movement from town to castle to room. Now that we can guess what Hubert and the executioners intend to do with their hot 'irons', how might the sense of increasing constriction suggested by that movement pattern inform an audience's response to the terrible act of violence that is about to be perpetrated against Arthur? Think about this individually for a few moments and then share your thoughts with the whole group.
- The introduction of the term 'audience' prepares the ground for an examination of a major visual sign: the *physical frame of the acting space* itself. Divide the group into research teams as before. Invite them to discover what they can about the different ways in which a performance can be framed, literally. Brown's (1968) description of four kinds of stage – *open*, *thrust*, *arena* and *traverse* – might be a useful starting point. The groups should compare the affordances and the constraints offered by each type of stage researched. The following questions may be helpful:

  o *What will the audience find easier or more difficult to see and hear?*
  o *What is the spatial relationship between actors and audience?*
  o *What affordances and/or constraints are offered to actors in terms of voice projection, actions, gestures and interaction with the audience?*
  o *What kind of acting style or theatre performance is most suitable in this acting space?*
  o *What affordances and/or constraints are offered in terms of costume, lighting and sound effects, make-up and hairstyle, props and scenery?*

- Depending on how far teacher and students wish to take this work, the research could be extended to explore the ways in which performance spaces differ throughout history and culture. An obvious starting point would be the Elizabethan and Jacobean theatres of Shakespeare's day (with a physical or virtual visit to *The Globe* included). Students might also consider the raked semicircles of classical theatre in Ancient Greece, or the mobile, cart-borne performances of the medieval mystery plays, or the temple theatres of Kerala, India, in which *kutiyattam* is performed.

- Call the whole group together and introduce them to Mackey and Cooper's (2000) *overall design concept*: how can the various aural, physical, verbal and visual signs of the theatre combine to present a coherent interpretation of a play text? Move back into your research groups and explore on-line accounts of recent performances of *The Life and Death of King John*. A quick trawl of the Internet reveals that there were at least four significant and very different productions of the play in 2012 – including a performance at *The Globe* by an Armenian theatre company as part of the *World Shakespeare Festival*. Read the on-line publicity blurb for the productions and compare this material with what the reviewers say. How do the productions differ? Has anything you have read made you think about the play in a new light? Do any of the interpretations excite you more than others? Share your findings with the whole group, projecting the relevant pages from the Internet sites on a large screen.

- This activity could also be extended so that it becomes an historical study. Students might research early productions of the play, such as those staged by the director and theatre manager John Rich in 1737 or the intriguing silent film version made by the actor Herbert Beerbohm Tree in 1899. Two different productions of the play appeared in London in 1745, the year of the second Jacobite Rebellion: how might the audience of the time have responded to a play that explores issues of power and the consequences of political instability in ways that they could recognise only too well?

Working at whole text level

- Working in pairs, ask the group to read the rest of Act Four Scene One together. When you have finished, consider the following questions:

  o *Given what you have learned about Hubert and his relationship with Arthur so far, does the ending of the scene surprise you?*
  o *Compare Shakespeare's use of the foot-stamping signal to your own: how effective is it in bringing the tension of the scene to a climax?*
  o *A narrative of despair ends as a narrative of hope: what seems to cause the change and, knowing what you do about human nature, do you feel it rings true?*
  o *At what point in the scene do you feel Hubert makes his decision to spare Arthur?*
  o *What did Arthur say or do to make Hubert change his mind?*
  o *What is significant about the fact that Arthur does most of the talking in the scene and Hubert most of the listening? What challenges does this pose for the actors playing these parts?*
  o *What image patterns does Arthur draw upon to support his plea for mercy?*

- ○ *What is the dramatic function of the executioners in the later part of the scene?*
- ○ *How do the publicity statements and reviews for the various productions of the play that you studied for your on-line research accord with or differ from your response to the scene?*

- Move into groups of four and compare your answers with the questions above. Choose the acting space that you feel would be most appropriate for a performance of Act Four Scene One from *The Life and Death of King John* (think about the play's title as you work). Choose an *overall design concept* and create on paper (or, if you have the necessary software, on computer) a setting for the scene, including props and scenery if appropriate (one of the 2012 productions mentioned earlier used an upturned table to double as the castle battlements). Which actors of the small or big screen might be cast in the parts of Hubert, Arthur and the executioners? Given that you have not met him yet in the play but will have formed some kind of impression, who do you feel might play the part of King John?
- Think about how lighting can be used to *create mood*, *atmosphere* and *emphasis*, to reveal and conceal and even to advance the plot (Pilbrow, 1970). Create a lighting plan for the opening of Act Four Scene One.
- Share your designs with the whole group. Are there areas of similarity and/or difference?
- If funds will allow, buy three shop mannequins (tops only – they can be bought relatively cheaply second-hand). Split the group into three and provide them with (or, better, ask them to use their imaginations and scavenge for) old clothes, scarves and jewellery, wigs, make-up and so on. One mannequin represents Hubert; one Arthur; and one an executioner. Choose one of the overall design concepts and dress the mannequin accordingly. Take photos of the results in different light settings and from different angles: which seem to be most effective? Share the results and use the mannequins and photos to create an installation response to Act Four Scene One of *The Life and Death of King John*.

Opportunities for work in the English classroom

Reading

References to the *New London Group's* reconfiguration of literacy in terms of *tools of design* occur frequently throughout the book. Drawing upon the work of semioticians like Kowzan and Elam, this particular set of sequence activities offers numerous opportunities to appreciate that a 'text' can be visual, aural and multi-modal. Activity Sequence 5, for example, shows how an understanding of *kinesics* can enrich interpretation. The important concept of *textual framing* is also explored throughout these activity sequences, not least in Activity Sequence 7, where the students have to 'frame' their interpretation of the play text by devising an overall design concept. To do this, they have to think again about *intertextuality*: how have earlier interpretations of the play informed their own? These framing concepts could be applied to any reading activity requiring *higher order* reading skills. Just to take a sentence as an example: think about how our interpretation of the statement GIANT

WAVES DOWN CHIMNEY differs depending on whether it is framed by the page of a newspaper or the stage directions for a pantomime. Framing activities like these can be used to make powerful ideological points. Students might consider, for example, how a canonical literary text (like a play by Shakespeare) is framed by so many scholarly opinions throughout the centuries that it is difficult to encounter it today with an unbiased mind or a clear eye. Why are some texts framed in this way when others are not?

The activity sequences also provide models for higher order reading, which can be applied to any text. The informing principle throughout is that the reader is actively engaged in the construction of meanings by speculating, predicting, filling in the gaps and reconfiguring an original response in the light of new information. Starting with a small section of text and working outwards encourages the reader to look with fresh eyes by making the familiar 'unfamiliar', as Shklovsky noted, and by reinforcing the importance of context and frame. Stage directions (Activity Sequence 3) are particularly powerful texts to work with in this way because they are so open to interpretation and compress significant amounts of information into a small number of words (sometimes, as at the start of Act Four Scene One of *The Life and Death of King John*, doing so without the use of sentences – an important point worth following up). Many other genres could be explored in similar fashion. One interesting way in which the reading strategies used in this sequence of activities might be enhanced is by taking students on a literacy 'tour' of the local environment so that they have opportunities to study signage in all its wonderful and bizarre manifestations. A favourite for me is this statement written in English on the door of an airport terminal in Siberia: THIS DOOR IS NOT PRESENT. What surreal and philosophical connotations do those words evoke! Even texts that appear to be firmly 'closed' raise ideological and cultural issues, as well as being highly evocative in themselves: IN CASE OF FIRE, BREAK GLASS comes to mind.

Activity Sequence 2 raises several issues that could be explored further in the English classroom. It attempts to make Shakespeare more of a living presence by describing the human story behind the production of the *First Folio*. A useful text to work with in this context might be Susan Cooper's historical novel *King of Shadows*. Activity Sequence 2 also explores the economic structures that underpin the production of texts: we think of the *First Folio* as belonging to Shakespeare; but, as the research undertaken for this sequence of activities makes clear, he had died by the time it was published and a diverse number of other people – acting from a range of motives – were responsible for its appearance. Interesting follow-up work could be undertaken into issues of ownership and copyright and how these have changed over time. Changing perspective slightly, the activity sequence could provide an opening for an exploration of communication channels in general: who are the 'gatekeepers' that police the relationship between text and reader and why do they do it?

References

Drama and related pedagogy

Abbs, P. (1987a) 'Towards a Coherent Arts Aesthetic'. In P. Abbs (ed.) *Living Powers: The Arts in Education*. London, New York and Philadelphia: The Falmer Press.

Abbs, P. (1987b) (ed.) *Living Powers: The Arts in Education*. London, New York and Philadelphia. The Falmer Press.

Anderson, M. (2012) *MasterClass in Drama Education: Transforming Teaching and Learning*. London and New York: Continuum.

Anderson, M., Hughes, J. and Manuel, J. (2008) (eds) *Drama and English Teaching: Imagination, Action and Engagement*. Melbourne: Oxford University Press.

Arnold, R. (2004) 'Recasting Drama in English Education'. In W. Sawyer and E. Gold (eds) *Reviewing English in the 21st Century*. Melbourne: Phoenix Education.

Arts Council of Great Britain (1992) *Drama in Schools: Arts Council Guidance on Drama Education*. London: ACGB.

Birdwhistell, R.L. (1970) *Kinesics and Context: Essays on Body Motion Communication*. Philadelphia: University of Pennsylvania Press.

Boal, A. (1995) *The Rainbow of Desire: The Boal method of Theatre and Therapy*. New York: Routledge.

Bolton, G. (1984) *Drama as Education: An Argument for Placing Drama at the Centre of the Curriculum*. Harlow, Essex: Longman.

Brown, J.R. (1968) *Drama*. London: Heinemann Educational Books.

Caldwell Cook, H. (1917) *The Play Way: An Essay in Educational Method*. London: William Heinemann.

Cameron, D. (2009) 'Mashup: Digital Media and Drama Conventions'. In M. Anderson, J. Carroll and D. Cameron (eds) *Drama Education with Digital Technology*. London and New York: Continuum.

Cameron, D. and Anderson, M. (2009) 'Potential to Reality: Drama, Technology and Education'. In M. Anderson, J. Carroll and D. Cameron (eds) *Drama Education with Digital Technology*. London and New York: Continuum.

Clipson-Boyles, S. (1998) *Drama in Primary English Teaching*. London: David Fulton.

Courtney, R. (1989) (4th Edition, Revised) *Play, Drama & Thought: The Intellectual Background to Dramatic Education*. Toronto, Ontario, Canada: Simon & Pierre Publishing.

Csíkszentmihályi, M. (1999) 'Implications of a Systems Perspective for the Study of Creativity'. In R. Sternberg (ed.) *Handbook of Creativity*. Cambridge: Cambridge University Press.

Department for Education (DfE) (2010) *Developing Drama in English: A Handbook for English Subject Leaders and Teachers*. Available at: www.nationaldrama.org.uk/nd/assets/File/Developing%20Drama%20in%20English.pdf [Accessed 27 November 2013.]

Dunn, J. and O'Toole, J. (2009) 'When Worlds Collude: Exploring the Relationship Between the Actual, the Dramatic and the Virtual'. In M. Anderson, J. Carroll and D. Cameron (eds) *Drama Education with Digital Technology*. London and New York: Continuum.

Elam, K. (2002, 1980) *The Semiotics of Theatre and Drama*. London: Routledge.

Esslin, M. (1978) *An Anatomy of Drama*. London: Abacus Sphere Books.

Esslin, M. (1987) *The Field of Drama: How the Signs of Drama Create Meanings on Stage and Screen*. London and New York: Methuen.

Finlay-Johnson, H. (1912) *The Dramatic Method of Teaching*. Boston, New York, Chicago and London: Ginn and Company.

Fleming, M. (1994) *Starting Drama Teaching*. London: David Fulton Publishers.

Fleming, M. (1997) *The Art of Drama Teaching*. London: David Fulton Publishers.

Havell, C. (1987) 'The Case of Drama'. In P. Abbs (ed.) *Living Powers: The Arts in Education*. London, New York and Philadelphia: The Falmer Press.

Heathcote, D. and Bolton, G. (1995) *Drama for Learning: Dorothy Heathcote's Mantle of the Expert Approach to Education*. Portsmouth, NH: Heinemann.

Hodgson, J. (1972) *The Uses of Drama: Acting as a Social and Educational Force*. London: Methuen.

Hornbrook, D. (1989) *Education and Dramatic Art*. Oxford: Basil Blackwell.

Hornbrook, D. (1998) *On the Subject of Drama*. London and New York: Routledge.

Hughes, J. and Arnold, R. (2008) 'Drama and the Teaching of Poetry'. In M. Anderson, J. Hughes and J. Manuel (eds) *Drama and English Teaching: Imagination, Action and Engagement*. Melbourne: Oxford University Press.

Johnston, R. and Watson, J. (2007) *Teaching Synthetic Phonics*. Exeter: Learning Matters.

Kempe, A. (1998) 'Reading Plays for Performance'. In D. Hornbrook (ed.) *On the Subject of Drama*. London and New York: Routledge.

Kempe, A. and Ashwell, M. (2000) *Progression in Secondary Drama*. Harlow: Heinemann.

Kidd, D. (2011) 'The Mantle of Macbeth'. *English in Education*, 45(1), 72–85.

Kirby, M. (1987) *A Formalist Theatre*. Philadelphia: University of Pennsylvania Press.

Kowzan, T. (1968) 'The Sign in the Theater: An Introduction to the Semiology of the Art of the Spectacle. (S. Pleasance, trans.) *Diogenes*, 16(61), 52–80.

Langer, S. (1953) *Feeling and Form: A Theory of Art Developed from 'Philosophy in a New Key'*. London: Routledge & Kegan Paul.

Lewis, M. and Rainer, J. (2005) *Teaching Classroom Drama and Theatre: Practical Projects for Secondary Schools*. London and New York: Routledge.

Manuel, J. (2008) 'Invigorating the Teaching of Fiction through Drama'. In M. Anderson, J. Hughes and J. Manuel (eds) *Drama and English Teaching: Imagination, Action and Engagement*. Melbourne: Oxford University Press.

McCullough, C. (1998) 'Building a Dramatic Vocabulary'. In D. Hornbrook (ed.) *On the Subject of Drama*. London and New York: Routledge.

Mackey, S. and Cooper, S. (2000) *Drama and Theatre Studies*. Cheltenham: Stanley Thornes.

Neelands, J. (1984) *Making Sense of Drama*. Oxford: Heinemann Educational Books.

Neelands, J. (1996) 'Reflections From an Ivory Tower: Towards an Interactive Research Paradigm'. In P. Taylor (ed.) *Researching Drama and Arts Education*. London: Falmer Press.

Neelands, J. (2008) 'Drama: The Subject that Dare not Speak its Name'. *ITE English: Readings for Discussion January 2008*. Available at: www.ite.org.uk/ite_readings/drama_180108.pdf [Accessed 2 August 2013.]

Neelands, J. (2011) 'Editorial'. *English in Education*, 45(1), 1–5.

Neelands, J. and Goode, T. (2000) *Structuring Drama Work: A Handbook of Available Forms in Theatre and Drama*. Cambridge: Cambridge University Press.

Nussbaum, M. (2010) *Not for Profit – Why Democracy Needs the Humanities*. New York: Princeton University Press.

O'Neill, C. (1995) *Drama Worlds*. Portsmouth, NH: Heinemann.

O'Neill, C. and Lambert, A. (1982) *Drama Structures: A Practical Handbook for Teachers*. Cheltenham: Nelson Thornes.

O'Toole, J. (2008) 'Process, Dialogue and Performance: The Dramatic Art of English Teaching'. In M. Anderson, J. Hughes and J. Manuel (eds) *Drama and English Teaching: Imagination, Action and Engagement*. Melbourne: Oxford University Press.

O'Toole, J. and O'Mara, J. (2007) 'Proteus, the Giant at the Door: Drama and Theatre in the Curriculum'. In L. Bresler (ed.) *International Handbook of Research in Arts Education* (pp. 203–218). Dordrecht, The Netherlands: Springer.

Pascoe, R. and Sallis, R. (2012) 'Perspectives on Drama Teacher Education in Australia'. *Asia-Pacific Journal for Arts Education*, 11(6), 126–158.

Piaget, J. (1951/1976) 'Mastery Play'. In J.S. Bruner, A. Jolly and K. Sylva (eds) *Play: Its Role in Development and Education* (pp. 166–171). Harmondsworth: Penguin Books.

Piaget, J. (1951/1976) 'Symbolic Play'. In J.S. Bruner, A. Jolly and K. Sylva (eds) *Play: Its Role in Development and Education* (pp. 555–569). Harmondsworth: Penguin Books.

Pilbrow, R. (1970) *Stage Lighting*. London: Studio Vista.

Rainer, J. and Lewis, M. (2012) *Drama at the Heart of the Secondary School: Projects to Promote Authentic Learning*. London and New York: Routledge.

Sayers, R. (2011) 'The Implications of Introducing Heathcote's *Mantle of the Expert* Approach as a Community of Practice and Cross Curricular Learning Tool in a Primary School'. *English in Education*, 45(1), 20–35.

Schechner, R. (1993) *The Future of Ritual: Writings on Culture and Performance*. Routledge: London and New York.

Schiller, F. (1795/1967) *On the Aesthetic Education of Man in a Series of Letters* (E.M. Wilkinson and L.A. Willoughby, eds and trans.). Oxford: Clarendon Press.

Sharpe, L. (2006) *Friedrich Schiller: Drama, Thought and Politics*. Cambridge: University Press.

Slade, P. (1954) *Child Drama*. London: University of London Press.

Spencer, H. (1855) 'Aesthetic Sentiment'. In *The Principles of Psychology*, Volume II. London: Williams and Norgate.

Sutton, P. (2009) 'Lip sync: performance placebos in the digital age'. In M. Anderson, J. Carroll and D. Cameron (eds) *Drama Education with Digital Technology*. London and New York: Continuum.

Thompson, J. (1999) *Drama Workshops for Anger Management and Offending Behaviour*. London: Jessica Kingsley Publishers.

Urian, D. (1998) 'On Being an Audience: A Spectator's Guide'. In D. Hornbrook (ed.) *On the Subject of Drama*. London and New York: Routledge.

Veltruský, J. (1964) 'Man and Object in the Theatre'. In P.L. Garvin (ed.) *A Prague School Reader on Esthetics, Literary Structure and Style*. Washington: Georgetown University Press.

Vygotsky, L. (1966/1976) 'Play and its Role in the Mental Development of the Child'. In J.S. Bruner, A. Jolly and K. Sylva (eds) *Play: Its Role in Development and Education*. Harmondsworth: Penguin Books.

Vygotsky, L. (1967/2004) 'Imagination and Creativity in Childhood' (M.E. Sharpe, trans.), *Journal of Russian and Eastern European Psychology*, 42(1), 7–97.

Way, B. (1967) *Development Through Drama*. London: Longman.

Wilhelm, J. (2002) *Action Strategies for Deepening Comprehension: Role Plays, Text Structure Tableaux, Talking Statues, and Other Enrichment Techniques That Engage Students*. New York: Scholastic Teaching Resources.

Wilkinson, E.M. and Willoughby, L.A. (1967) Introduction. In F. Schiller, *On the Aesthetic Education of Man in a Series of Letters* (E.M. Wilkinson and L.A. Willoughby, eds and trans.) (pp. xc–xcvi). Oxford: Clarendon Press.

English and related pedagogy

Alexander, R. (2005) 'Culture, Dialogue and Learning: Notes on an Emerging Pedagogy'. Paper delivered at the 10th international conference of the *International Association for Cognitive Education and Psychology (IACEP)* University of Durham, United Kingdom, 10–14 July.

Andrews, R. (2001) *Teaching and Learning English: A Guide to Recent Research and its Applications*. London and New York: Continuum.

Appleyard, J.A. (1991) *Becoming a Reader: The Experience of Fiction from Childhood to Adulthood*. Cambridge: University Press.

Assessment and Qualifications Alliance (AQA) (2008) *GCSE Specification 2011: English Literature 3711*. Manchester: AQA.

Bakhtin, M. (1973) *Problems of Dostoevsky's Poetics* (C. Emerson, ed. and trans.). Manchester: University Press.

Baron, N.S. (2000) *Alphabet to Email: How Written English Evolved and Where It's Heading*. London and New York: Routledge.

Barthes, R. (1982) *Selected Writings*. London: Fontana Collins.

Britton, J. (1970) *Language and Learning*. Harmondsworth: Penguin.

Bruner, J. (1986) *Actual Minds, Possible Worlds*. Cambridge, MA: Harvard University Press.

Cox, B. (1991) *Cox on Cox: An English Curriculum for the 1990s*. London: Hodder & Stoughton.

Dentith, S. (1995) *Bakhtinian Thought: An Introductory Reader*. London and New York: Routledge.

Dixon, J. (1967) *Growth Through English: A Report Based on the Dartmouth Seminar 1966*. Oxford: Oxford University Press.

Fish, S. (1980) *Is There a Text in This Class? The Authority of Interpretive Communities*. Cambridge, MA, and London: University of Harvard Press.

Grice, H. P. (1975) 'Logic and Conversation'. In P. Cole and J. Morgan (eds) *Syntax and Semantics: Speech Acts*. Volume 3. New York: Academic Press.

Hawkes, G. (1964) *Dramatic Work with Backward Children*. In D. Holbrook (ed.) *English for the Rejected: Training Literacy in the Lower Streams of the Secondary School*. Cambridge: Cambridge University Press.

Holbrook, D. (1964) *English for the Rejected: Training Literacy in the Lower Streams of the Secondary School*. Cambridge: Cambridge University Press.

Hourd, M.L. (1949/1968) *The Education of the Poetic Spirit: A Study in Children's Expression in the English Lesson*. Melbourne, London and Toronto: Heinemann.

Irish, T. (2011) 'Would You Risk it for Shakespeare? A Case Study of Using Active Approaches in the English Classroom'. *English in Education*, 45(1), 6–19.

Iser, W. (1978) *The Act of Reading: A Theory of Aesthetic Response*. Baltimore, MA and London: The Johns Hopkins University Press.

Jeffcoate, R. (1992) *Starting English Teaching*. London: Routledge.

Kress, G. and Bezemer, J. (2009) 'Writing in a Multimodal World of Representation'. In R. Beard, D. Myhill, J. Riley and M. Nystrand (eds) *The SAGE Handbook of Writing Development*. London: SAGE Publications.

Kristeva, J. (1970) *Le Texte du roman: approche sémiologique d'une structure discursive transformationelle*. The Hague: Mouton.

Leitch, V.B, Cain, W.E., Finke, L., Johnson, B., McGowan, J., Sharpley-Whiting, T.D. and Williams, J.J. (2010) (eds) *The Norton Anthology of Theory and Criticism*. Second Edition. New York and London: W.W. Norton & Company.

Lemon, L.T. and Reis, M.J. (1965) (eds and trans.), *Russian Formalist Criticism: Four Essays*. Lincoln, Nebraska: Nebraska University Press.

Medway, P. (1989) 'Argument as Social Action', in R. Andrews (ed.) *Narrative and Argument*. Milton Keynes: Open University Press.

The New London Group (1996) 'A Pedagogy of Multiliteracies: Designing Social Futures'. *Harvard Educational Review*, 66(1), 60–92.

Propp, V. (1928/1958) *Morphology of the Folktale* (L. Scott, trans.). Bloomington: Indiana University Press.

Rosenblatt, L. (1970) *Literature as Exploration*. London: Heinemann.

Saussure, F. de (1916/2010) *Course in General Linguistics*. In V.B Leitch, W.E. Cain, L. Finke, B. Johnson, B., J. McGowan, T.D. Sharpley-Whiting and J.J. Williams, (eds) *The Norton Anthology of Theory and Criticism*. Second Edition. New York and London: W.W. Norton & Company.

Shklovsky, V. (1917/1965) 'Art as Technique'. In L.T. Lemon and M.J. Reis (eds) *Russian Formalist Criticism*. Lincoln: University of Nebraska Press.

Van Riel, R. and Fowler, O. (1996) *Opening the Book: Finding a Good Read*. Leeds: Peepal Tree Press.

Webb, E. (1987) 'The Case of English: English as Aesthetic Initiative'. In P. Abbs (ed.) *Living Powers: The Arts in Education*. London, New York and Philadelphia: The Falmer Press.

Whitehead, F. (1966) *The Disappearing Dais: A Study of the Principles and Practice of English Teaching*. London: Chatto & Windus.

General pedagogy and pedagogical issues

Bronfenbrenner, U. (1979) *The Ecology of Human Development: Experiments by Nature or Design*. Cambridge, MA: Harvard University Press.

De Corte, E., Verschaffel, L., Entwistle, N. and Merriënboer, J. (2003) *Powerful Learning Environments: Unravelling Basic Components and Dimensions*. Oxford: Elsevier Science.

Dewey, J. (2007, 1916) *Democracy and Education. An Introduction to the Philosophy of Education*. Teddington: Echo Press.

Gibson, J.J. (1977) *The Theory of Affordances*. In R. Shaw and J. Bransford (eds) *Perceiving, Acting and Knowing*. Hillsdale, NJ: Erlbaum.

Guardian UK (2001) 'Towards a national debate.' http://education.theguardian.com/thegreatdebate/story/0,9860,574645,00.html [Retrieved 12 July 2013].

Krathwohl, D. (2002) A Revision of Bloom's Taxonomy: An Overview. *Theory into Practice*, 41(4), 212–218.

Lave, J. and Wenger, E. (1991) *Situated Learning: Legitimate Peripheral Participation*. Cambridge: University of Cambridge Press.

Lombardi, M.M. (2007) *Authentic Learning for the 21ˢᵗ Century: An Overview*. Educause Learning Initiative Paper 1, May.

Steger, M.B. (2003) *Globalisation: A Very Short Introduction*. Oxford: Oxford University Press.

Sutherland, M. (1971) *Everyday Imagining in Education*. London: Routledge and Kegan Paul.

Government policy statements on drama and English

Australian Curriculum, Assessment and Reporting Authority (ACARA) (2011) *Shape of the Australian Curriculum: The Arts*. Sydney, NSW: ACARA.

Department of Education and Science (DES) (1963) *The Newsom Report (1963) Half Our Future: A Report of the Central Advisory Council for Education (England)*. London: Her Majesty's Stationery Office.

Department of Education and Science (DES) (1967) *Education Survey 2: Drama*. London: Her Majesty's Stationery Office.

Department of Education and Science (DES) (1975) *A Language for Life: Report of the Committee of Inquiry Appointed by the Secretary of State for Education and Science under the Chairmanship of Sir Alan Bullock F.B.A.* London: Her Majesty's Stationery Office.

Department of Education and Science (DES) (1989) 'Drama From 5 to 16'. *Curriculum Matters, 17*. London: Her Majesty's Stationery Office.

Office for Standards in Education (OFSTED) (2009) *English at the Crossroads* (080247) www.ofsted.gov.uk/publications/080247 [Accessed 17 August 2013].

Office for Standards in Education (OFSTED) (2011) *Excellence in English: What we can Learn from 12 Outstanding Schools* (100229) www.ofsted.gov.uk/resources/excellence-english [Accessed 17 August 2013].

History of education

Lawrence, E. (1952) (ed.) *Friedrich Froebel and English Education*. London: The University Press.

Locke, J. (1693) *Some Thoughts Concerning Education*. London: A & J Churchill.

Mathieson, M. (1975) *The Preachers of Culture*. London: George Allen & Unwin.

Richardson, A. (1994) *Literature, Education, and Romanticism: Reading as Social Practice, 1780–1832*. Cambridge: Cambridge University Press.

Slight, J.P. (1952) 'Froebel and the English Primary School of Today'. In E. Lawrence (ed.) *Friedrich Froebel and English Education*. London: The University Press.

Stone, L. (1977) *The Family, Sex and Marriage in England, 1500–1800*. New York: Harper & Row.

Walsh, D.J, Chung, S. and Tufekci, A. (2001) 'Friedrich Wilhelm Froebel'. In J.A. Palmer (ed.) *Fifty Major Thinkers on Education from Confucius to Dewey*. London and New York: Routledge.

Wollstonecraft, M. (1792/1975) *A Vindication of the Rights of Women* (C.H. Poston, ed.). New York: WW Norton.

Woodham-Smith, P. (1952) 'The Origin of the Kindergarten'. In E. Lawrence (ed.) *Friedrich Froebel and English Education*. London: The University Press.

Studies of childhood

Bottigheimer, R.B. (1994) 'The Child-Reader of Children's Bibles, 1656–1753'. In E. Goodenough, M.A. Heberle and N. Sokoloff (eds) *Infant Tongues: The Voice of the Child in Literature*. Detroit, MI: Wayne State University.

Bühler, C. (1931) 'The Social Behavior of Children'. In C. Murchison (ed.) *Handbook of Child Psychology* (pp. 374–416). Worcester, MA: Clark University Press.

Coveney, P. (1957) *Poor Monkey: The Child in Literature*. London: Rockliff.

Cunningham, H. (1995) *Children & Childhood in Western Society Since 1500*. London and New York: Longman.

Donaldson, M. (1978) *Children's Minds*. London: Fontana.

Froebel, F. (1826/2005) *The Education of Man* (W.N. Hailmann, Trans.) Mineola, NY: Dover Books.

Freud, A. (1827/1967–1981) 'Four Lectures on Child Analysis'. In A. Freud, *The Writings of Anna Freud*. New York: International Universities Press.

Frost, J.L. (2010) *A History of Children's Play and Play Environments: Towards a Contemporary Child-Saving Movement*. Abingdon and New York: Routledge.

Grasberger, L. (1864) *Erzeihung und Unterricht im klassichen Alterthum*, Volume I. Würzburg: Stahel.

Groos, K. (1898) *The Play of Animals* (E.L. Baldwin, trans). London: Heinemann.

Groos, K. (1901) *The Play of Man* (E.L. Baldwin, trans). London: Heinemann.

Hall, G.S. (1907) *Aspects of Child Life and Education*. London and Boston: Ginn & Co.

Isaacs, S. (1930) *The Intellectual Growth of Young Children*. London: Routledge and Kegan Paul.

Klein, M. (1932) 'The Psycho-Analysis of Children'. In *The International Psycho-Analytical Library*, 22, 1–379. London: The Hogarth Press.

Lowenfeld, M. (1935/1991) *Play in Childhood*. Oxford: Blackwell, New York: Cambridge University Press.

Mitchell, E.D. (1937) *The Theory of Play*. Baltimore, MD: Penguin Books.

More, H. (1799) *Strictures on the Modern System of Female Education*, Volume 1. London: Cadell and Davies.

Opie, I. and Opie, P. (1960) *The Lore and Language of Schoolchildren*. Oxford: Oxford University Press.

Preyer, W.T. (1882) *Die Seele des Kindes: Beobachtungen über die geistige Entwicklung des Menschen in den ersten Lebensjahren*. Grieben: Leipzig.

Roopnarine, J.L., Johnson, J.E. and Hooper, F.H. (1994) (eds) *Children's Play in Diverse Cultures*. New York: State University Press.

Rousseau, J-J. (1762/1911) *Emile* (B. Foxley, trans.) London: J.M. Dent & Sons.

Rousseau, J-J. (1762/1979) *Emile* (B. Bloom, trans.) New York: Basic Books.

Sully, J. (1896) *Studies of Childhood*. London and New York: Appleton.

Works of literature

Almond, D. (2009) *Skellig*. London: Hodder Children's Books.

Bennett, A. (2007) *Talking Heads*. London: BBC Books.

Blake, W. (1794/2011) *Songs of Innocence and Experience*. Oxford: Oxford University Press.

Causley, C. (2000) *Timothy Winters*. In *Collected Poems 1951–2000*. London: Picador.

Coleridge, S. T. (1895) *Anima Poetae*. In E.H. Coleridge (ed.) *Anima Poetae: From the Unpublished Notebooks of Samuel Taylor Coleridge*. London: William Heinemann.

Cooper, S. (2000) *King of Shadows*. London: Puffin Books. *The Dream of the Rood*. Available at www.dreamofrood.co.uk [accessed 7 December 2013].

Eliot, G. (1876/1892) *Daniel Deronda*. Edinburgh and London: William Blackwood & Sons.

Goscinny, R. and Uderzo, A. (1963/2005) *Asterix and Cleopatra*. London: Orion.

Greene, G. (1954/2000) *The Destructors*. In *Complete Short Stories*. London: Penguin.

Heaney, S. (1966/2006) *Death of a Naturalist*. London: Faber & Faber.

Heaney, S. (1972) *Wintering Out*. London: Faber & Faber.

Housman, A.E. (1896/2010) *A Shropshire Lad and Other Poems: The Collected Poems of A.E. Housman*. London: Penguin Classics.

Hughes, T. (1963/2011) *How the Whale Became: and Other Stories*. London: Faber & Faber.

Hughes, T. (1990) *Tales of the Early World*. London: Faber & Faber.

Hughes, T. (2004) *The Dreamfighter and Other Creation Tales*. London: Faber & Faber.

Kipling, R. (1902/2009) *Just So Stories for Little Children*. Oxford: Oxford Paperbacks.

Lee, Li-Young. (2008) *A Hymn to Childhood*. In *Behind my Eyes*. London: WW Norton.

Lessing, D. (1955/1980). *Through the Tunnel*. In *Stories*. New York: Vintage Books.

Macdonald, S. (1987) *Not About Heroes*. London: Samuel French Ltd.

McGough, R. (1973) *The Identification*. In *Gig*. London: Jonathan Cape.

Miller, A. (1949/2000) *Death of a Salesman*. London: Penguin Classics.

Miller, A. (1953/2000) *The Crucible: A Play in Four Acts*. London: Penguin Classics.

Milne, A.A. (1928/2009) *The House at Pooh Corner*. London: Egmont.

Milton, J. (1667/2008) *Paradise Lost*. Oxford: Oxford University Press.

Morpurgo, M. (2004) *Private Peaceful*. London: HarperCollins.

Nicholls, J. (1994) *Bluebottle*. In *Storm's Eye*. Oxford: Oxford University Press.

Plato (2005) *Phaedrus* (Penguin Classics). London: Penguin.

Plutarch (1704) 'Of Hearing'. *Plutarch's Morals, translated by several hands. The Fourth edition, Corrected and Amended*. London and Westminster: Thomas Braddyll.

Potter, D. (1979/1990) *Blue Remembered Hills*. London: Samuel French Ltd.

Raine, C. (1979) *A Martian Sends a Postcard Home*. Oxford: Oxford Paperbacks.

Scannell, V. (1965/2010) *A Case of Murder*. In *Collected Poems 1950–1993*. London: Faber & Faber.

Sedley, D. and Long, A. (Eds) (2010). *Plato: Meno and Phaedo* (Cambridge texts in the history of philosophy). Cambridge: Cambridge University Press.

Senior, O. (1985) *Birdshooting Season*. In *Talking of Trees*. Kingston, Jamaica: Calabash.

Shakespeare, W. (2005) *Antony and Cleopatra*. London: Penguin.

Shakespeare, W. (1992) *Hamlet*. London: Wordsworth Editions.

Shakespeare, W. (1992) *Julius Caesar* (Wordsworth Classics). Ware, Hertfordshire: Wordsworth Editions.

Shakespeare, W. (eds M. Bell, E. Dane and J. Dane, 1993) *King Henry V*. Cambridge: Cambridge University Press.

Shakespeare, W. (ed. C. McEachern, 2000) *The Life and Death of King John*. Harmondsworth: Penguin.

Shakespeare, W. (1992) *Macbeth*. London: Wordsworth Editions.

Traherne, T. (1903) *The Poetical Works of Thomas Traherne 1636–1674* (edited by Bertram Dobell) London: Dobel.

Wordsworth, W. (1807/2012) *Intimations of Immortality: An Ode* (Classic Reprint). Hong Kong: Forgotten Books.

Index